THE COMPLETE GUIDE TO

CONTRACTING YOUR HOME
2nd Edition

THE COMPLETE GUIDE TO

CONTRACTING YOUR HOME

2nd Edition

A Step-by-Step Method for Managing Home Construction

DAVE McGUERTY & KENT LESTER

BETTERWAY BOOKS

Cincinnati, Ohio

Cover photograph by D. Altman Fleischer
Cover design by Angela Lennert and Clare Finney
Typography by TechType

Other fine Betterway Books are available from your local bookstore or direct from the publisher.

96 95   8   7   6

Every precaution has been taken in preparing *The Complete Guide to Contracting Your Home* to make your home construction project as safe and successful as possible. However, neither the publisher nor the authors assume any responsibility for any damages incurred in conjunction with the use of this manual.

Library of Congress Cataloging-in-Publication Data
McGuerty, Dave
        The complete guide to contracting your home : a step-by-step method for
        managing home construction / Dave McGuerty and Lester.—2nd ed.
            p. cm.
        Includes index.
        ISBN 1-55870-229-6 (pbk).
        1. House construction—Amateurs' manuals. I. Lester, Kent.
            II Title.
TH4815.M27   1992
690'.83—dc20   91-40075

Dedicated to you:

THE HOMEBUILDER

That rare breed of individual with determination,
perseverance, demand for quality,
and the desire to save lots of money.

ACKNOWLEDGMENTS

To Thomas Harrison
and
The Georgia Institute of Homebuilding
for their contribution and support.

Many illustrations in this edition appear courtesy of the
United States Department of Housing and Urban Development
and the United States Department of Agriculture.
We wish to thank many of its members for being so helpful.

Contents

SECTION III: APPENDICES

Introduction

Welcome to the exciting world of homebuilding. Whether you are a homebuilder or an individual planning to build your own home, this manual will be a great step in helping you to achieve your goal. The fact that you have come this far indicates that you have the desire to do things in an efficient, organized manner and to save money on your project.

Homes have existed as long as man himself. Over centuries, homes have evolved from simple dwellings to complex structures combining state of the art skills and materials from many industries. Such rapid advancement has made the task of building a home increasingly difficult and complex. What the residential builder needs is a simple and complete method covering all of the activities involved in completing a construction project from beginning to end. That's what this book is all about.

WHO CAN BE A HOMEBUILDER?

A homebuilder is anyone who wants to be one. Many states have no examinations or licensing requirements for builders. Check with local building authorities in your area to determine if you must meet any special requirements. The homebuilder, or contractor, is the person in charge of overseeing the entire construction project, coordinating the efforts of professional subcontractors and labor, and managing materials. The term "Homebuilder" is somewhat of a misnomer since a homebuilder normally does not even have to raise a hammer to build a home. His efforts are best concentrated on managing the project. A professional homebuilder is anyone who builds for a living.

BEING YOUR OWN CONTRACTOR

Many would-be homebuilders are discouraged from attempting to build their own homes because of fear due to the "mystique" of modern construction practices and the profusion of available reference materials. Although many steps covered in this book provide you with information on what is happening at a specific point in time, you are usually not the person doing it. The steps you choose to perform are up to you. This book provides concise step-by-step instructions for residential construction. Building a home requires a sound knowledge of contracting. Contracting is the process of coordinating the efforts of skilled tradesmen (carpenters, masons, electricians, plumbers, etc...) and materials in an efficient manner. This book will show you how to work with subcontractors and material suppliers to become a successful homebuilder, whether you plan to build one house or a hundred.

CONTRACTING OBJECTIVES

- Save Time
- Save Money
- Reduce Frustration

Save Time

This book provides you with a complete detailed master plan that will help keep your project organized by dividing the work into discrete, manageable tasks. Efficiency will be gained by only doing necessary tasks - and doing them only once.

Save Money

This book can easily help save you from 25% to 42% on the home you build over a comparable home purchased through a real estate agent. Here are the major ways:

Real estate commission	up to 7%
Builder markup	up to 20%
Savings on material purchases	up to 4%
Cost saving construction	up to 2%
Doing work yourself	up to 9%
Total	**up to 42%**

This book will also provide you with a wealth of instantly usable knowledge equivalent to many other books on construction. This book can also save you from numerous, costly pitfalls associated with residential construction. After all, learning from bad experiences doesn't mean they have to be your own!

Reduce Frustration

This book will:

■ EQUIP you with the knowledge to effectively manage a residential construction project.

■ HELP you avoid major problems and pitfalls.

■ PROVIDE you with the benefit of years of experience.

■ ADVISE you when to avoid tackling tasks which are best left to specialists.

■ SHOW you how to specify and inspect the work performed by others.

HOW THIS BOOK DIFFERS FROM OTHER CONSTRUCTION MANUALS

There are more than enough books on the market covering construction techniques such as how to frame a home, lay bricks, mix concrete, cut beveled miter joints, etc. However, most fail to cover the important, practical day-to-day details of managing a construction project. Remember, you are not building the home per se; you are managing the building of the home. Also, many other publications fail to provide the necessary forms and sequenced, step-by-step instructions helpful in guiding you through the day to day details of a construction project.

OVERVIEW

THE COMPLETE GUIDE TO CONTRACTING YOUR HOME is composed of two major sections:

■ Concepts

■ Project Management

Concepts

Certain aspects of construction do not deal with specific construction steps, but are important to understanding successful homebuilding. Concepts such as lot and plan selection, financial and legal issues,

dealing with members of the construction industry and other topics are important in gaining a proper orientation to this environment. Much of the CONCEPTS material will be helpful throughout the PROJECT MANAGEMENT section of your manual.

Project Management

Residential construction involves the orderly coordination of some two dozen specialty trades each with their own special instructions, specifications, inspection requirements, detailed steps and special terms. The PROJECT MANAGEMENT section will cover each trade one at a time in the order in which the project normally proceeds.

HOW TO USE THIS BOOK

This book is designed to be easy to use and straight forward. It has been carefully sequenced to provide you with the right information at the right time. Before beginning your project:

■ READ this book thoroughly.

■ FAMILIARIZE yourself with all material in the PROJECT MANAGEMENT section.

During Your Project:

■ FOLLOW the STEPS outlined in the PROJECT MANAGEMENT section. Certain steps may not pertain to your project. For example, if you are building on a slab foundation, excavating a basement will not be applicable. However, be very careful not to skip steps that do apply to your project. Some common sense and judgement are obviously essential in this respect. Interpretation of the execution of many steps will naturally vary from project to project. **Do not even think of starting your project until you are familiar with the steps covered in this book.**

■ REFER to the sample specifications for ideas on what to include in your specifications when dealing with tradesmen. These are primarily intended to remind you of items easily overlooked and to illustrate the level of detail you should use.

■ REFER to the INSPECTION checklists for ideas on how and what to inspect to help insure you are getting good workmanship as your project progresses. It may take ten years to learn how to lay bricks properly, but only ten minutes to check the work for quality craftsmanship.

- ■ USE the FORMS provided when applicable. Most of these forms are included in the Appendices:
  - • House plan evaluation checklist
  - • Lot evaluation checklist
  - • Lien waivers
  - • Home construction contract
  - • Material and labor take-off sheets
  - • Purchase orders
  - • Sub-contractor specification form
  - • Change order

EXCUSES FOR NOT BUILDING

If you decide not to contract your own home, here are a few excuses you can use:

- ■ I have plenty of money. I don't need to save money by contracting myself.
- ■ I'm not particular about getting exactly what I want in a home, representing the single largest financial commitment of my life.
- ■ I don't know how.
- ■ It seems too complicated — I don't know where to begin.
- ■ I can't even hammer a nail straight.
- ■ It's not worth the trouble.
- ■ I don't have the time.
- ■ It's not my bag.

The last excuse is the only valid one. Building isn't for everyone. Many will use one of the above excuses or custom make their own. To make up an excuse is to rationalize why one pays "retail" for a home. Sadly enough, the money saved by contracting your own home can make all the difference in affording one or not.

The second most valid excuse is:

"I Don't Have the Time"

Most of us who can afford to contemplate building a home have full-time jobs. So how can one build a home in the evenings and on weekends? This is resolved in the "How to Be a Builder" section.

HELPFUL PERIODICALS

The magazines listed below are some of many you may wish to use as a source of ideas:

Fine Homebuilding
Better Homes & Gardens
New Shelter
Architectural Digest
Southern Homes
Southern Living
Country Living
House & Garden
Fine Homes
Town & Country
Southern Accents
Home

ADDITIONAL HELPFUL MATERIAL

In conjunction with your manual, several other documents will provide you with a wealth of information, while minimizing your expenditures on reference material. They are:

YOUR LOCAL BUILDING CODE — These are the rules you must abide by while building in your area. Obtainable from your county building inspector.

THE ESTIMATOR — A paperback full of tables and graphs to help you estimate the quantity of each building material you will use. Available from THE HOME BUILDING PLAN SERVICE, 2235 N.E. Sandy Boulevard, Portland, Oregon 97232.

THE LABORATOR — A counterpart to "The Estimator". This book shows time in hours and minutes required to perform various construction activities. Same publisher as above.

MODERN CARPENTRY — A general purpose text with over 1400 excellent illustrations covering the actual techniques of construction. By Willis H. Wagner. 1973. 480 Pages. THE GOODHEART-WILLCOX CO., INC. South Holland, Illinois. ISBN 0-87006-208-5.

MINIMUM PROPERTY STANDARDS FOR SINGLE FAMILY HOUSING — HUD guidelines that FHA and VA officials use to evaluate homes. Document number 999999. May 1979. 325 pages. U.S. Department of Housing and Urban Development. Available from the Superintendent of Documents, U.S. Government Printing Office, Washington, D.C. 20402.

MANUAL OF ACCEPTABLE PRACTICES — Extensive manual covering most aspects of residential construction. Document number 4390.1. U.S. Department of Housing and Urban Development. 1973. 420 pages. Available from the Superintendent of Documents, U.S. Government Printing Office, Washington, D.C. 20402.

SECTION I: CONCEPTS

How to Be a Builder

INTRODUCTION

A lot of people incorrectly believe that builders must know everything about building a house and must pass several tests to become licensed. Many states do not require small homebuilders to be licensed, and in states that do, building your own home is exempt from licensing requirements.

Few working people can afford the time to build their house themselves by hand. This book is directed at the person wanting to function as the CONTRACTOR. The contractor can be thought of as manager of the project, making sure that sub-contractors and materials show up at the site when needed. Leave the difficult and tedious tasks to the experts: They have spent years learning their trade.

Homebuilding may challenge your abilities in ways yet untested. It will test your ability to:

■ Get people to do what you want and when you want

■ Be fair, yet tough

■ Save money in creative ways

■ Manage an exciting, major project. You are the *BOSS*

Before you embark on this major project, you must become educated. Just as important, after you have studied this manual, you must decide whether you can handle all the details, people, surprises, insanity and periodic frustration associated with homebuilding. Building is not for the squeamish. This book will not necessarily make homebuilding a bed of roses for you. Homebuilding favors hard work, perseverance, guts, the ability to "horse trade", common sense and anything else you can muster to get the job done. To get yourself on the right path to being a builder, get your mind set for doing three things right from the beginning:

■ Act like a builder

■ Keep good records

■ Keep a builder's attitude

Act Like a Builder

Remember: Unless special licensing is required in your area, you are just as much a builder as the next guy. But check with your county Building Inspection Department for a copy of the local building code and information on licensing. If you are building your own house, even areas with licensing requirements will probably not require you to have a license.

Get comfortable using building terms and present yourself in a self-confident and professional manner. Trade-specific terms are covered in the respective sections in the PROJECT MANAGEMENT SECTION. The respect of your subs, labor and suppliers is essential to your effectiveness as a builder. The better you relate to those you work with, the easier your job will be. As good practice, get in your jeans, construction boots and your favorite plaid shirt and walk around a few construction sites. Get some mud on your shoes. This is a dress rehearsal. What you see is probably similar to what you'll have when you break ground. Get used to the smell of lumber, lots of mud and nails by the box. Talk to subs and imagine they're working for you. Figure out what makes them tick; and keep telling yourself you're a builder!

How you are perceived by others in this industry can make a difference. Much of a contractor's job is human relations, so acting like a builder will help you in getting along with others involved with your project. Order a set of business cards. It is amazing how many doors a simple business card will open. The business card will help convince suppliers that you are indeed a "professional". The only time you should wear a suit while working on this project is when you're at the bank polishing apples.

Keep Good Records

If this manual accomplishes anything, it should be to emphasize the need for keeping track of costs and expenses. You will be at a distinct advantage over the common builder if you keep good records. Some of the primary records are:

COST TAKE-OFF — The single most important tool you can use to save money on your project is the cost take-off. The cost take-off will tell you approximately what your house will cost before starting the project. It also gives you that checklist of materials necessary to make sure that all essential materials are ordered at the proper time. The take-off has a further advantage of giving you a cost goal to strive for when purchasing materials. When bargaining with materials suppliers don't hesitate to point out that "I've got to stay within my cost take-off budget!"

PURCHASE ORDERS — Make sure to use purchase orders when ordering materials. This will eliminate possible future confusion over whether certain items were ordered and from whom. Purchase orders and invoices are ESSENTIAL when figuring the house's cost basis for the IRS.

INVOICES — Most of the checks you write will be initiated by invoices. It is your responsibility to make sure they are accurate and that you pay them on time, especially if discounts apply. Match your purchase orders to invoices to control payments.

RECEIPTS AND CANCELED CHECKS — Lots of money is going to flow out on invoices. Keep them in a book. You'll need to compare them against purchase orders to avoid paying for things you didn't order and paying for things twice. Compare what was delivered with the invoice. Keep all proofs of payments together in an organized manner. Try to get a receipt — not just a canceled check. Your canceled check may take a month to get back to you as proof of payment.

PHOTOGRAPHS — Consider taking photographs of your home at various times during construction. This allows you to see changes take place and record them visually. Use a tripod and mark three spots on the ground. This way, you will always be taking a picture from exactly the same location.

CONTRACTS — Nothing will make or break the project like being able or unable to lay your hands on a good, sound written contract when a dispute arises. A man's memory is only as good as the paper it's written on. Contracts and their related specifications can almost never be too detailed. You can specify anything you want; but if you don't specify it, don't count on it being done.

WORKER'S COMPENSATION RECORDS — You must keep track of which subs have their own worker's compensation policy. For all those who don't, you should retain approximately six percent of the total charges. For subs with their own worker's compensation, you should make note of their policy number and its expiration date.

A SMALL PILE OF BANK LOAN PAPERS — These papers will vary from one lender to another, but will include all or some of the following:

- Loan documents
- Draw schedules
- Funds drawn
- Original take-off
- Surveys and plats
- Title search and insurance

Keep a Builder's Attitude

Your attitude and that of others working on your project is important. You may not always be able to see it, but a poor attitude can cause:

- Delays
- Liens
- Poor workmanship
- Additional costs due to carelessness
- Lots of frustration and headaches

Undertaking such a bold project takes a special frame of mind. And once you break ground, there is no turning back. Here are some important attitudes you'll need to build successfully:

■ PERSEVERE. Don't let anything get you down. When problems arise; tackle them immediately. Keep the project moving forward as close to schedule as possible. Realize that time is money and that you are responsible.

■ BE FIRM. When you have a dispute with a sub over sloppy work or a high bid, stick to your guns.

You are the BOSS. Don't let anyone talk you up against a wall. Remember the golden rule: "He who has the gold makes the rules".

■ DON'T BE A PERFECTIONIST. You want the work done on your home to be of high quality, but don't be upset every time you see a bent nail (provided you don't see too many of them). Chances are, the flaws you see in your home will not be noticeable by others when completed.

■ BE FRUGAL. Always look for new and creative ways to save money on anything pertaining to the project. Small savings can really add up in a project of this size.

■ BE THOROUGH. Think your ideas through and be meticulous. Pay attention to detail. Have the desire to keep detailed records organized and up to date.

■ DON'T GET MAD. Avoid chiding your subs on the job as this will reduce their desire to cooperate with you.

■ DON'T WORRY TOO MUCH. Instead of worrying, do something about the problem.

THE BUILDER'S RESPONSIBILITIES

The laborers and sub-contractors on your project are responsible for performing quality work and providing materials as specified and when specified by written contracts. That is their single most important responsibility. As the contractor, your responsibilities include the following:

■ PROVIDE clear, detailed specifications for those who work for you.

■ PAY laborers and sub-contractors promptly.

■ SCHEDULE material to arrive when or just before needed.

■ SCHEDULE labor and subs to work when needed.

■ MINIMIZE costs while maximizing quality.

■ PROVIDE a safe site at which to work.

■ MAINTAIN control of the project and the subs.

■ INSPECT work as it proceeds and is completed.

■ MAINTAIN accurate, up-to-date records on all

project matters such as:

• Insurance
• Drawings and plans
• Inspections
• Bank papers
• Purchase orders and invoices
• Legal documents such as variances, permits and licenses
• Payments, receipts, bank documents and other financial matters.

HOW TO BE A PART-TIME BUILDER

Most people have a full-time job and cannot take time off to construct a house. How can you have your cake and eat it too? There are two good options available.

Option I - Hire a Supervisor

Check the want ads for retired carpenters or builders who would like some light work in the construction industry. They have the time and experience to do things right, and chances are, they've been in the building industry most of their lives. Even if they are too old to do physical work, they can spot good work — and bad. This is also a great source for subs and the occasional use of a pickup truck.

Arrangements can probably be made on an hourly, daily or even monthly basis. The supervisor can be around at three o'clock in the afternoon when the concrete is about to be poured or a load of bricks needs to be delivered when you are at work or out of town. These individuals can play an important part in your project. Without them, you may not be able to build at all. If this route is chosen, involve the individual early in the process, when designs and project are being planned. This will allow you time to determine the individual's credibility, skill and honesty. If you would like more control over your project, consider getting a pager, so that you can reach the supervisor at all times.

Most subs can do work unsupervised when not being paid by the hour. Your "supervisor" only needs to confirm that they are doing the proper work, answer questions and assist in inspecting the work. He's there to keep the job rolling along and answer questions that would otherwise bring work to a halt.

Option II — Pay a Builder for His Assistance

Another option is to pay another builder to help run your project. This allows you:

■ Use of his subs. This saves you the time and hassle of finding reputable subs. In return, let him put up his building sign at your site.

■ Assistance during your work hours. If you can be at the site before and after work, this can be a helpful bridge during those unattended hours.

■ Assistance in securing a construction loan.

In return there may be a number of favors you can do for the builder when you don't have anything to do at your site. Also, your site may attract another prospective buyer for your builder. Let him keep a copy of your plans if he likes them.

THE HOMEBUILDING PROCESS

Regardless of what size home you are building or where you build, there are certain inevitable characteristics your project will have.

Your Project Will Proceed with Decreasing Degrees of Risk

For example, the first steps such as digging the foundation and pouring footings will have more impact if done improperly than if a door is hung to swing in the wrong direction. Hence, your utmost care should be taken at the beginning of the project when every step is critical — particularly through the framing stage.

Your Project Will Proceed Erratically

As the result of unforeseen circumstances, many weeks may pass with no progress on the project. Material shortages, poor weather, or subcontractor scheduling can all contribute to delays. Then for no apparent reason, three different subs and all your materials will show up at the site at one time.

You Will Make Changes and Unplanned, Impromptu Decisions

You will probably change the position of a door, window, wall, or major appliance. You may put in a dormer, a skylight or a screen porch. A prefab fireplace may be substituted for a masonry one at the last minute. There is no limit to the things that can change once a project is started. Don't let this frighten you. Details not necessarily shown on your plans will unfold before your very eyes. These trivial issues are normal and always occur when an idea on paper is converted to reality.

You Will Spend Lots of Money and Use It as a Tool

Until you have paid a sub you have his undivided attention. If he doesn't fix those squeaky stairs, that leaky pipe, or that crooked window, you simply won't pay him. Once you have paid too much, too early, you have killed his incentive to return and you have failed to use a builder's most important tool.

You Will Make The Difference

Small jobs will appear with no one assigned to do them. Replacing a bad piece of plywood or sturdying up the floor with a few nails — the list is endless. You make the difference. You may sacrifice a lazy morning in bed to pick up some brick, test out paint samples, or get a free load of slate somewhere. If you are determined to get the job done, you will get up at five AM if that's what it takes. You will crawl in bed some nights aching — but knowing you did what had to be done to make a lasting contribution to a structure that may well last a hundred years.

COMMON PROBLEMS FOR BUILDERS

Being a builder means handling problems. Every project is different and has its peculiar quirks, but there are several problems that occur to some degree on just about all construction projects. Although you may not be able to avoid these problems altogether, it may be helpful for you to know what some of them are now so that you take precautions to minimize their adverse impact on your project. The most common problems are:

Subs are often late.

■ Let subs tell you when they'll be there.

■ Call the sub the day before he is scheduled to arrive at the site.

■ Meet the sub at the site at a certain time.

■ Give incentives for early completion. Cash talks.

Subs don't show at all.

■ Let them know up front that you expect prompt attendance and that you will spread the word around if they cancel with no warning.

■ Have other subs as backups.

Subs proceed slowly.

■ Give subs a bonus for finishing work on or before schedule. A cash bonus makes a great incentive.

Subs do work incorrectly or disagree on work to be done.

■ Ask them to repeat instructions back to you.

■ Have detailed specifications and drawings where needed.

■ Don't let too much work get done without checking on it. Visit the site daily.

■ Discuss detailed drawings with sub and make sure he understands it.

■ Have a site phone so that the sub can call you when questions arise.

■ Have detailed specifications and drawings where needed.

Dispute arises over amount to be paid, especially when changes are involved.

■ Put payment amount and payment schedule in writing and have it signed by both parties.

■ All changes to the original plans should be written on a change order form and signed by both parties.

■ Use lien waivers to control your liability.

■ Pay with checks to insure proper records.

Materials not available when needed.

■ Order custom pieces early to insure that they are on site when needed.

■ Confirm delivery dates with suppliers and have them notify you of delays several days in advance.

■ Determine which suppliers deliver after hours and on weekends.

■ Get friendly with the delivery men and schedulers at your supply houses.

Wrong material or wrong quantity of material is delivered.

■ Use detailed descriptions or part numbers on all purchase order items.

■ Print legibly.

■ Don't order over the phone unless extremely urgent.

■ Have materials delivered early so they can be exchanged or corrected before they are actually needed.

■ Have your subs help you to determine actual quantities and materials.

■ Get to know your salespeople and work with the same person every time.

Bad weather.

■ Don't begin project during or just before the rainy season.

■ Get roof up as soon as possible.

■ Make the most of good weather.

■ Provide a drive area of #57 crusher run to avoid muddy areas.

■ Get a roll of poly (plastic sheet) to cover materials.

Theft and vandalism.

■ Visit site each day.

■ Call the local police department and have your site put on surveillance.

■ Don't always visit site at a routine time. Make unannounced visits, especially near quitting time.

■ Don't keep too much material on site. This is especially true for windows, doors, millwork, good plywood, and expensive tubs and appliances. Some builders even put a 3" screw in the top corners of a stack of plywood.

■ Get builder's risk and theft insurance with a low deductible.

■ Install locks as soon as possible and use them.

RULES FOR SUCCESSFUL BUILDERS

- PUT EVERYTHING IN WRITING — *not written, not said.*

- BE PREPARED *before* breaking ground and don't get behind.

- KEEP PROJECT BINDER current with all project details.

- BE FAIR with money. Pay subs what was agreed, when agreed.

- ALWAYS GET REFERENCES and check out three on each major sub. You must see their work.

- DON'T TRY TO DO TOO MUCH of the actual physical work yourself. Your time and skills are often better used managing the job.

- SHOP CAREFULLY for the best material and labor prices. Don't hesitate to insist on builder discounts.

- USE CASH to your maximum advantage.

- RELY ON YOUR CONTRACTORS for advice in their field. But above all, use common sense.

- DON'T ASSUME anything. Material is not on site unless you see it. Subs are not on site unless you see them there. Don't expect subs to know what you want unless it's in writing.

- USE AS FEW SUBS AS POSSIBLE without sacrificing cost or quality.

- USE THE BEST MATERIALS you can afford.

- KEEP CHANGES TO A MINIMUM and budget funds for them carefully.

- ESTIMATE ON THE HIGH SIDE and have a contingency fund.

- KEEP MONEY UNDER CONTROL and track progress versus your original budget.

- RELY ON YOUR LOCAL BUILDING CODE as a primary reference for specifications, inspection criteria, material guidelines and settling of disputes. Learn to use it comfortably.

- STAY AT LEAST A WEEK OR TWO AHEAD of the game. Staying ahead will allow you time to compensate for material delays or time needed to replace unreliable or unsatisfactory subs.

- USE THE BEST MATERIALS you can afford.

- LET YOUR FINGERS DO THE WALKING. If it looks like rain, call the roofer. If something can't be delivered, advise your subs.

PROVERBS FOR BUILDERS

Below are a few sayings very appropriate to the building industry. As a builder, you are bound to encounter times when one or more of them apply.

MURPHY'S LAW — If anything can go wrong, it will.

If there is a possibility of several things going wrong, the one that will cause the most damage will be the one to go wrong.

If you perceive that there are four possible ways in which a procedure can go wrong, circumvent it, then a fifth way will promptly develop.

It is impossible to make anything foolproof, because fools are so ingenious.

DAVE'S CONSTANT — Matter will be damaged in direct proportion to its value.

If you explain so clearly that nobody can misunderstand, somebody will.

Do not believe in miracles — rely on them.

LESTER'S FIRST LAW — Everything put together falls apart sooner or later.

LESTER'S SECOND LAW — No matter what goes wrong, it will probably look right.

If only one bid can be secured on any project, the price will be unreasonable.

KING'S LAW — No matter how long or how hard you shop for an item, after you've bought it, it will be on sale somewhere, for less.

Everything takes longer than you think.

THE GOLDEN RULE — He who has the gold makes the rules.

The Eighty-Twenty Rule of Project Schedules: The first twenty percent of the task takes eighty percent of the time and the last twenty percent of the time takes the other eighty percent.

Once you have exhausted all possibilities and fail, there will be one solution, simple and obvious, that is highly visible to everyone else.

All delivery promises must be multiplied by a factor of 2.0.

HARRISON'S LAW — The most vital dimension of any plan or drawing stands the greatest chance of being omitted.

COMMONER'S LAW — Nothing ever goes away. When things just can't get any worse, they will. Left to themselves, things tend to go from bad to worse.

Nothing is as easy as it looks.

WHY CONSTRUCTION PROJECTS FAIL

As a builder, it is up to you to make your project a success, but along with all the glory comes all the responsibility! Listed below are a number of common reasons why construction projects fail and/or encounter severe difficulties:

■ Costs are underestimated.

■ Lack of budget control. Excessive design changes are made late in the game.

■ Project manager not organized; letting things get out of control.

■ Lack of understanding of contracting.

■ Acts of vandalism, arson or natural catastrophes not adequately covered by insurance.

■ Lack of enthusiasm.

■ Workers paid before careful inspection was made of work and materials.

■ Legal complications due to careless handling of business transactions, such as double invoice pay-ment or payment for work uncompleted or unde-livered, damaged or inferior goods.

■ Conflicts with spouse or partner.

BUILDING FOR YOURSELF VS. BUILDING FOR OTHERS

One of the first questions that any of your workers are going to ask you is whether you are building this home for yourself or to sell. The difference can be subtle, but more likely the difference will change the house dramatically in terms of workmanship and materials used.

Those who build for a living learn quickly that the only way to make a fair profit is to build into a home ONLY those features and the level of quality that is necessary to sell the house and nothing more. Quality materials such as hardwood floors, marble, custom millwork, brickwork, fancy lighting and fancy bath fixtures are used sparingly or not at all.

However, you may defeat at least part of the purpose of building your own home if you don't outspend the neighborhood builder in a few areas. Perhaps you want a skylight, nice brass faucets, fancy wallpaper or better grade appliances. This is your prerogative. You should add a few special touches that will make your house stand out and easier to sell.

WHEN YOU GET NERVOUS

Nervous because you've never done anything so am-bitious? Nervous because the carpenter hasn't re-turned your call yet? Or maybe you just can't put a finger on the source of your uneasiness. RELAX.

Remember:

Fear is a natural response to the uncertain and the unknown. A goal of this book is to replace uncer-tainty with clear, concise knowledge — to remove those cloudy uncertainties. Some individuals main-tain a certain level of fear as a natural defense mech-anism — to always remain cautious and alert of the situation and possible problems.

Individuals with little or no formal education build houses every day — and they do it for a living!

A certain degree of fear is typical when doing anything for the first time. Chances are, after you have built your first home, you'll want to do it again!

Your construction project is staffed by many knowledgeable, professional sub-contractors each specializing in his area. It is their job to do the work properly. Don't worry if you don't know everything they do. That is not a requirement of a builder. If the job is not done right you can refuse to pay until the items in question are fixed.

The construction approach presented in this book has been time-tested. Many homes have been built using material in this book. Using this book puts you way ahead of many individuals who may either try to brave it alone or otherwise push ahead without adequate knowledge and/or preparation.

Assure yourself that you are doing everything you can to protect your project against the pitfalls described in "WHY CONSTRUCTION PROJECTS FAIL."

Assure yourself that you are using the STEPS, SPECIFICATIONS and INSPECTION checklists provided.

WHEN YOU GET DISCOURAGED

You're into the project and things aren't going along perfectly. Your framing crew made some mistakes, you've had four straight days of rain, your roofing sub won't return your call and the price just went up on storm windows. So what else is new? Getting discouraged?

Did you ever hear of any project proceeding from beginning to end without a hitch or two — or twenty? Below are a few things to ponder when you wonder why you didn't just throw this book away and cut your losses short.

LOOK at the money you're saving. You probably have a good idea how much. Just look at that figure for a moment. That's the money you would have paid someone else to do the work you're doing right now. If someone else were performing your job, they'd run into the same kind of problems. When the interest costs are figured in, you will probably be saving one or more year's salary by contracting yourself. Aren't a few months of challenge worth it?

LOOK at all the problems and solutions you're encountering. One day when your home is completed, you'll look back at them and laugh. You'll tell of some of your experiences the rest of your life.

LOOK at your accomplishment! Your friends, associates and family look upon you with admiration. You can honestly say that you built your home. Only you will know how much physical work and skill you didn't put in.

REMEMBER — Bad days are always followed by better ones. Hang in there!

Legal and Financial Information

FINANCIAL ISSUES

Obtaining financing for your home will be one of the most critical and demanding phases of your building project. You must be bookkeeper, financier and salesman. The lender will want evidence that you know what you are doing and that you can finish your project within budget.

THE CONSTRUCTION LOAN

Unless you are one of the few who build with cash, the construction loan is a necessity. The construction loan process will be a trying one, entitling you and a friend to a night out upon loan approval. It is typical for interest on a construction loan to be a few points higher than a permanent loan. This gives you further incentive to finish the project as quickly as possible. WARNING: When you apply for your loan, apply for all the money you will need — and then some. Don't plan on getting extra money later. You are headed for a disaster of mammoth proportions if you run out of money before your project is over. Your lender will likely foreclose on your project and you'll end up with next to nothing. This also means that once you've done your take-off and are into construction, don't make expensive changes and upgrades unless you can pay for them out-of-pocket.

The Financial Package — Applying for Your Loan

Make sure that your financial package is complete before visiting the lender. The package should be neat, informative, well organized, and comply with all of the lender's requirements. Your lender will want to be sure that you can keep good records. Your financial package should include the following:

■ Personal financial statement

■ Resume or personal biography

■ Total cost estimate of the project

■ Description of materials

■ Survey of the proposed building site showing location of dwelling

■ Set of blueprints

THE PERSONAL FINANCIAL STATEMENT should include all your assets and liabilities. Make sure to include everything of value you own, including personal property. Many people tend to underestimate the value of items like furniture and clothing. Your liabilities should include any loans, charge accounts and credit balances. Ask your lender for one of their own standard forms.

THE RESUME is designed to sell yourself to the lender. Start with a standard job resume but be sure to emphasize any construction interests or experience.

THE COST ESTIMATE will be very important, as your construction loan will be based on it. Make sure to include a 7 to 10% cost overrun factor in your estimates as a cushion for unexpected expenses. Many lenders can provide you with a standard cost sheet for you to fill out. If not, use the one included in this book.

THE DESCRIPTION OF MATERIALS form will aid the lender's appraiser in estimating the appraised value of your property. Many lenders use the standard FHA form for this purpose, but check to see if your lender uses their own special form.

THE SURVEY should be obtained from the seller of the property or from the county tax office. If the property is very old, you may have to request that a new survey be done. Indicate on a copy of the survey the approximate location of the house.

A SET OF BLUEPRINTS complete with all intended changes should be submitted. Give your lender the set without the coffee stains.

START-UP MONEY

You will need to put up a lot of your own money before you can expect to receive your first draw. Typically your initial outlay will include:

■ Lot cost to be paid before the construction begins

■ Closing costs (construction loan closing)

■ Permits (building, water, sewer, etc.)

■ Site preparation (clearing, grading & excavation)

■ Foundation

If you can't do this out of your pocket before going to the lender, you aren't ready to begin building.

About Draws

Unlike a car loan where you receive all your cash at once; construction loans are almost always handled on a draw basis. The lender will make you earn the money that you borrowed — bit by bit. Each time the lender sees that you have completed say, 5% of the project, you are allowed a "draw" of 5% of the construction loan. This nuisance is, in fact, a way of making sure that money isn't wasted carelessly up front. Whenever you would like a loan draw, you must contact the lender and request one. The lender has an inspector who will visit the building site to see what work has been completed. The lender will normally have a fixed draw schedule which allows a certain amount of money to be "drawn" for each major phase of construction. Many lenders inspect on Thursdays and distribute draws on Fridays. Builders are usually allowed only five draws free of charge. If you desire more draws than allowed per project, you are usually charged a nominal fee per draw.

Money is drawn after proof is shown that such money is deserved. Hence, you must go into the project with some start-up money of your own. The need for this "pocket money" can't be underesti-

mated. It will be used to buy permits and licenses, dig your foundation and perhaps get your foundation built before money is drawn. It will also be used to cover unexpected expenses, such as price increases, last-minute additions you may want to make and underestimates. Be aware that draw schedules are normally back ended, meaning that you will spend more than you can draw up front, while receiving a 5% draw for painting your mailbox near the end.

The Construction Permanent Loan

When possible, apply for a Construction Permanent Loan (also known as a convertible loan). This type of loan eliminates one of two closing costs related to separate loans for construction and permanent financing. This is done by putting both the construction loan and the permanent loan in your name. When the permanent loan is ready to close, the construction loan is "converted" to a permanent mortgage. Shop loans carefully. Time here is well spent. Many institutions now offer 15-year payoffs that only cost a little extra each month over a standard 30-year loan. Charging points, a lump-sum cost when you originate a loan, is only a way for lenders to get a little bit more money out of you without raising the interest rate.

Dealing with the Lender

When going to the lender, be prepared:

■ Have your financial package ready.

■ Know exactly how much money you need.

■ Have all requested information typed.

■ Dress up (preferably dark suit).

■ Show up at the scheduled time.

■ Don't mention how much pocket money you have on the side — the lender will want you to put it into the construction loan.

■ Don't talk too much. Answer questions only when asked and don't volunteer any information not asked for.

■ Have a list of your subs and backups.

■ Have all lender forms typed.

The Appraisal

The lending institution will have its capital at risk. As

such, they will want to be assured that the house you are planning to build is worth more than the construction loan. They will also test your skill at estimating costs.

The lender will appraise your home in one of two ways; the Market Approach (most likely) or the Cost Approach.

MARKET APPROACH — This method of appraisal bases the value of the home on "comparables" in the area. The appraiser will look for comparable houses to yours in the surrounding neighborhood that have similar features, style, square footage and property values. Therefore, it is advantageous to build your house near a neighborhood with homes similar but higher in price than yours. Don't get too far-fetched with your design. The appraiser may not be able to find suitable comparables and may have to guess at the value; usually to your disadvantage.

COST APPROACH — This is similar to the cost take-off or a determination of value by square footage.

After the value is determined, the lender will then loan you a fixed percentage of the appraised value, usually up to 70 or 80%, to build the house. Very seldom will the lender give you a loan based totally on what you claim your construction costs to be. However, you should easily be able to build a house for less than 75% of its appraised value.

THE LEGAL ISSUES

Real estate laws have evolved over thousands of years. Needless to say these issues are complex and are best left to the experts. Make sure to consult the appropriate authorities about any legal issue in order to avoid unpleasant surprises. The professionals you will need to deal with are attorneys, insurance agents and financial lenders. The key legal issues affecting your building project are:

- Filing in the public record
- Free and clear title to the property
- Land survey
- Easements
- Covenants
- Zoning

- Variances
- Liens
- Sub-contractor contracts
- Builder's risk insurance
- Building permits
- Worker's compensation

FILING IN THE PUBLIC RECORD — Because of the importance and complexity of real estate law, all real estate transactions concerning the transfer of property, liens, and loans are normally filed in the public records at your county's local courthouse. This way you are announcing to the public what property you own. Anyone has access to these records and may research the history of your property to see who owned it before you and if there are any mortgages, judgments or liens on the property. This is for your protection; because you can do the same research on any property you intend to buy. Go to your local courthouse and familiarize yourself with the records. Ask one of the title lawyers in the room (there are always a few attorneys there) to help you learn how to search the records. This will give you an idea of the process of real estate transactions.

FREE AND CLEAR TITLE concerns your bundle of rights to a piece of property, whether it is land or improved property. Before closing on a property, your lawyer will do a "title search" of the property in the public record to determine its ownership history. Most real estate records are kept at the county courthouse and are accessible to anyone. If the lawyer finds someone with an "interest" in the property or a confusion over rights, this will create a "cloud on the title" which must be removed before title can transfer. A title search is required by all lenders and is usually done for a standard fee. *NEVER BUY A PIECE OF PROPERTY WITHOUT DOING A TITLE SEARCH!* Many so called "bargains" are properties with title problems that the present owner is hoping to "pawn off" on some unsuspecting buyer. Don't be that buyer! You should also get title insurance, protecting your claim to the land.

A LAND SURVEY is another required item that must be done before title can be transferred. This survey can usually be arranged by your lawyer or financial lender. The survey will describe the exact location of your land in a written legal description and scale drawing of the property called a "plat map." These descriptions will be attached to the deed and filed in the public record.

EASEMENTS on the property will normally be discovered during the survey and title search. Easements give rights of traverse on your property to others such as local governments (sidewalk easement), utility companies (sewer or electric company easements) or individuals. Make sure to check the location of your construction in relation to the easements to avoid any conflicts.

COVENANTS are building restrictions or requirements placed on construction in certain subdivisions, such as minimum square footage of the building or the type and style of construction. These restrictions are usually placed on the property by the developer of the subdivision in order to protect the value of the homes in the subdivision. Ask your lawyer to check for any building restrictions in the public record before buying a building lot. You may not be able to build the house of your dreams if the design is not allowed in the neighborhood! Watch out for any restriction stating that the home can only be built by a specific set of builders or in a specific time frame.

ZONING RESTRICTIONS, like covenants, control use of land in an area and the type of structures built. These restrictions are placed on property by the local government planning board in order to protect the value of land in the area. Check with your local planning office if you are unsure of the zoning of your property. A zoning map of the county can usually be purchased for a nominal fee and can be very helpful in searching for property. Zoning laws also define the area of the lot that the structure can actually occupy. The builder is required to place the structure a certain minimum distance from neighboring homes. This requirement is called the minimum setback. In many planned subdivisions, these boundaries are closely adhered to in order to make the homes in the area appear consistent and planned. You may also have requirements for a backyard of a certain depth and a minimum side yard of 20'. It is important to find out where your baselines are before you break ground. If you build outside a baseline and are caught, you may be in for a hefty fine.

VARIANCES allow you to "vary" from standard state and local zoning ordinances within prescribed, approved limits. For example, if you want to build your home 30' from the front curb and the local zoning ordinance requires a 40' set back, you must apply for a 10' set back variance. Unless your request adversely affects neighborhood appearance or safety, your variance will normally get approval. To obtain a variance, you must normally pay an application fee and go before a panel of county zoning officials at a variance hearing, where you or your representative describe or illustrate your intentions and the reasons for them. Normally a notice of your variance request will be posted on your lot so that the public is aware of your intent to get a variance. They have a right to appear at the variance hearing to either support or fight against your variance.

LIENS can become extremely important to a home builder because of the effect they can have on the construction project and the subsequent closing of the property. A lien places an interest in a property that will create a cloud on the title, preventing the close of the sale until resolved. For example, if the plumbing contractor does not feel that he was fully paid for his work, he may file a lien in the public record on the property involved. This lien can stay attached to the property until the disagreement is resolved. Many states do not require that the owner be notified of the lien, but you will know about it at closing! The lien will prevent sale or mortgaging of the property until the disagreement is resolved.

To avoid the pitfalls of liens to potential homebuyers, many states now require contractors to sign an affidavit guaranteeing to the purchaser that the contractor has paid all his bills due to suppliers and sub-contractors. If any parties then file a lien, the contractor can become criminally or legally liable not only to the lien holder, but also to the purchaser! Builders or subs can be thrown in jail in many states for this offense!

If you are building for yourself or others, you can protect yourself from liens by requiring your suppliers and sub-contractors to sign a sub-contractor's affidavit. This agreement works like the contractor's affidavit. The sub-contractor agrees that all bills have been paid and that the contractor has no legal claim against your property. This will prevent the sub-contractor from filing any liens on the property. Make everyone you deal with sign this agreement for your own protection!

SUB-CONTRACTOR CONTRACTS, like affidavits, protect you from surprises. Get everything important in writing no matter how good your sub's memory or integrity. Subs may have a contract amnesia if a problem comes up. Make sure to include the specifications for the work done as well as a schedule of how payment will be made. It is wise to use a statement such as "Final payment will be made when work is satisfactorily completed."

BUILDER'S RISK INSURANCE is another "ounce of prevention" necessary before starting your project. This insurance will protect against liability if someone should be injured on the building site. Theft of building materials is sometimes covered also. Risk insurance may only cover theft after the dwelling can be locked. Be aware of very high deductibles.

BUILDING PERMITS must be obtained from your County Building Inspector's office before construction can begin. This will notify the city or county of your project so that the building inspector can schedule the required inspection of the property during construction. This permit must be displayed in a prominent location at the site. Check your local county for details. Normally, building permits cost a certain amount per $1000 of construction value or per square foot. Obviously, this value is somewhat intangible. You may have to accept the authority's estimated value.

WORKER'S COMPENSATION is required in every state to provide workers with hospitalization insurance for job-related injuries. This accident insurance must be taken out by any person or company with hired employees. Most states also have special statutes that require builders, even when using subcontractors, to have this insurance protection for anyone working on the building site. At the end of each year, the insurance company does an audit to determine the amount of insurance to be paid. Each building trade is assessed an insurance rate depending on the relative risk involved in the trade. For instance, roofing trades will be charged a higher rate than trim carpenters. Since you are providing insurance to cover these workers on your site, make sure to deduct the amount of the insurance from the price paid to the sub-contractor.

Many of the subs who work for you will have their own worker's compensation policies since they may have employees working for them. If a sub has a policy, make sure to obtain the policy number and expiration date. Most insurance companies allow you a credit on your own rate if the sub-contractor has his own policy. This credit will be applied at the insurance audit. Contact your local insurance agent for more information about worker's compensation in your state.

Don't underestimate the importance of this policy. You are liable for any work-related injuries that occur on your property. Without this policy, a negligence lawsuit could take your life savings. Look for any situations that can void worker's compensation coverage. For example, in some states, drywall subs experiencing accidents while using drywall stilts are not covered. Better safe than sorry!

The Lot

The lot you purchase will be a part of the home. It's a location and setting you had better be comfortable with. There's an old saying about the three most important factors when buying a lot: location, location and location. While this stretches the truth, it does make an important point.

CONSIDERATIONS

If you have not purchased your lot yet, you may wish to ask yourself the following questions:

Would you prefer to build in a planned development (subdivision), where home values will be more stable and controlled, or on a one-of-a-kind lot? If you are purchasing a lot in a subdivision, make sure that the building covenants work for you; not against you. Do the covenants allow you to build the home you want? When you want? Do the covenants allow you to subcontract the home yourself? Do they protect against low priced homes which could affect your resale value? Don't build in an area where homes are more than 15 or 20% lower in value than your planned home.

Would you prefer a large lot, which may require lots of time and money in maintenance, or a smaller one that may cost less and involve less maintenance?

Are the lot and surrounding area suitable for the type home you are planning to build? Consider this from both a physical and an esthetic point of view.

Will the lot support a basement, slab or crawl space if you plan to have one? A better location is almost always worth spending a little more money.

ADVICE

Don't attempt to save money by buying a "less desirable" lot. Curb appeal can affect the value of your home by 25% or more. Saving $2,000 in lot costs could cost you $10,000 in home resale value. (Don't step over a dollar to pick up a dime!) Don't overbuild for the area; build in an area of comparable value. Make sure that the lot and the neighboring homes are WORTHY of the home you plan to build.

Obtain a title search of the property before purchasing to ensure free and clear title to the land. Make sure that there is public sewer access on the lot if the seller says it is available. Don't take his word for it.

It is wise to first determine the style and size home you plan to build before looking at lots. It would be a shame to find out that the home you want to build won't even fit on the lot after considering baselines. Also, you may want to build near homes of comparable value. To do this, you need to know what size home to build. This is the subject of the next chapter.

LOT EVALUATION

Review the following checklists of strengths and weaknesses, although many of them may already be obvious to you. Each weakness provides grounds for negotiating a lower offering price. Once you own the land, each weakness is your problem.

When evaluating a lot, you must walk the lot to check for soft spots, drain pipes, lay of the land, etc. Realize that all the trees on a lot may well disappear after the foundation area is cleared.

Corner Lots — Good or Bad?

Although some homeowners enjoy corner lots, they are generally not preferred by speculative homebuilders because they lack backyard privacy and often have a front setback even on the side. The "non-square" shape complicates the design and placement of the house.

STRENGTHS: CHECKLIST

☐ Lot slopes to allow for basement (if desired).

☐ Lot has rear and side privacy.

☐ On sewer line. Check height of sewer line. Your lowest drain pipe should be slightly higher than the sewer line.

☐ On cul-de-sac or in other low traffic area.

☐ Well-shaped square, rectangular or otherwise highly usable.

☐ Trees and woods. Hardwoods and some larger trees.

☐ Good firm soil base. Important for a solid foundation.

☐ No large subterranean rocks that will require blasting.

☐ Not in flood plain.

☐ Safe, quiet atmosphere.

☐ Attractive surroundings such as comparable or finer homes and attractive landscaping.

☐ Level or gradual slope up from road.

☐ Good drainage.

☐ Lot located in stable, respected neighborhood.

☐ Just outside of city limits. May pay less local taxes.

☐ Easy access to major roadways, highways and thoroughfares.

☐ Convenient to good schools, shopping centers, parks, swiming/tennis, firehouse and other desirable amenities.

☐ Situated in an area of active growth.

☐ Provides attractive view from dwelling site.

☐ Fully usable. No ditches, ruts or irregular surfaces.

☐ Seller will finance partially or in full.

☐ In area zoned exclusively for single family dwellings.

☐ Underground utilities. Phone, electrical, cable TV.

☐ Natural features in areas that will remain undisturbed.

☐ Swim, tennis, golf and other amenities.

☐ Private back yard area. If there are no trees to block the neighbor's house, check for room to plant trees or shrubs.

WEAKNESSES: CHECKLIST

☐ No sewer, must install septic tank. Must pass a percolation test.

☐ On or very near major thoroughfare. Yellow or white lines down the center of the road. Speed limit over 35 mph.

☐ Odd-shaped (too narrow or too shallow). Either will cause limited front or side yards.

☐ No trees or barren.

☐ Rocky. May have large rocks to excavate or dynamite.

☐ Sandy soil. May require special foundation work. May not support a large foundation. Excavation difficult.

☐ In flood plain. Normally involves expensive flood insurance and difficult resale.

☐ Near airport, railroad tracks, landfill, exposed electric power facilities, swamps, cliffs or other hazardous area. Near large power easements, commercial properties or radio towers.

☐ Slopes down from road and/or steep yard. Hard to mow. Difficult access by car when iced over. Water drains toward home. May require excessive or unusual excavation and/or fill dirt.

☐ Flat yard. Less than 2% slope may be difficult to drain.

☐ Water collects in spots. May require expensive drainage landscaping and/or fill dirt. May result in a wet/damp basement.

☐ Lot located in or near unstable/declining neighborhood.

☐ Just inside city limits. May have to pay more local tax.

☐ Relatively inaccessible by major roadways.

☐ Isolated from desirable facilities such as shopping centers, swimming/tennis, parks, etc.

☐ Lot provides unattractive views, either from prospective dwelling site or from road.

☐ Shallow lots leaving a small area for the back yard.

☐ Lot located in flood plain area. (Check local county plats.)

☐ Creek, gully or deep valley running near center of lot.

☐ Area zoned commercial, duplex, quadruplex or other high-density, multi-family dwelling.

☐ Area populated by less expensive homes.

☐ Utilities above ground or not yet established. Unsightly electrical wires.

FINDING A LOT

Finding the right lot may involve approaching lots from any of the sources below and others as well:

■ Local real estate agents and/or multiple listing services

■ For sale ads in newspapers

■ For sale signs on land

■ Legal plats in county courthouses or other local government offices.

PURCHASING THE LOT

Review the considerations and the checklists on the previous pages. Check for problems and weaknesses. REMEMBER: "Once you buy it, it's YOUR problem!"

Request the seller to provide a legal description of the lot, prepared by a registered surveyor, showing all legal easements and baselines (you may not be able to build just anywhere on the lot). Negotiate legal and other closing costs to be paid by or split with the seller. If you must pay all or part of the legal fees, INSIST on appointing an attorney of YOUR choice.

Cash talks — especially when purchasing from an individual rather than an organization. Look for owner financing.

Insist on and pay for a title search and title insurance. Title insurance is important if there is ever a dispute over land ownership. Litigation could cost you lots of time and money. When applying for a construction loan at a local lending institution, you must have "free and clear title" to the land. This insures that no dispute over title will interfere with the completion of a successful construction project. All financial institutions insist on you having free and clear title before negotiating a loan.

House Plans

Before you can build or purchase your "dream home" you must determine what features you can realistically afford. Many future homeowners start out by designing a dream home with all the features they have ever wanted. Unfortunately, reality tends to get in the way of many people's dreams. Before you spend valuable dollars on blueprints and architects' fees, determine the exact amount of home you can afford to purchase.

HOW MUCH HOME CAN YOU AFFORD?

The standard rule of thumb used by most banks is that your principal and interest (P&I) payments should not exceed 25% of your Gross annual income. With interest rates fluctuating, many banks will now allow up to 35% of your income. To find the total amount of home you can afford, use the following equations. Look up the mortage amount in Table 1 to determine the total amount of mortgage your monthly salary will allow you to cover financially.

Example:

John earns $37,000 per year and has just bought a subdivision lot for $12,000. How much can he spend on house construction and still meet the bank's loan requirements? The bank is willing to finance 80% of the value of the house. The interest rate is 12% and the mortgage term is 30 years.

Since the bank will only approve a mortgage payment of about 25% of John's monthly income, divide John's yearly income by 12 to obtain the monthly income and then divide it by 4 (25%). This will give you the total payment amount available to put toward monthly mortgage payments.

$$\frac{Monthly \ Gross \ Income}{4} = Monthly \ \ Mortgage \ Payment$$

$$\frac{\$37,000}{12} = \frac{\$3,083.33}{4} = \$770.83$$

Look up the payment amount in Table 1 for a 30 year loan at 12% interest to determine the amount of the mortgage your monthly payments will cover. The table gives figures on a $100 per month payment. Multiply this by your available monthly payment to obtain the total mortgage amount.

$$\frac{\$770.83}{\$100} = 7.71 \ x \ \$9,722 = \$74,956$$

Since the bank will finance this much mortgage at 80%, the total price of the house will be the mortgage amount plus the 20% down payment John must contribute to the purchase. Work backwards to obtain the total house value.

$$\frac{Mortgage \ amount}{Percentage \ financing} = Total \ value \ of \ house$$

$$\frac{\$74,956}{.80} = \$93,700$$

Many times you will be able to secure 100% financing on your own construction once you have free and clear title to the land. In this example, however, we will use 80%.

Now take the total value of the house and subtract the cost of the land, construction loan cost and closing costs to determine the total amount of money you can afford to spend on the construction of your home. As a rule of thumb, the minimum cost of your home, excluding land, will be roughly $40.00 per square foot of heated space (excludes garage) if you contract the work yourself. For expensive brickwork, appliances, cabinets, etc., costs can exceed $55.00 per square foot. You should check with local building associations to find out the typical cost per square foot in your area.

Total cost of home	$93,700
Land cost	- 12,000
Construction interest	- 2,500
Closing costs	- 1,800
	————
Construction cost	$ 77,400
	=========

This amount should be the upper limit that you are willing to spend to secure a home of your own in this example. Next, determine what it is costing builders to build in your area. One way of doing this is to ask a few builders what they would sell their homes for direct. Deduct about 15 to 25 percent profit for them and then divide by the square footage. This will give you the cost per square foot. Another way is to ask experienced salesmen at a large building supply outlet. They always talk to builders and know what's going on. Remember, the cost per square foot does not include the cost of the lot.

Back to our example: the total cost of the home less the cost of the lot, interest and closing is $77,400. Assuming that the cost per square foot is $41.25, you could build a 1,935 square foot home. This is quite a bit of house at your cost! Your actual cost per square foot will obviously depend on the quality of your materials and the extras that you include. Only after your cost take-off will you know what your house will cost, but this figure will give you an idea of the size house you can afford. Keep your square footage figure in mind when deciding on a house design.

BUILDING VS. REMODELING

If you're looking to save money, you might be considering remodeling an old home instead of building a new one. This can be especially attractive if a low interest loan can be assumed on the property. Examine this option carefully. Remodeling can have many pitfalls! Virtually all information in this manual, except for the discussion of buying land, is useful to remodelers.

Advantages of Remodeling

- Low interest rates can sometimes be assumed on older homes.

- There is potential for finding good bargains.

- The property can usually be occupied sooner than new construction can.

- Tax laws provide numerous incentives for remodeling, especially in areas designated as historical districts.

- Additional money can be saved by doing much of the work yourself.

AMOUNT OF MORTGAGE PER $100 MONTHLY PAYMENT						
	10 YR. LOAN	15 YR. LOAN	20 YR. LOAN	25 YR. LOAN	30 YR. LOAN	35 YR. LOAN
5.5%	9,214	12,239	14,537	16,284	17,612	18,621
6.0%	9,007	11,850	13,958	15,521	16,679	17,538
6.5%	8,807	11,480	13,413	14,810	15,821	16,552
7.0%	8,613	11,126	12,898	14,149	15,031	15,653
7.5%	8,424	10,787	12,413	13,532	14,302	14,831
8.0%	8,242	10,464	11,955	12,956	13,628	14,079
8.5%	8,065	10,155	11,523	12,419	13,005	13,389
9.0%	7,894	9,859	11,114	11,916	12,428	12,755
9.5%	7,728	9,576	10,728	11,446	11,893	12,171
10.0%	7,567	9,306	10,362	11,005	11,395	11,632
10.5%	7,411	9,047	10,016	10,591	10,932	11,134
11.0%	7,260	8,798	9,688	10,203	10,501	10,673
11.5%	7,113	8,560	9,377	9,838	10,098	10,245
12.0%	6,970	8,332	9,082	9,495	9,722	9,847
12.5%	6,832	8,113	8,802	9,171	9,370	9,476
13.0%	6,697	7,904	8,536	8,867	9,040	9,131
13.5%	6,567	7,702	8,282	8,579	8,730	8,808
14.0%	6,441	7,509	8,042	8,307	8,440	8,506
14.5%	6,318	7,323	7,813	8,050	8,166	8,223
15.0%	6,198	7,145	7,594	7,807	7,909	7,957
15.5%	6,082	6,974	7,386	7,577	7,666	7,707
16.0%	5,970	6,809	7,188	7,359	7,436	7,471
16.5%	5,860	6,650	6,998	7,152	7,219	7,249
17.0%	5,754	6,498	6,818	6,955	7,014	7,040
17.5%	5,650	6,351	6,645	6,768	6,820	6,841
18.0%	5,550	6,210	6,480	6,590	6,635	6,654
18.5%	5,452	6,073	6,322	6,421	6,460	6,476
19.0%	5,357	5,942	6,170	6,259	6,294	6,307
19.5%	5,264	5,816	6,025	6,105	6,135	6,147
20.0%	5,174	5,694	5,886	5,958	5,984	5,994

Table 1. Affordable mortgage amounts

Disadvantages of Remodeling

- Many sub-contractors are hesitant to do remodeling because of the hassles involved. Good remodeling contractors are hard to find and many require payment by the hour.

- The cost of remodeling may be hard to determine before starting the project due to hidden factors (rotten wood, air infiltration, foundation flaws, poor wiring, poor plumbing, etc.).

- The improvements on the house may raise its value above that of the surrounding neighborhood. The value of neighboring homes may hold down the resale value of your home. Consider though that this can also work in your favor if you buy the smallest home in the area.

- Appraisers have a hard time determining the final value of a home before remodeling is done.

- Future utility costs are usually higher due to inferior insulation. This can be difficult or impossible to improve.

- Remodeling is more suited to someone who plans to do much of the work himself.

- If you plan to remodel an existing home, get several bids from remodeling subs and have the house inspected carefully before making your purchase offer. Then make your sales contract contingent on a good appraisal, approval of the remodeling loan and the discovery of no hidden defects.

Estimating Remodeling Costs

If you contract a "remodeling specialist", you are paying retail costs. He will be his own general contractor on your project. Often, their bids will range from 2-3 times the sum of material and labor costs. By doing your own contracting, your cost will normally be a fraction of this.

WHAT TYPE OF HOME SHOULD YOU BUILD?

Fit the Home to Your Lifestyle

Up front, some people choose their home based on what they believe other people like. Of course, this defeats the purpose of "having your own castle". Make sure that you consider what you want based on the way you live.

Before deciding on a plan, make a list of those features you find most valuable to your own style of living. This will be your set of criteria for evaluating plans. Do you like a formal setting or a more rustic

environment? Is a formal dining room or living room important to you? What are your family considerations? Listed below are some suggestions to keep in mind when making your planning decision.

- Eliminate as many hallways and walls as possible. Hallways waste building materials and add to heated space while making a house seem smaller.

- Combining living and dining rooms into one room will make a smaller home seem more spacious and will cut down on building materials needed for separating walls.

- Place the kitchen near the garage or driveway for easy access when bringing in groceries.

- Two story and split level homes are generally less expensive to build than ranch style houses of the same square footage because there is less roof and foundation to build.

- Make sure the inside of the kitchen cannot be seen while entering or sitting in the living area.

- Use closets as sound buffers between rooms.

- Avoid house plans that have many different sizes of windows. During purchasing, delivery and installation, many mismatches can occur.

Energy Considerations

The energy efficiency of a home can be greatly improved with a little advance planning. Listed below are a few energy considerations:

- A window's insulating ability is much lower than that of a typical wall. Reducing the amount of window coverage will increase insulating efficiency. This can be done by reducing the number of windows (which also saves money) or the size of each window. Wooden windows, although more expensive, tend to insulate better than metal ones. Choose double or triple pane windows or use storm windows for the best insulation possible.

- Make sure insulation has a vapor barrier — either foil-backed insulation or a sheet of plastic placed between the interior drywall and insulation. The vapor barrier prevents condensation from building up in the wall.

- Framing your exterior walls with 2x6's 24" on center will allow 6" batts of insulation in exterior walls, but will cost more in lumber costs. Also, framing doors and windows can be a problem with 6" walls. Another way to achieve a higher insulation value is to use thinner walls but more efficient exterior sheathing such as foil backed urethane.

■ Orient your building site so that the exterior walls with the smallest window area face north. Southern exposure to sunlight will allow more solar heat gain during the day.

■ Planting hardwoods near the house will provide shade in the summer, but will allow the sun to shine through in the winter when the leaves fall. Don't plant trees too close to foundations, driveways, patios or walkways to prevent cracks.

■ The two most efficient heating systems are gas heat and heat pumps. Gas heaters are cheaper to install and are simpler to maintain; however, heat pumps use less energy to operate. As gas prices are deregulated, heat pumps will become an even greater bargain. Heat pumps lose their efficiency where winter temperatures stay below 30 degrees. In this type of climate, gas heat may be better.

■ The importance of caulking air leaks cannot be over-emphasized. Air infiltration can contribute up to 40% of a home's heat loss. Buy a can of urethane spray insulation and caulk around doors, windows, electrical outlets, switch plates and pipes during construction.

SAVING ON FOUNDATIONS

Choosing the proper foundation can save money. The foundations listed below are the four major foundation types. They are listed in order from the least expensive to the most expensive. See the section on foundations for further information.

All Wood Foundation

An all wood foundation can be installed at any time of the year and saves labor costs because only one sub-contractor (carpenter) is used. Acceptable for crawl spaces and full basements.

Monolithic Slab

A monolithic slab is the least expensive concrete foundation and a good choice for quality and savings. Work can be completed quickly for additional savings. Care must be taken to position plumbing accurately before casting in concrete.

Cinder Block

Cinder block is somewhat cheaper than concrete but requires the use of several different sub-contractors. This causes a longer completion period and more complications. Not as strong as concrete and more vulnerable to leaks.

Poured Concrete

Poured concrete is the best choice for full basements due to high strength and resistance to leakage. It is the most expensive type, but time and money can be saved because only one sub-contractor is used.

COORDINATING SUB-CONTRACTORS

The task of timing and coordinating subs can be difficult but can yield savings by reducing construction time. In some instances, promoting cooperation between subs can make their jobs easier and give you a reason to bargain for a lower price. One example would be coordinating the painter and trim carpenter. If trim and walls are to be of a different color, then have the painter put on his primer coats before trim and doors are installed. Primer coats can also be put on trim and doors before they are set. This will save the painter considerable time and effort and will speed up the construction process.

HOUSE PLANS

How many copies? Regardless of how you arrived at a design, you will need plenty of copies of your plan. Plans refer to a standard set of blueprints showing basic elevations of the home and a layout of each floor. Special detail plans will be covered later in this section. The following is a representative list of the copies you may likely need:

Personal Copies	2
Bank Copy	1
County Inspector	1
HVAC	1
Plumbing	1
Electrical	1
Framing	1
Total	**8**

Sound crazy? Copies are cheap. Normally $10 each after the first one. Don't scrimp here. Get what you need. It's always nice to have that extra clean copy when your originals become ragged from use. You cannot directly make a blueprint from a blueprint.

GENERAL ADVICE

When building your first home, consider using a standard plan, preferably a popular one designed by a reputable architect or plan company. Plans drawn by architects are generally engineered better but are more expensive. If you are staying with a simple, standard layout, home planners and draftsmen's plans are usually fine and much cheaper. Go to the architect if you plan any special layouts such as special foundations or vaulted ceilings. Their expertise will be well worth it. Always use plans with a standard scale such as ¼" to 1'.

If you build again, consider using the same plan again. You'll learn from your mistakes and probably do an even better job. You will also know exactly how much materials are needed. Your costs will be more accurate.

Critically review the kitchen and kitchen cabinet layout. Cabinet layouts are normally there just to meet minimum requirements. You can probably do better. The kitchen design itself may not be the best either.

For sources of house plans, check with builder plan services, architects, draftsmen and new home magazines. Architects and draftsmen usually charge a certain fee per square foot of house.

For an additional charge, your plan supplier may be able to provide you with a material takeoff. But DO NOT assume it to be accurate.

If you change interior partitions, be careful of any impact on load-bearing walls. Consult an architect if you are in doubt. If you want to finish the basement, opt for a 9' basement ceiling to allow for a dropped ceiling to hide heating ducts.

PLAN CONTENTS

How do you know if your plans are complete? At a

minimum, a set of plans should include the following diagrams:
- Front elevation
- Side elevations (one for each side of home)
- Rear elevation
- Top view of each floor (floor plan)
- Detailed layout of kitchen cabinets
- Detailed foundation, footings and framing specifications

Special Detail Plans

Although you have a set of blueprints, they may not include the following:
- Mechanical layout (HVAC and ductwork)
- Electrical layout
- Plumbing layout

These are normally done by the respective subs, based in part on your specific lifestyle, tastes and ideas. Your blueprints may also include:
- Detail cabinetry layout
- Trim detail layout
- Detail tile plan
- Window and door schedule
- Detail roof plan

DETAIL CABINET LAYOUT — This should include a final layout of each specific cabinet you plan to have in the kitchen, including style, finish and placement. All cabinetry in bath areas, such as vanities, must also be spelled out.

TRIM DETAIL LAYOUT — This should include a room-by-room schedule of what trim is used where. Base, chair rail, crown and other decorative molding as well as paneling should be described in detail. Specific material finishes should also be covered. Trim detail layouts are not usually included with most standard plans.

DETAIL TILE PLAN — This should include diagrams showing areas to be covered with particular types of tile. All tiled shower stalls, bathtub areas, tiled walls and floors should be covered. Also, all fixtures such as mirrors, soap dishes, safety rails, towel racks, tissue roll holders, toothbrush and tumbler holders, medicine cabinets and related fixtures. Grout types and colors also need to be determined.

WINDOW AND DOOR SCHEDULE — Itemized list of all window types and dimensions. Make sure that if you plan to have shutters you have adequate room between window sets for the shutters (normally 12" or 15"). Also make sure you have symmetrical spacing between windows where applicable. Check before construction and during the construction process.

DETAIL ROOF PLAN — This plan is helpful, especially with complicated hip roofs. It consists of a framing diagram showing opening dimensions, hips, valleys, ridges, roof pitch, ridge venting and skylights.

CHANGES

After you have selected your plans, consider special changes such as zoned heating/AC, passive solar, special wall partitions, window modifications, special cabinetry, etc. Your original drawings should provide the basis for any details, refinements or other changes you wish to make. When you decide to change a plan, mark the change on the plan with a red permanent marker. (This will keep the change from smearing if the plans get wet.) Make sure when making changes on plans that you mark ALL the sets of plans to eliminate costly problems later. Many lenders require that houses be built exactly as the plans indicate.

OTHER DETAILS

- Look for 42" wide halls when possible.

- If you are installing a basement, specify a 9' ceiling. This will make it easier to finish later.

- Make sure the room layout accents large furniture fixtures that will be present in the room, ie., dining room table or master bed.

- Make sure the space left for stairs allow the proper number of steps. A 9' ceiling needs several more steps in the stairway than an 8' ceiling.

Figure 1. Kitchen layouts: A, U-type; B, L-type; C, "parallel wall" type; D, side wall type.

PLANS AND SKETCHES
1 SQUARE = ¼"=____

PLANS AND SKETCHES
1 SQUARE = ¼"=____

Dealing with Material Suppliers

DEALING WITH LARGER COMPANIES offers advantages due to potential savings passed on as a result of volume purchasing. Larger companies may offer wider selections than their smaller counterparts. Larger companies have a larger reputation to protect. Hence your satisfaction is of great importance.

DEAL DIRECT WITH MANUFACTURERS when possible. Companies that specialize in windows, doors, carpet, bricks or other such items may provide you with merchandise at close to wholesale prices. Be prepared to pick many of these purchases up yourself since delivery may be costly or unavailable.

LIMIT THE NUMBER OF VENDORS YOU DEAL WITH in order to reduce confusion, building accounts and persons you must deal with. Dealing with a few vendors may mean special discounts due to larger volume purchasing.

OPEN BUILDER ACCOUNTS at your suppliers. You are a builder! And builders get discounts. Also, builders don't deal with retail sales personnel. Most large material supply houses have special contract sales personnel in the back of the store. Builder accounts often imply special payment schedules. For example, in one case you may pay the open balance on the first of each month. In this case it is to your advantage to purchase your materials early in the month to gain a full month's use of the money. The time value of money is on your side in this case. Paying accounts within a specified period is a sure-fire way to earn early payment discounts. Keep track of them and earn them. That's money in your pocket.

INSPECT MATERIAL as it arrives on site. If something is damaged or just doesn't look right, insist on having it returned for exchange or credit. This is normal and expected: you're paying good money and

you should expect good quality material in good condition. Indicate returned items on the bill of lading as proof. Generally, once installed, the materials are your responsibility. This includes such items as doors, tubs, sinks, etc.

GET SEVERAL BIDS on all expensive items or whenever you feel you could do better. The old saying "Only one thing has one price: a postage stamp" is alive and well in the building material business. Shop around and chances are, you'll find a better price. Check with the local builders in your area and ask them where they buy their materials.

DETERMINE WHAT IS RETURNABLE. In the normal course of construction, you will more than likely order too many of certain items accidentally or on purpose to avoid delays due to shortages. Find out what overages can be returned to suppliers. Ask for written return policies. Certain cardboard cartons, seals, wrapping or steel bands may need to be intact for an item to be returnable. There may be minimum returnable quantities for such items as bricks in full skids (1000 units). Restocking charges may also be incurred when returning materials.

MANAGE YOUR PURCHASES WITH PURCHASE ORDERS. Explain to your suppliers up front that you plan to control purchases with "P.O.s" and that you will not pay any invoice without a purchase order number on it. Purchase orders help to ensure that you receive what you ordered and no more. Make sure to use two-part forms. This makes it impossible for someone to create or alter a form. Pre-numbered purchase orders are available at most local office supply stores.

MINIMIZE INVENTORY and schedule your material deliveries with the project schedule as best you can. This is easier said than done. Minimizing the materials on site minimizes your investment and exposure to theft or damage. Most material suppliers will be glad to store purchased items for you and deliver them when ready for use. Fragile materials such as drywall and windows are good examples of items not to have lying around too long. Try to be on site when material is delivered. Write special delivery instructions on purchase orders. You're the customer; you make the rules.

HAVE MATERIALS DROPPED CLOSE TO WHERE THEY WILL BE USED in order to save time. Bricks, loads of sand and gravel are good examples. Place bricks around the house to reduce handling. Have delivery men move plywood, drywall and other heavy items to the second floor if that is where they will be used. Make sure to write your delivery instructions and directions to the site on the purchase order.

KEEP MATERIALS PROTECTED from weather by covering them with plastic or keeping them inside whenever possible. The garage is a great place to keep millwork, doors, windows and other valuable items that shouldn't get wet. Lumber, especially plywood, is susceptible to water damage. Lumber should be covered with heavy-duty plastic and should be ordered shortly before it will be used. Bricks and mortar should be covered carefully with plastic. Wet mortar is ruined and is difficult to throw away. Many suppliers will allow you to purchase materials and keep them in their warehouses until you need them. Rocks, brick or scrap wood should be used to hold the plastic down on windy days.

PROTECT MATERIALS FROM THEFT. You should not have material suppliers deliver until shortly before the material is needed. With stacks of plywood, some builders put a long wood screw through the top corners of the top sheet. If someone wants a sheet, he'll have to haul off four at a time. This usually stops kids. Make sure to lock up all movable items in a storeroom or basement. You will want to install the locks on your house as soon as possible to protect interior items from theft. Instead of giving subs keys, unlock in the morning and lock in the evening.

GET DISCOUNTS from early payments. Many suppliers give a percentage discount if full payment is made by the end of the month, the beginning of the month or within 30 days of purchase. Make sure you don't lose these discounts. Take advantage of them because they can really add up. Deal with lumber yards and other suppliers who provide payment discounts.

USE FLOAT as much as possible. Many suppliers will invoice you at a certain period each month and will only charge you a finance charge thirty days later. If you pick up materials at the beginning of the month and they invoice you for them at the end of the month, you have had thirty days' free use of their money.

ORDER EARLY FOR PROMPT DELIVERY. Orders are normally queued up for next day delivery. The earlier in the day you get your order in, the earlier your shipment should arrive the next day. Ask each supplier for a reliable delivery time.

GIVE PLANS TO YOUR LUMBER SUPPLIER. In many areas, you can arrange for your supplier salesman to drop by the site every other day or so to keep your framing crew properly stocked.

Dealing with Labor and Subs

Labor generally refers to employees who are working for you and have employment tax and withholding taken from their pay. If you use employees, get a good bookkeeping service to figure withholding taxes for you. The sub-contractors you use are in business for themselves and withhold their own taxes. Your subs may consist of workers who supply labor only, such as framers and masons, or businesses that provide materials and labor, such as heating and air conditioning contractors. Use contractors whenever possible to avoid the paperwork headaches that go along with payroll accounting. Using contract labor will also save you money because you are not paying their withholding taxes. The IRS may require you to file a "1099" form on your subs. This form shows the amount you paid your subs so that the IRS can be sure that they are paying their share of taxes. Check with a Certified Public Accountant to obtain the proper forms.

LOCATING WORKERS

Finding good subs and labor is an art. The following is a surefire list of sources for locating subs and getting you on the right track of determining which is the best combination of skill, honesty and price:

- JOB SITES—(an excellent source because you can see their work.) As your building site shows progress, it will act as a billboard, attracting all sorts of subs looking for work.

- REFERENCES FROM BUILDERS AND OTHER SUB-CONTRACTORS

- THE YELLOW PAGES—Look under specific titles. Do this only when you are in a pinch because these folks always seem to charge a bit more.

- CLASSIFIED ADS—Here you can normally bargain more than when you meet them at a job site.

- ON THE ROAD—Look for phone numbers on trucks — busy subs are normally good subs.

- MATERIAL SUPPLY HOUSES keep lists of approved subs. Many of them keep a bulletin board where subs leave their business cards.

References are essential in the homebuilding business. Nobody should earn a good reputation without showing good work and satisfied customers. Insist on at least three references; one of them being their last job. If their last reference is four months old, it may be their last good reference. Some feel that companies which use a person's name as the title, such as "A. J. SMITH'S ROOFING" will tend to be a "safe" choice over "XYZ ROOFING" under the premise that a man's name follows his reputation. But this obviously cannot be taken at face value. Contact references and inspect the work. You may even wish to ask the customer what he paid for the job, although this may sometimes be awkward. A good local standing is essential.

BACKGROUND INFORMATION

Acquiring reference information should be a rule. It is not a bad idea to have your "candidate" sub-contractors fill out a brief form in order for you to find out a little about them. By asking the right questions, you can get a fairly good idea of what type of character they are.

ACCESSIBILITY

It is important to be able to reach your subs. Try not to hire subs who live too far away. If they need to make a quick visit to fix something, it may not be worth their time. Your subs must have a home phone where they can be reached.

PAYING SUBS

When you have your checkbook out to pay your subs, remember LESTER'S LAW—"The quality of a man's work is directly proportional to the size of his investment." If you want your subs to defy human nature and do the best job possible, then give them motivation. *Do not pay any sub-contractor until you are completely satisfied with his work and materials.* Once you have paid him, you have killed all his incentive to perform for you. After you have paid him, do not expect to see him again in your life. Subs make money by getting lots of jobs, not by taking time on one job. Make each of your subs earn his pay. Below is a suggested schedule for payment:

■ 45% after rough-in.

■ 45% after finish work complete and inspected.

■ 10% retainage held for about two weeks after finish work. (This is to protect yourself if something is detected a bit later.)

Let them know your pay schedule in writing before you seal the deal.

PAYING CASH

Paying with cash gets results. Telling a sub that "you will pay him in cash upon satisfactory completion of his job" should be ample incentive for him to get the job done — and may motivate him to do a good job to boot! Make sure when obtaining cash for work that you keep documentation of the work done for the IRS! Write a check in the sub's name and have him cosign it. Then cash the check. This way you will have an "audit trail" to prove that you paid the sub for work done.

BE FAIR

Be fair with money. Pay what you promise. Be discretionary with payments. Pay your subs and labor as work is completed. Not everyone can go a week or two without a little money. It is customary to pay major subs, such as plumbers, HVAC subs and electricians, 40% after rough-in and the remaining 60% after final inspection and approval. This keeps the "pot sweet". If you pay subs too much too early their incentive to return may diminish. If he doesn't return you'll have to pay another sub a healthy sum to come in and finish the job. Some subs may not even guarantee work they didn't do completely. NEVER PAY SUBS FOR MORE THAN THE WORK THAT HAS ALREADY BEEN DONE. Give them a reason to come back and finish the job.

SPECIFICATIONS

Don't count on getting anything you don't ask for in writing. *REMEMBER: NOT WRITTEN, NOT SAID.* A list of detailed specifications reduces confusion between you and your sub and will reduce call backs and extra costs. Different subs have different ways of doing things. Make sure they do it YOUR way.

PAPERWORK

Remember that many subs live from week to week and despise paperwork. You will have difficulty getting many subs to present bids or sign affidavits. Many are stubborn and believe that "their word is their bond". You must use discretion in requiring these items. Generally your more skilled trades such as HVAC, Electrical and Plumbing will be more business-like and will cooperate more fully with your accounting procedures. These trades are the most important to get affidavits from because they purchase goods from other suppliers that become part of your house. Labor-only subs need not sign affidavits. Make sure that all your subs provide you with an invoice for work done and have them sign it PAID IN FULL. This practice will save you many headaches later.

LICENSES

Depending upon who you have work for you, you may want them to furnish a business license. If required, make sure that plumbers, electricians, HVAC subs and other major subs are licensed to work in your county; if not, have them pay to obtain the license or get another sub.

ARRANGEMENTS FOR MATERIALS

Material arrangements must be agreed upon in a signed, written specification. If subs are to pay for all materials or some of the materials, this must all be spelled out in detail. If a sub is supposed to supply materials, make sure he isn't billing the materials to your account, expecting you to pay for them later. (Refer to Lien Waivers in the Legal section.) If you are to supply the materials, make sure they are at the site ahead of time and that there is sufficient material to do the job. This will be appreciated by the subs and will generate additional cooperation in the future.

Ask your sub about any special materials he needs. For instance, many framers use nail guns, which require special nails. Make sure to take this into consideration when ordering materials.

KEEP YOUR OPTIONS OPEN

Don't count on one excavator, framing crew, plumber or anyone for that matter. Have at least one or two back-up subs who can fill in when the primary doesn't show up or does not please you. It is best to be up front with your primaries; let them know that you plan to count on them and expect them to live up to their word. If they can't be there to do the work, skip to your second string subs.

BE FLEXIBLE WITH TIME

Because of variables in weather, subs and their work, expect some variation in work schedule. Chances are, they are doing four or five other jobs at the same time. Expect some problems in getting the right guy at exactly the right time.

EQUIPMENT

Your work specifications should specify that subs are to provide their own tools including extension cords, ladders, scaffolding, power tools, saw horses, etc. Before hiring a sub, make sure he has all the tools. Don't plan on furnishing them. Defective tools you supply can make you liable for injuries incurred when using them. If you don't have sawhorses available for your framing crew and if they didn't bring any, count on them spending their first ten minutes cutting up your best lumber to make a few.

WORKER'S COMPENSATION

Make sure your sub's worker's compensation policy is up to date before the job is started and get a copy for your records. If the sub doesn't have worker's compensation make it clear to him that you intend to withhold a portion of his payment to cover the expense. This can be a sore spot later if you forget to arrange this in advance.

Worker's compensation should be deducted from each check when paying a sub more than once. Typically, you must set a deduction percentage that matches the rate for the particular sub. Check with your insurance agent to determine the proper percentage.

POOR WORKMANSHIP

This can be one of your worst headaches. A sub you've contracted is halfway through a job and you notice poor workmanship. The work will have to be completely redone, so you fire the sub. He may file a lien on the project, halting or hindering further progress. Make sure you inspect often and well; and know your subs!

STANDARD BIDDING PROCESS

Most of the steps below will apply to the effort of reaching final written agreements with the subs you will be using. These steps will be referred to in each of the individual trade sections.

BD1 REVIEW your project scrapbook and locate potential sub-contractors.

BD2 FINALIZE all design and material requirements affecting sub-contractor.

BD3 PREPARE standard specifications for job.

BD4 PREPARE sub-contractor packages (Sub-contractor Information Sheet, Standard Contract Terms and Specification Sheet).

BD5 CONTACT sub-contractor and discuss plans. Mention any forms to be completed and specify deadline (should be written on forms). Get a good understanding of who will provide what.

BD6 RECEIVE and evaluate completed bids.

BD7 SELECT the best three bids, based on price and your personal assessment of the sub.

BD8 COMPARE bids against budget.

BD9 NEGOTIATE with prospective sub. Ask him what his best "CASH" price is. When you can't get the price any lower, get more service out of the same cash by asking him to do other items in lieu of a cash discount.

BD10 SELECT sub. Make it clear that he has been selected and that he needs to commit a specific period of time for the job. Explain that you are fair with money but expect good, timely work according to a written contract.

BD11 CONTACT subs and tell them when you expect them at the site. Discuss upcoming schedule and keep in touch with them or you will lose them. If the building schedule changes, let the sub know as soon as possible so that he can make other plans. This courtesy will be returned to you when you need the sub at the last minute.

Making Changes

Changes are second nature. Most people can't even order lunch without changing their minds. We all see things and perceive how they could be made better. That's where a good imagination and careful thought are important. The idea here is to *make changes on paper, then freeze the design.* The cost of ripping out walls, adding windows or "that breakfast counter" can be staggering. In many cases, the cost of making a change after construction makes the change economically impractical. Making changes late in the game is a good way to wreck your budget. So be good to yourself; plan ahead and make all those modifications and additions to your plans, while you're still just using an eraser.

Let's look at three examples. Suppose you have decided to have a bay window in the kitchen as opposed to the original idea of a flat window. For the sake of simplicity, let's assume the two windows are of the same dimensions.

CHANGE DURING PLANNING

You think the change over and decide that the $110 material differential is well worth the money. You take out your eraser and update your drawings, take-off and contract specifications. Not bad.

CHANGE PRIOR TO INSTALLATION

The flat window has been delivered to the site but is uninstalled. Now you will have to negotiate with the sub-contractor who already signed the contract to install the flat window. The sub may charge you a little extra; that's just part of the game. But now you hope that the material supplier will exchange a bay window for a flat one (provided it is still in new condition). You also pay the $110 differential and a restocking fee which was not in your original budget; this is an out-of-pocket expense. The change will cost you money, but at least you aren't undoing work.

CHANGE AFTER INSTALLATION

The flat window has been installed. NOW you (or your spouse) decide to change to a bay window. This could be expensive for several reasons:

- You may have to damage the flat window to remove it so it may not be returnable.

- You have to purchase the bay window, say $700, out-of-pocket. You or the bank didn't count on this.

- You will have to pay to have the flat window removed and the bay window installed. Pray that you didn't paint or wallpaper yet.

In addition, you have to prepare the change order form. Note that in this case you are at the mercy of the sub-contractor. He knows you want the bay window and may charge you heavily for it. If his price is too high, you have three alternatives:

- Pay the man and try to forget this ever happened.

- Do it yourself. This can be dangerous if you don't know what you're doing. If the sub damages the bay window during installation, it's his problem. If you damage it, that bay window may cost you another $200-300.

- Live with the flat window. (This is frustrating. So long as you live in that home, that flat window will be a constant reminder of a careless mistake.)

ADVICE

Think changes over carefully on paper. Really take the time and picture what that drawing represents in real life. Is it what you want?

If you must make changes, decide to act as early as possible. If you make a change, pay for it out-of-pocket; that is, with funds you had not earmarked for the project.

COMMON PITFALLS WHEN MAKING CHANGES

■ When changing ceiling heights, pay close attention to stairs. Added ceiling height changes the number of steps used in a staircase. Make sure you have room for the extended length of the staircase.

■ When walls are moved, play close attention to the effect on load bearing. Load bearing walls cannot be moved easily without providing some other means of supporting the wall. Even small changes in walls can make a big difference. Most walls are located directly above and below each other. If you move a wall one or two feet, the floor between them may sag over time.

■ Any changes to walls in the house can affect the roof framing. Check with a home designer or an architect when moving any wall.

■ When adding shutters to windows, make sure that the window spacing will allow it without changing the balance or symmetry of the house.

■ Examine the door swing of each door in the house. Moving a door may cause the door to block entrances or other doors when open.

■ Adding brick to the outside of a house designed for siding will change the spacing and size of the foundation and roof overhang. Take this into consideration.

Saving Money

Aside from the obvious ways to save money on a home, such as building yourself and reduction of square footage, other measures can be taken to minimize the cost of your home without compromising on quality. Let's look at a few ways to save more money before, during and after construction.

SAVING MONEY BEFORE CONSTRUCTION

The most effective means here are:

- Shop for prices aggressively

- Plan your home to minimize waste (modular construction)

- Plan for extras later

- Plan your home without extras

- Build closer to the street

- Minimize the house's "footprint"

Shop for Prices Aggressively

This means not accepting bids as being the best job for the best price until you are satisfied. Use your take-off to help keep prices down. Subs are out there to earn a living; and they will try to get the best price possible. If you say the price is right, it's a done deal. Don't be too anxious to give in. The more you save over your estimate early in the game, the more "cushion" you'll have later for unexpected expenses.

Plan Your Home to Minimize Waste

This means going below the surface. Here is an example:

Carpet normally comes in 12' rolls. In estimating your job, a carpet sub will charge you for any and all scrap necessary to carpet designated areas. When possible, plan rooms to be twelve feet wide or 24' long. This reduces waste significantly.

Use Modular Construction

Blueprints are often designed with esthetic purposes in mind. That's O.K., but remember that many materials, lumber especially, are designed around 16", 24" and 48" units. To a reasonable extent, plan your home to be composed of 24" or 48" units, eliminating waste and cutting time. Refer to the framing section, which describes this approach in more detail.

Plan for Extras Later

Almost anyone would like to have all or some of the following items in their home:

- Built-in microwave
- Intercom system
- Central vacuum system
- Electronic alarm/security systems
- Skylights
- Finished bonus room(s)
- Patio or deck
- Swimming pool and hot tub
- Electric garage door opener
- Crown and other fancy molding
- Wallcoverings
- Sidewalk or other paved area
- Expensive landscaping
- Den paneling and built-in bookcases
- Wet bars (stub in plumbing)
- Paved driveway/garage door
- Gas grill

But these items, and many others, are not essential to getting a Certificate of Occupancy. Don't strain to pay for items you can easily add later. Minimize that mortgage! Smarter individuals learn to live without certain luxuries and add them later when a little cash is available. The trick is to prepare for extras by doing work that is difficult or impossible to add later.

If you want a gas grill, run the gas line NOW and cap it. Gas lines, plumbing and wiring are fairly inexpensive to put in during construction and will wait for you until you are ready to add those extras.

Plan Your Home Without Extras
Still, certain other extras can be avoided altogether. These include such items as basements, bay windows, brick veneer, an extra room or a fireplace, expensive cabinetry, etc. While it may be nice to have them, they may be the difference between a lesser home and no home at all.

Basements, for example, can easily cost you 5 to 7% of the cost of your home. Do you want a basement? Do you need a basement? Many only have one for possible resale purposes. No basement is better than a leaky, damp and smelly one.

Build Closer to the Street
Moving the house closer to the street will reduce the cost of the driveway and front yard landscaping. The additional benefit will be a bigger backyard — an added plus with modern houses. Just make sure that you meet the minimum setback requirements.

Reduce the Footprint of the House
The smaller the footprint of the house, the smaller (and less expensive) the foundation. How do you reduce a house's footprint without reducing its size? By using cantilevers. Bay windows, breakfast areas and fireplaces can all be extended out from the house 4' or more. These cantilevers also serve to break up the straight lines of the house — adding more stylistic variety.

Watch for Extra Costs of Larger Houses
Larger homes carry with them additional hidden costs. If a 2,000 square foot house built at $40 per sf. costs $80,000, then why doesn't a 4,000 square foot home cost over $160,000? Home costs aren't directly related only to square footage. The additional size of larger rooms in large houses is mostly made up of air and does not add costs linearly. However, many other factors contribute to adding extra costs to larger houses:

■ Larger homes typically require larger rooms with corresponding longer spans for floor and ceiling joists. Longer pieces of lumber cost more per board foot than shorter pieces. Longer spans may also require thicker lumber in order to carry the weight over the longer spans.

■ Larger homes tend to have higher ceilings — 9', 10', 12' and up. Longer studs cost more per square foot. Taller rooms use more drywall, paint, trim, etc.

■ Larger homes tend to have more structural weight, which often means thicker joists, steel support and I-beams; all of which add to the cost.

■ Larger homes have larger and fancier doors, windows and trim.

■ Larger kitchens mean more and fancier cabinetry.

SAVING MONEY DURING CONSTRUCTION
The most effective ways here are:

• Do work yourself
• Economize with framing
• Make pre-fabricated substitutions
• Downgrade

Do Work Yourself
This can be lots of fun. You'll feel (and be) helpful, while saving even more money. In most cases, every hour you spend productively on site can save you 10 to 15 dollars. Great! But be careful. There are two main reasons why you shouldn't get carried away with doing too much of the work yourself:

■ There are many jobs you shouldn't even consider doing. Remember, where special skills are needed, skilled tradesmen serve an important purpose: they accomplish professional results and save you from injury, expensive mistakes, frustration and wasted time. Certain jobs may only appear easy. You can ruin your health sanding hardwood floors or drywall. You can ruin a den trying to put up raised paneling and crown molding.

■ Work can distract from your more important job of overseeing the work of others. Your most valuable skill is that of BOSS — scheduler, inspector, coordinator and referee. Saving $50 performing a small chore could cost you even more than that in terms of problems caused by oversight elsewhere on the site. Doing lots of work yourself invariably extends your project timetable. Let the pros do the job quickly.

Jobs to Consider Doing Yourself

- Paint, sand and fill
- Wallpaper
- Install door and light fixtures
- Install mailbox
- Light landscaping
- Light trimwork
- Clean-up
- Organizing materials and locating them where needed (stack bricks where masons will use them, etc.)

Jobs Better Left to Pros

- Framing
- Masonry
- Electrical
- HVAC
- Roofing
- Cabinetwork
- Plumbing
- All others not listed

Economize With Framing

Since framing is hidden, appearance is not an issue — only workmanship and safety. You can use utilty grade lumber for many non-loadbearing parts of the house, such as window and door jacks and cripples. Look for used lumber from a demolition project. Sometimes this older lumber is superior to new lumber and can be used for other trim work where a "rustic" effect is desired.

Make Prefab Substitutions

Many items, such as fireplaces, can be purchased as pre-fabricated units. This saves you labor costs. When pre-fabricated items are used, make sure the sub knows of this and takes it into consideration in his bid. One-piece fiberglass shower and tub enclosures, attic staircases and pre-hung doors are other examples.

Downgrade If Necessary

Certain items can make a major impact on cost reduction without making a visible impact on your home. Consider hollow vs. solid core doors, pre-fabricated cabinets vs. custom cabinets, pre-fabricated doors and windows vs. custom doors and windows to name a few of your options. Another example is trim. Trim that will be stained will show all imperfections, so it should be as high a grade as possible. But if you plan to paint the molding, use "finger-joint" grade. This is molding made of lots of little scrap pieces glued together. It costs less, but will serve the purpose.

Windows with true divided panes are more expensive than solid pane windows with "fake" wood pane inserts. In most cases the fake panes look just as good and have the added benefit of easier window cleaning and better insulation.

Brick provides a great look to the house but is very expensive. If you use brick, consider bricking only the front of the house — that part visible from the street. Use siding on the back side.

SAVING MONEY AFTER CONSTRUCTION

Here, savings are small, but every little bit helps:

- Clean up yourself
- Move in yourself as early as possible

Cleaning Up

Cleaning up yourself can save you money. Normally, a cleaning crew works on a home for hours before it goes on sale. This is work you can do yourself for sure. Treat yourself (and your family) to dinner out after finishing this one. Scraping windows with razor blades, paint touch-up and trash hauling will take days.

Burn or bury trash if you can. It is cheaper than hauling off the material. Check your local county ordinances for rules of burning and burying. Save small lumber pieces that may be used by trim carpenters, plumbers or electricians.

If you burn material in your yard, follow proper safety procedures. Don't burn on dry or windy days.

Don't burn roofing materials or plastics. Don't leave the fire unattended and keep a source of water handy for spot fires.

Moving In

Most likely, you will build in the same city (or nearby) where you live during the project. Moving yourself can save hundreds of dollars. You can save yourself a little rent if you move in early and "finish up" while you're at home. You should ask the local building inspector about minimum requirements for occupancy.

Safety and Inspections

INSPECTIONS AND INSPECTORS

During the course of your project, you will probably run into two primary type of inspectors:

■ County and local officials

■ Financial institutions

In general, inspectors are on your side. They are there to help ensure that critical work meets minimum safety and structural standards. Hence, in many cases, an approved inspection does not assure you that a job has been done properly. If certain work fails inspection, you will be required to correct it, re-schedule the inspection and probably pay a re-inspection fee.

County and Local Officials

A certain number of inspections are normally required by state or county officials during the construction process. When you apply for your building permit, ask for a schedule of required inspections. Although actual inspection points will vary from place to place, your inspections will probably include some of the critical inspection points listed below in order of occurence:

■ Before pouring concrete footings

■ Before pouring concrete foundation

■ After framing rough-in

■ After electrical, HVAC and plumbing rough-in

■ After laying sewer or septic tank lines and before filling in

■ Final completion

Financial Institutions

If you borrowed money from a financial institution for your project, they have an active interest in seeing that the money is being spent properly, as intended,

and at a rate such that the money is used up just as the project is being completed. In addition to requiring approval of state and local inspections, bank inspectors will normally want to examine the site each time a loan draw is requested. As your financial institution sees certain phases of work completed, they will release a certain amount of loan money based on the percentage of completion of the project. Hence, they will make sure that you have "earned" the right to use their money as intended. Each lender sets up their own "draw schedule" allowing a certain percentage for each construction task.

Pre-inspection

Nobody enjoys unpleasant surprises. Before you have anyone show up for an inspection, make sure that you are ready to pass the inspection. Check the work yourself. Use checklists and your subs. This will insure that the formal inspection turns out to be a mere formality. This eliminates rejected inspections, embarrassment, re-inspection fees and a bad builder reputation. Inspectors will see you in a favorable light if you are always fully prepared for their inspections. Your major subs — plumbers, HVAC and electricians — normally schedule their own inspections, but you should follow up.

GUIDELINES FOR WORKING WITH INSPECTORS

■ MAKE sure the work to be inspected is ready for inspection.

■ DETERMINE how much advance notice is required and always give proper advance notice.

■ NOTIFY the inspector to cancel or reschedule the inspection if work is not ready.

■ BE present for the inspection so that you can determine exactly what is incorrect and what must be done to correct it if necessary. If you don't proceed in this manner, you may have to wait for a form letter in the mail and then follow up.

■ STAY on good terms with all your inspectors. Be friendly and courteous. Don't argue when they ask for something to be fixed. They can give you good advice. Cooperate!

■ HAVE the site looking clean. This will put your inspector in a good frame of mind and will let him know that you are organized and efficient.

PROJECT SAFETY

Few disasters can affect your project more adversely than the death or severe injury of you, one of your subs, a neighbor's child or a building partner on site. As they say, "Project safety is no accident". Hence, project safety should play a MAJOR part in your overall project planning and routine supervision. The best way to make sure that serious accidents don't happen is to make safety a big issue with your subs. Remain aware of safety and emphasize this to your workers and site visitors.

You should have builder's risk insurance covering your building site and accidents that may occur there.

SITE SAFETY CHECKLIST

☐ Site safety rules communicated to all subs.

☐ First aid kit available? Familiar with basic first aid practices.

☐ Phone numbers for police, ambulance and fire-house available.

☐ Temporary electrical service grounded.

☐ All electrical tools grounded.

☐ All electrical cords kept away from water.

☐ Warning and danger signs posted in appropriate areas.

☐ Hard hats and steel-tipped shoes worn where needed.

☐ Other protective gear available and used. Goggles, gloves, etc. Always use protective goggles when flying fragments are possible.

☐ Set a good example as a safety-minded individual.

☐ Adequate slope on edges of all ditches and trenches over 5' deep.

☐ Open holes and ditches fenced properly.

☐ Open holes in sub-floor properly covered or protected.

☐ Scaffolding used and secure where needed.

☐ Workers on roof with proper equipment.

☐ Excess and/or flammable scrap not left lying around.

☐ No nails sticking up out of boards or other materials.

☐ Gas cans have spark arrest screens.

☐ Welding tanks shut off tightly when not in use. Stored upright.

☐ Area where welders working checked for smoldering or slow burning wood. Houses have burned down because of this!

☐ Proper clearance from all power lines.

Estimating Costs

The cost estimate or "take-off" will be one of the most time-consuming and important phases of your construction project. Jumping into your first construction project without a realistic estimate of your costs could spell financial disaster. Spend a lot of time working on this one before continuing with your project.

"How in the world do I do a take-off with no previous experience?" A fair question indeed. The information in this section should help you along quite a bit. In addition, *Estimating Home Building Costs* (W.P. Jackson, Craftsman Book Company, 6058 Corte del Cedro, P.O. Box 6500, Carlsbad, CA 92008-0992), is an invaluable and time-saving paperback. Also, this is the time to study your construction books in detail to get a feel for the structure of the building and the amount of materials used in each phase.

The first "materials list" you may come in contact with may be included with your construction plans. These lists are usually offered as an extra at an additional price. As reliable documents, these lists are practically worthless. Many will be inaccurate or based on outdated construction techniques. There is no way of telling whether the list is accurate or not. The best use of this type of take-off is as a checklist while running your own figures.

Another important source of information will come from the sub-contractors you plan to use. These subs are familiar with the type of construction in your area and will be very knowledgeable in calculating the amounts of materials needed. In fact, most of your subs will offer to calculate the amount of materials needed for you. This can be very valuable, especially for framing, because of the sheer number of different materials used. Don't rely solely on your sub's estimate! Make sure to run your own figures to compare against their estimate. Subs have a tendency to overestimate just to be on the safe side. They hate to run out of material and

have to sit around while you run to the supplier for reinforcements. Just make sure that you do add in at least 5-10% waste factor to each estimate.

Another good source of estimating information is your local materials supplier. In previous years, suppliers used to do quite a bit of estimating for their customers. If you can find a supplier who still does this, he is worth his weight in gold.

When figuring your take-off, use the enclosed materials sheet as a checklist to make sure that you don't forget any necessary items. As you figure each item, enter it onto your purchase order forms, taking care to separate materials ordered from different suppliers onto different invoices.

EXCAVATION

Excavation is usually charged by the hour of operating time. Larger loaders rent for higher fees. Determine whether clearing of the lot is necessary and whether or not refuse is to be buried on the site or hauled off. Below are approximate times for loader work. Remember, these are only approximations. Every lot is different and may pose unique problems. Your grader may supply chain saw labor to cut up large trees.

One Half Acre Lot:	Small ldr.	Large ldr.
Clearing trees & shrubs	2-5 hrs.	1-4 hrs.
Digging trash pit	2-4 hrs.	1-3 hrs.
Digging foundation	2-3 hrs.	1-3 hrs.
Grading building site	1-5 hrs.	1-3 hrs.
Total	7-17 hrs.	4-13 hrs.

Larger loaders can be an advantage and can be cheaper in the long run, especially if the lot is heavily wooded or has steep topography. If the lot is flat and sparsely wooded, use the smaller loader for the best price.

CONCRETE

When calculating concrete, it is best to create a formula or conversion factor that will simplify calculations and avoid having to calculate everything in cubic inches and cubic yards. For instance, when pouring a 4" slab, a cubic yard of concrete will cover 81 square feet of area. This is calculated as follows:

1 Cubic Yard = 27 Cubic Feet = 46,656 Cubic Inches

1 Sq. Ft. of Concrete 4" thick = 576 Cubic Inches (12"x12"x4")

46,656 Cu. In. / 576 Cu. In. = 81 Sq. Ft. of Coverage

By doing this equation only once, you now have a simple formula for calculating slabs 4" thick that you can use for driveways, basement floors and slab floors. For instance, to determine the concrete needed for a 1200 sq. ft. slab simply divide by 81.

1200 Sq. Ft. / 81 = 14.8 Cu. Yds. of concrete

NOTE: Always make sure to add a 5 to 10% waste factor to all calculations.

Use this same principle of creating simple formulas for footings, calculating blocks, pouring concrete walls, etc. Just remember to calculate your own set of formulas based on the building codes in your area. For your convenience, refer to the concrete tables to determine the conversion factors for your project.

Footings

Footing contractors will be hired to dig the footings and to supervise pouring of the footings. Footing subs generally charge for labor only and will charge by the lineal foot of footing poured. Pier holes will be extra. You must provide the concrete. These subs may charge more if they provide the forms. If you use a full service foundation company, they will charge you for a turn key job for footing, wall and concrete. This makes estimating easy.

Footings generally must be twice as wide as the wall they support and the height of the footing will be the same as the thickness of the wall. The footing contractor will know the code requirements for your area. Ask him for the dimensions of the footing and then figure an amount of concrete per lineal foot of

Cu. Yds. Concrete needed per lineal foot of footing							
Depth ins.	Width of footing in inches						
	4"	6"	8"	10"	12"	14"	16"
4"	0.004	0.006	0.008	0.010	0.012	0.014	0.016
6"	0.006	0.009	0.012	0.015	0.019	0.022	0.025
8"	0.008	0.012	0.016	0.021	0.025	0.029	0.033
10"	0.010	0.015	0.021	0.026	0.031	0.036	0.041
12"	0.012	0.019	0.025	0.031	0.037	0.043	0.049
14"	0.014	0.022	0.029	0.036	0.043	0.050	0.058
16"	0.016	0.025	0.033	0.041	0.049	0.058	0.066

Table 2. Concrete needed for footings

footing. (See the section on calculating concrete.) Here is a typical calculation for supporting an 8" block wall:

Footing dimension: 8" high x 16" wide

8" x 16" x 12"(1 ft. of footing) = 1536 Cu. In.

46,656 Cu. In. / 1536 Cu. In. = 30.38 lineal ft. of footing per Cu. Yd.

With this size footing, figure one cubic yard of concrete for every 31 lineal feet of footing. Make sure to include 4 extra feet of footing for every pier hole. Add 10% for waste. Refer to the footing table for concrete factors.

Concrete Floors or Slabs

Use the conversion factor of 81 sq. ft. for 4" slabs or basement floors. If your slabs must be more or less than 4" make sure to calculate a new conversion factor or refer to the table.

Monolithic Slabs

Break a one piece slab into two components — the slab and the footing sections; then figure the items separately using the tables.

Block Foundations and Crawl Spaces

Concrete blocks come in many shapes and sizes; the most common being 8"x8"x16". Blocks that are 12" thick are used for tall block walls with backfill in order to provide extra stability. Blocks 8" deep and 12" deep cover the same wall area: .888 sq. ft.

To calculate the amount of block needed, measure the height of the wall in inches and divide by 8" to

Square footage of slab that 1 cu. yd. of concrete will fill			
Slab	**S.F.**	**Slab**	**S.F.**
1 "	324	7 "	46
1 1/2 "	216	7 1/2 "	43
2 "	162	8 "	41
2 1/2 "	130	8 1/2 "	38
3 "	108	9 "	36
3 1/2 "	93	9 1/2 "	34
4 "	81	10 "	32
4 1/2 "	72	10 1/2 "	31
5 "	65	11 "	29
5 1/2 "	59	11 1/2 "	28
6 "	54	12 "	27

Table 3. Cu. Yds. of concrete in slab

find out the height of the wall in numbers of blocks. The height of the wall will always be in even numbers of blocks plus a 4" cap block or 8" half block (for pouring slabs). Cap blocks are solid concrete 4"x8"x16" blocks used to provide a smooth surface to build on. If you are figuring a basement wall, take the perimeter of the foundation and multiply by .75 (3 blocks for every 4 ft.); then multiply this figure by the number of rows of block. To calculate the row of cap block multiply the perimeter of the foundation by .75. Always figure 5-10% waste when ordering block.

If your foundation is a crawl space, your footing is likely to have one or more step downs, or bulkheads, as they are called. Step downs are areas where the footing is dropped or raised the height of one block. This allows the footing to follow the contour of the land. As a result, sections of the block wall will vary in height; requiring more or fewer rows of block. Take each step down section separately and figure 3 blocks for every 4 feet of wall. Multiply the total number of blocks by the total number of rows and then add all sections together for the total number of blocks needed.

Poured Concrete Walls

Your poured wall sub-contractor will charge by the

lineal foot for setting forms. Usually, the price quoted for pouring will include the cost of concrete; but if not, you must calculate the amount of concrete needed. Determine the thickness of the wall from your poured wall sub and find the square foot conversion factor for the number of square feet coverage per cubic yard. Divide this factor into the total square footage of the wall. Example:

8' Poured Concrete Wall x 12" x 12" = 1152 cubic inches per square foot of wall

46656 cubic inches / 1152 cubic inches = 40.5 square foot per cubic yard of concrete

Refer to the concrete wall table to quickly calculate the concrete needed.

Cu. Yds. concrete needed per lineal foot of wall							
Height of wall	**Width of wall in inches**						
	4 "	**6 "**	**8 "**	**10 "**	**12 "**	**14 "**	**16 "**
4 '	0.049	0.074	0.099	0.123	0.148	0.173	0.198
5 '	0.062	0.093	0.123	0.154	0.185	0.216	0.247
6 '	0.074	0.111	0.148	0.185	0.222	0.259	0.296
7 '	0.086	0.130	0.173	0.216	0.259	0.302	0.346
8 '	0.099	0.148	0.198	0.247	0.296	0.346	0.395
9 '	0.111	0.167	0.222	0.278	0.333	0.389	0.444
10 '	0.123	0.185	0.247	0.309	0.370	0.432	0.494
11 '	0.136	0.204	0.272	0.340	0.407	0.475	0.543
12 '	0.148	0.222	0.296	0.370	0.444	0.519	0.593
13 '	0.160	0.241	0.321	0.401	0.481	0.562	0.642
14 '	0.173	0.259	0.346	0.432	0.519	0.605	0.691
15 '	0.185	0.278	0.370	0.463	0.556	0.648	0.741
16 '	0.198	0.296	0.395	0.494	0.593	0.691	0.790
17 '	0.210	0.315	0.420	0.525	0.630	0.735	0.840
18 '	0.222	0.333	0.444	0.556	0.667	0.778	0.889

Table 4. Concrete needed for concrete walls

Brick

To figure the amount of brick needed, figure the square footage of the walls to be bricked and multiply by 6.75. (There are approximately 675 bricks per 100 square feet of wall.) Add 5-10% for waste.

Mortar

Mortar comes premixed in bags of masonry cement, which consist of roughly one part portland cement and one part lime. Each bag requires about 20 shovels of sand when mixing. To calculate the amount of mortar needed for brick, figure one bag of cement for every 125 bricks. For block, figure one bag of cement for every 28 blocks. Make sure to use a good grade of washed sand for a good bonding mortar. Most foundations will require at least 10 cubic yards of sand.

FRAMING

Estimating your framing lumber requirements will be the most difficult estimating task and will require studying the layout and construction techniques of your house carefully. Be sure to have a scaled blueprint of your home as well as a scaled ruler for measuring. Consult with a framing contractor before you begin for advice on size and grade of lumber used in your area.

This is the time you will want to pull out your books on construction techniques and study them to familiarize yourself with the components of your particular house. Local building code manuals will include span tables for determining the maximum spans you are allowed without support. Your blueprints will also list the sizes of many framing members and may include construction detail drawings, which can be especially helpful in determining the size and type of lumber needed for framing.

Floor Framing

Determine the size and length of floor joists by noting the position of piers or beams and by consulting with your framing contractor. Floor joists are usually spaced 16" on center. Joists spaced 12" on center are used for extra sturdy floors. If floor trusses are used, figure 24" on center spacing. Calculate the perimeter of the foundation walls to determine the amount of sill and box sill framing needed.

Calculate the square footage of the floor and divide by 32 (square footage in a 4x8' sheet of plywood) to determine the amount of flooring plywood needed. If the APA Sturdifloor design is used, order ¾" or ⅝" Tongue & Groove Exterior Plywood.

Bridging between floor joists is used to reduce twisting and warping of floor members and to tie the floor together structurally. Bridging is calculated by taking the total number of floor joists and multiplying by

three. This is the lineal feet of bridging needed for one course of bridging. Most floors will require at least two courses of bridging, so double this figure.

If you are using a basement or crawl space, you will probably be using a steel or wood beam to support the floor members. If floor trusses are used, this item may not be needed since floor trusses can span much greater distances. Consult with your local truss manufacturer.

Wall Framing

When calculating wall framing lumber, add together the lineal feet of all interior and exterior walls. Since there is a plate at the bottom of the wall, and a double plate at the tip, multiply wall length by three to get the lineal feet of wall plate needed. Add 10% for waste. For precut wall studs (make sure to get the proper length if precut studs are used, there are many sizes), allow one stud for every lineal foot of wall and 2 studs for every corner. Count all door and window openings as solid wall. This will allow enough for waste and bracing.

Headers are placed over all openings in load bearing walls for structural support and are doubled. Add together the total width of all doors and windows and multiply by two. Check with your framing sub for the proper size header.

The second floor can be calculated the same way as the first floor, taking into consideration the different wall layouts, of course. The second floor of a two story house can be figured the same as a crawl space floor with the exception that the joists will be resting on load bearing walls instead of a beam. This will require drawing a ceiling joist layout.

Roof Framing

If roof trusses are to be used, figure one truss for every 2' of building length, plus one truss. If the roof is a hip roof or has two roof lines that meet at right angles, extra framing for bridging must be added.

The roof truss manufacturer should calculate the actual size and quantity of roof trusses at the site or from blueprints to insure the proper fit. Get him to do this and present a bid and material list during the estimating process.

"Stick building" a roof is much harder to calculate and requires some knowledge of geometry to figure all the lumber needed. A "stick built" roof is one that is built completely from scratch. The simplest way of finding the length of ceiling joists and rafters is to measure them from your scaled blueprints. Always round to the nearest greater even length, since all lumber is sold in even numbered lengths.

If you can't measure the length of the rafter from your plans, you can calculate rafter length and roof area using a conversion factor similar to the one used for concrete. Think of a roof as two identical triangles back-to-back. If you know the length of the triangle base, you can calculate the length of the long side of the triangle (the rafter) by using trigonometry. We have spared you this headache by providing a conversion factor for each roof slope (rise/run). See the accompanying table for this multiplication factor. A 10" slope roof means that the roof rises ten inches for every foot of run (distance). This term is sometimes mistakenly refered to as "10 pitch slope".

To use this table, measure the total width of the house (including roof overhang) from the peak of the roof to the cornice edge. Multiply this by the conversion factor to obtain the rafter length. Don't forget to add in waste for lumber cut from the ends of each rafter (see illustration). This same conversion factor can also be used to calculate roof area for shingles and tar paper. Calculate the total area of the ceiling plus overhang and multiply by the conversion factor to obtain the total roof area. By the way, a 10" slope roof is very steep!

Figure 2.   Length of rafter and area of roof calculated by using conversion factor for a 10" slope roof.

When calculating ceiling joists, draw a joist layout with opposing joists always meeting and overlapping above a load bearing wall. Figure one ceiling joist for every 16" plus 10% extra for waste.

Rafters are also spaced 16" on center. The length of the rafters can be determined by measuring from blueprints, making sure to allow for cornice overhang. Where two roof lines meet, a valley or hip rafter is necessary. Multiply the length of a normal rafter by 1.5 to get the approximate length of this rafter.

Pitch (slope)	Conversion Factor	Pitch (slope)	Conversion Factor
1 "	1.01	9 "	1.26
2 "	1.02	10 "	1.31
3 "	1.04	11 "	1.36
4 "	1.06	12 "	1.42
5 "	1.09	13 "	1.48
6 "	1.12	14 "	1.54
7 "	1.16	15 "	1.61
8 "	1.21	16 "	1.67

Table 5. Conversion factors for roofs

Gable studs will be necessary to frame in the gable ends. The length of the stud should be equal to the height of the roof ridge. Figure one stud per foot of gable width plus 10% waste. This will be enough to do two gable ends since scrap pieces can be used in the short areas of the gable.

Decking for the roof usually consists of ½" CDX exterior plywood. Multiply the length of the rafter times the length of the roof to determine the square footage of one side of the roof. Double this figure to obtain total square footage area of the roof. Divide this figure by the square footage of a sheet of plywood (32). Add 10% waste. This is the number of sheets of plywood needed. Remember the square footage of the roof for figuring shingles.

ROOFING SHINGLES

Roofing shingles are sold in "squares" or the number of shingles necessary to cover 100 sq. ft. of roof. First, find the square footage of the roof, adding 1 ½ square feet for every lineal foot of eaves, ridge, hip and valley. Divide the total square footage by 100 to find the number of squares. Shingles come packaged in one third square packages, so multiply the number of squares by three to arrive at the total number of packages needed.

Roofing felt is applied under the roof shingles as an underlayment and comes in 500 sq. ft. rolls. Divide the total square footage of the roof by 500 and add 20% for overlap and waste to determine the number of rolls needed.

Flashing is required around any chimney or area where two roof lines of different height meet and comes in 50 ft. rolls. Measure the length of the ridge if installing roof ridge vents.

SIDING AND SHEATHING

Multiply the perimeter of the outside walls by the height to obtain the total square footage of outside walls. If gables are to be covered with siding, multiply the width of the gable by the height (this figure is sufficient for both gable ends) and add this to the square footage of the outside walls. This figure is the total square footage of area to be sided.

Different types of siding are sold in different manners. Sheathing and plywood siding are sold in 4x8' sheets (32 sq. ft.). Divide this figure into the total square footage to determine the number of sheets needed. Add 10% for waste. Lap siding, on the other hand, is sold by squares or 1,000's. Make sure to ask if siding is sold by actual square footage or by "coverage area" (the amount of area actually covered by the siding when applied). Add 10% for waste or 15% if lap siding is applied diagonally.

Corner trim boards are generally cut from 1x2 lumber. Figure two pieces for every inside and outside corner; the length being equal to the height of the wall being sided.

CORNICE MATERIAL

To estimate cornice material, you must first determine the type or style of cornice and the trim materials to be used. Consult blueprints for any construction detail drawings of the cornice.

The following materials are generally used in most cornices:

- Fascia boards — 1x6" or 1x8"
- Drip mold (between fascia & shingles) — 1x4"
- Soffit — ⅜" exterior plywood
- Bed mold — 1x2"
- Frieze mold — 1x8"

Calculate the total lineal feet of cornice, including the gables, to find the total lineal feet of each trim material needed. Calculate the square footage of the soffit by multiplying the lineal feet of cornice by the depth of the cornice. Divide this by the square footage of a plywood sheet to determine the number of sheets needed.

INSULATION

Calculating the amount of wall insulation is easy — batts of insulation are sold by square footage coverage. Simply multiply the perimeter of the exterior walls to be insulated by the wall height to determine the total square footage to be insulated.

To calculate the amount of blown-in insulation

needed, first determine the type of insulation to be used. Each type — mineral wool, fiberglass, and cellulose has its own R-factor per inch. This must be known in order to determine the thickness of fill. Then multiply the depth in feet (or fraction thereof) by the square footage of the ceiling area to arrive at the cubic foot volume. Blown-in insulation is sold by the cubic foot. If batt insulation is used in the ceiling, it can be figured in the same manner as the wall insulation.

Most insulation contractors will quote a price including materials and labor when installing insulation. Ask the contractor to itemize the amount of insulation used, for comparison with your figures.

DRYWALL

Gypsum drywall is sold by the sheet (4x10, 4x12, etc.) but is estimated by square footage. To find the total amount needed for walls, multiply the total lineal feet of inside and outside walls by the wall height. Make sure to count each interior wall twice, since both sides of the wall will be covered. Count all openings as solid wall and add 10% for waste. Some subs will charge by the square foot for material and labor — then add extras for tray ceilings and other special work.

For the ceiling, simply take the finished square footage of the house. Add 10% for waste and then add this to the wall amount for the total amount of Drywall needed. If the house has any vaulted or tray ceilings, extra wallborad and labor must by figured in.

Joint finishing compound comes pre mixed in 5 gallon cans and joint tape in 250 ft. rolls. For every 1,000 sq. ft. of drywall, figure one roll of joint tape and 30 gallons of joint compound.

TRIMWORK

Base molding comes in many styles, with clamshell and colonial the most common, and will be run along the bottom of the wall in every room. Therefore, the lineal foot figure of walls used to calculate wallboard is equal to the lineal feet of baseboard trim needed. Add 10% for waste.

Make sure to measure the perimeter of any room that requires shoe molding or crown molding. Shoe mold (quarter round) is usually used in any room with vinyl or wood flooring to cover the crack between the floor and wall. Crown molding around the ceiling may be used in any room but is most common in formal areas such as foyers and living and dining areas. Add 10% for waste.

When ordering interior doors, you may want to purchase prehung doors with preassembled jambs. These doors are exceptionally easy to install and already have the jamb and trimwork attached. Study the blueprints carefully to be sure that the doors ordered open in the right direction and don't block light switches. (There are right-hand and left-hand doors.) To determine which door to order, imagine standing in front of the door, walking in. If you must use your right hand to open the door, it is a right-hand door. Most blueprints will have the size and type of each door marked in the opening.

FLOORING

Because of the complexity of laying flooring materials — carpet, hardwood floors, vinyl or ceramic tile — it is essential to get a flooring contractor to estimate the flooring quantities. An approximate figure would be equal to the square footage of the area covered plus 10% for waste. Carpet and vinyl are sold by the square yard, so divide by 9 to determine square yardage. Keep in mind, however, that carpet and vinyl are sold in 12' wide rolls. This dimension may affect the amount of waste in the estimate.

MISCELLANEOUS COVERINGS

This includes ceramic tile for bathrooms or floors, parquet, slate for foyers or fireplaces and fieldstone for steps or fireplaces. Virtually all these materials are sold by the amount of square footage area covered. Sub-contractors who install these items also charge by the square foot; sometimes with material included and sometimes without. Grouts and mortars used in installing these items (with the exception of rock) are premixed and indicate the coverage expected on the container.

PAINT

When hiring a painting contractor, the cost of paint should be included in the cost of the estimate unless you specify otherwise. If you should decide to do the painting yourself, you will need to figure the amount of paint needed. The coverage of different paints varies considerably, but most paints state the area covered on the container. Simply calculate the square footage of the area to be covered and add at least 15% for waste and touchup. Also figure the amount of primer needed. If colors are custom mixed, make sure that you have sufficient paint to finish the job. It is sometimes difficult to get an exact match of a custom color if mixed again at a later date.

CABINETS

Most blueprints include cabinet layouts with the plans. Use this layout if you are purchasing your own cabinets. If the cabinets are installed by a sub-contractor, he will take care of the exact measurements. Be sure that painting, staining and installation are included in the price.

WALLPAPER

One roll of wallpaper will safely cover 30 square feet of wall area including waste and matching of patterns. The longer the repeat pattern the more waste. Some European wallpapers vary in coverage. Be sure to check coverage area with the wallpaper supplier. When figuring the square footage of a room to wallpaper, count all openings as solid wall. Also be careful to note if you are buying a single or double roll of wallpaper. Most wallpaper is sold in a roll that actually contains 2 true rolls of wallpaper, or 60 sq. ft. of coverage. Always buy enough paper to finish the job. Buying additional rolls at a later time can cause matching problems if some of the rolls are from a different dye lot. Look for the same lot numbers (runs) on all rolls purchased to assure a perfect match. Use only vinyl wallpaper in baths and kitchen areas for water resistance and cleanup.

MILLWORK AND MISCELLANEOUS

The ordering of windows, lights, hardware and other specialty items will not be covered here as they are fairly straightforward to calculate. Other estimates such as heating and air, plumbing, electrical and electrical fixtures must be obtained from the contractors themselves since they provide the materials and labor.

The following section outlines the way most subcontractors charge for their services. Some subs may or may not include the cost of materials in their estimates. Make sure you know your particular sub's policy.

SUB-CONTRACTORS

FRAMING— Frame house, apply sheathing, set windows and exterior doors. Charges by the square foot of framed structure (includes any unheated space such as garage). Extras include bay windows, chimney chase, stairs, dormers, anything else unusual.

SIDING— Apply exterior siding. Charges by the square of applied siding. Extras: diagonal siding, decks, porches and very high walls requiring scaffolding.

CORNICE— Usually the siding sub-contractor. Applies soffit and fascia board. Charges by the lineal foot of cornice. Extras: Fancy cornice work, dentil mold. Sometimes sets windows and exterior doors.

TRIM— Install all interior trim and closet fixtures and set interior doors. Charges a set fee by the opening or by lineal feet of trim. Openings include doors and windows. Extras: stairs, rails, crown mold, mantels, book cases, chair rail, wainscoting and picture molding.

FOOTINGS— Dig footings, pour and level concrete, build bulkheads (for step downs). Charges by the lineal foot of footings. Extras: Pier holes.

BLOCK— Lay block. Charges by the block. Extras: Stucco block.

BRICKWORK— Lay brick. Charges by the skid (1000 bricks).

STONEWORK— Lay stone. Charges by the square foot or by bid.

CONCRETE FINISHING—Pour concrete, set forms, spread gravel and finish concrete. Charges by the square foot of area poured. Extras: Monolithic slab, digging footing.

ROOFING— Install shingles and waterproof around vents. Charges a set fee per square plus slope of roof. Ex.- $1 per square over slope on a 6/12 slope roof = $7/square. Extras: Some flashing, ridge vents, and special cutout for skylights.

WALLPAPER— Hang wallpaper. Builder provides wallpaper. Charges by the roll. Extras: High ceilings, wallpaper on ceilings, grass cloth.

GRADING— Rough grading and clearing. Charges by the hour of bulldozer time. Extras: Chain saw operator, hauling away of refuse, travel time to and from site (drag time).

POURED FOUNDATION— Dig and pour footings, set forms, and pour walls. Charges by the lineal foot of wall. Extras for bulkheads, more than four corners, openings for windows, doors and pipes.

PEST CONTROL — Chemically treat the ground around foundation for termite protection. Charges a flat fee.

PLUMBING— Install all sewer lines, water lines, drains, tubs, fixtures and water appliances. Charges per fixture installed or by bid. (For instance, a toilet, sink and tub would be three fixtures.) Installs medium grade fixtures. Extras: Any special decorator fixtures.

HVAC— Install furnace, air conditioner, all duct-work and gas lines. Charges by the tonnage of A/C or on bid price. Extras: Vent fans in bath, roof fans, attic fans, dryer vents, high efficiency furnaces and compressors.

ELECTRICAL— Install all switches and receptacles; hook up A/C compressor. Will install light fixtures. Charges by the receptacle. Extras: Connecting dishwasher, disposal, flood lights, door bells.

CABINETRY— Build or install pre-fab cabinets and vanities and apply Formica tops. Charges by the lineal foot for base cabinets, wall cabinets and vanities. Standard price includes Formica counter tops. Extras: Tile or marble tops, curved tops, pull-out shelves, lazy susans.

INSULATION— Install all fiberglass batts in walls,

ceilings, floors. Charges by square foot for batts, by the cubic foot for blown-in.

DRYWALL— Hang drywall, tape and finish, stipple. Charges by the square foot of Drywall. Materials are extra. Extras: Smooth ceilings, curved walls, tray and vaulted ceilings and open foyers.

SEPTIC TANK— Install septic tank. Charges fixed fee plus extra for field lines.

LANDSCAPING— Level with tractor, put down seeds, fertilizer and straw. Charges fixed fee. Extras: Trees, transplanted shrubs, pine straw, bark chips.

GUTTERS— Install gutters and downspouts. Charges by lineal foot plus extra for fittings. Extras: Half round gutters, collectors, special water channeling and gutters that cannot be installed from the roof.

GARAGE DOOR — Install garage doors. Fixed fee. Extras: Garage door openers.

FIREPLACE— Supply and install prefab fireplace and flue liner. Extras include gas log lighter, fresh air vent and ash dump.

PAINTING AND STAIN— Paint and stain interior and exterior. Charges by square foot of finished house. Extras: High ceilings, stained ceilings, painted ceilings.

CERAMIC TILE— Install all ceramic tile. Charges by the square foot. Extras include fancy bathtub surrounds and tile counter tops.

HARDWOOD FLOOR— Install and finish real hardwood floors. Charges by square foot. Extras include beveled plank, random plank and herringbone.

FLOORING— Install all carpet, vinyl, linoleum and prefinished flooring. Charges by the square yard. Extras include contrast borders and thicker underlayments.

BIDS BEAT ESTIMATES EVERY TIME

Now that you know how detailed an estimate can be, look at the other side of the coin. You can spend a day calculating how many cubic yards of concrete you will need and how many approximate hours of labor it will take; or you can call up a full-service foundation company and nail down a bid. The moral here is to use bids whenever possible in completing your take-off. The bottom line is what counts; if your estimate comes out to be $600 to tile a floor and your lowest bid is $750, you've obviously missed the boat — and wasted a little time.

COST ESTIMATE SUMMARY

DESCRIPTION	MATERIAL	LABOR	SUB-CONTR.	TOTAL
EXCAVATION				
PEST CONTROL				
CONCRETE				
WATERPROOFING				
FRAMING				
ROOFING				
PLUMBING				
HVAC				
ELECTRIC				
MASONRY				
SIDING & CORNICE				
INSULATION				
DRYWALL				
TRIM				
PAINTING				
CABINETRY				
TILE				
CARPET				
OTHER FLOORING				
GLAZING				
GUTTERS				
LANDSCAPING				
SUB-TOTAL				
APPLIANCES				
LUMBER				
OTHER MATERIALS				
TOOLS/RENTAL				
LOAN/LEGAL				
INSURANCE				
PERMITS/LICENSE				
SUB-TOTAL				
GRAND TOTAL				

CODE NO.	DESCRIPTION	QTY.	MATERIAL		LABOR		SUB-CONTR.		TOTAL
			UNIT PRICE	TOTAL MATL.	UNIT PRICE	TOTAL LABOR	UNIT PRICE	TOTAL SUB	
1	LAYOUT								
2	STAKES								
3	RIBBON								
4	ROUGH GRADE								
5	PERK TEST								
6	WELL AND PUMP								
7	Well								
8	Pump								
9	BATTER BOARDS								
10	2 X 4								
11	1 X 6								
12	Cord								
13	FOOTINGS								
14	Re-Rods								
15	2 X 8 Bulkheads								
16	Concrete								
17	Footings								
18	Piers								
19	FOUNDATION								
20	Block								
21	8"								
22	12"								
23	4"								
24	Caps								
25	Headers								
26	Solid 8's								
27	Half 8's								
28	Mortar Mix								
29	Sand								
30	Foundation Vents								
31	Lintels								
32	Portland Cement								

CODE NO.	DESCRIPTION	QTY.	MATERIAL		LABOR		SUB-CONTR.		TOTAL
			UNIT PRICE	TOTAL MATL.	UNIT PRICE	TOTAL LABOR	UNIT PRICE	TOTAL SUB	
33	WATERPROOFING								
34	Asphalt Coat								
35	Portland Cement								
36	6 Mil Poly								
37	Drain Pipe								
38	Gravel								
39	Stucco								
40	FOUNDATION								
41	(Poured)								
42	Portland Cement								
43	Wales								
44	TERMITE TREAT								
45	SLABS								
46	Gravel								
47	6 Mil Poly								
48	Re-Wire								
49	Re-Rods								
50	Corroform								
51	Form Boards								
52	2 X 8								
53	1 X 4								
54	Concrete								
55	Basement								
56	Garage								
57	Porch								
58	Patio								
59	AIR CONDITIONING								
60	House								
61	FRAMING SUB-FLOOR								
62	I-Beam								
63	Steel Post								
64	Girders								
65	Scab								

CODE NO.	DESCRIPTION	QTY.	MATERIAL		LABOR		SUB-CONTR.		TOTAL
			UNIT PRICE	TOTAL MATL.	UNIT PRICE	TOTAL LABOR	UNIT PRICE	TOTAL SUB	
66	Floor Joist								
67	Bridging								
68	Glue								
69	Plywood Sub Floor								
70	5/8" T&G								
71	3/4" T&G								
72	1/2" Exterior								
73	Joist Hangers								
74	Lag Bolts								
75	Sub-Floor								
76	FRAMING—WALLS								
77	Treated Plate								
78	Plate								
79	8′ Studs								
80	10′ Studs								
81	2 X 10 Headers								
82	Interior Beams								
83	Bracing								
84	1 X 4								
85	1/2" Plywood								
86	Sheathing								
87	4 X 8								
88	4 X 9								
89	Laminated Beam								
90	Flitch Plate								
91	Bolts								
92	Dead Wood								
93	FRAMING—CEILING/ROOF								
94	Ceiling Joist								
95	Rafters								
96	Barge Rafters								
97	Beams								
98	Ridge Beam								

CODE NO.	DESCRIPTION	QTY.	MATERIAL		LABOR		SUB-CONTR.		TOTAL
			UNIT PRICE	TOTAL MATL.	UNIT PRICE	TOTAL LABOR	UNIT PRICE	TOTAL SUB	
99	Wind Beam								
100	Roof Bracing Matl.								
101	Ceiling Bracing								
102	Gable Studs								
103	Storm Anchors								
104	Decking								
105	3/8" CDX Plywood								
106	1/2" CDX Plywood								
107	2 x 6 T&G								
108	Plyclips								
109	Rigid Insulation								
110	Felt								
111	15 #								
112	40 #								
113	60 #								
114	FRAMING—MISC.								
115	Stair Stringers								
116	Firing-in								
117	Chase Material								
118	Purlin								
119	Nails								
120	16DCC								
121	8DCC								
122	8" Glv.Roof.								
123	1 ½" Glv Rf.								
124	Concrete								
125	Cut								
126	ROOFING								
127	Shingles								
128	Ridge Vent								
129	End Plugs								
130	Connectors								
131	Flashing								

CODE NO.	DESCRIPTION	QTY.	MATERIAL		LABOR		SUB-CONTR.		TOTAL
			UNIT PRICE	TOTAL MATL.	UNIT PRICE	TOTAL LABOR	UNIT PRICE	TOTAL SUB	
132	Roof to Wall								
133	Roll								
134	Window								
135	Ventilators								
136	TRIM–EXTERIOR								
137	Doors								
138	Main Entrance								
139	Secondary								
140	Sliding Glass								
141	Doors								
142	Windows								
143	Fixed Window								
144	Glass								
145	Window Frame								
146	Material								
147	Corner Trim								
148	Window Trim								
149	Door Trim								
150	Flashing								
151	Roof to Wall								
152	Metal Drip Cap								
153	Roll								
154	Beams								
155	Columns								
156	Rail								
157	Ornamental Iron								
158	NAILS								
159	16d Galv. Casing								
160	8d Galv. Casing								
161	4D Galv. Box								
162	LOUVERS								
163	Triangular								
164	Rectangular								

CODE NO.	DESCRIPTION	QTY.	MATERIAL		LABOR		SUB-CONTR.		TOTAL
			UNIT PRICE	TOTAL MATL.	UNIT PRICE	TOTAL LABOR	UNIT PRICE	TOTAL SUB	
165	SIDING								
166	CORNICE								
167	Lookout Mat'l								
168	Fascia Mat'l								
169	Rake Mold								
170	Dentil Mold								
171	Cont. Eave Vent								
172	Screen								
173	3/8" Plywood								
174	DECKS & PORCHES								
175	MASONRY—BRICK								
176	Face								
177	Fire								
178	MORTAR								
179	Light								
180	Dark								
181	Sand								
182	Portland Cement								
183	Lintels								
184	Flue								
185	Flue								
186	Ash Dump								
187	Clean out								
188	Log Lighter								
189	Wall Ties								
190	Decorative Brick								
191	Lime Putty								
192	Muriatic Acid								
193	Sealer								
194	Under-hearth								
195	Block								
196	Air Vent								

CODE NO.	DESCRIPTION	QTY.	MATERIAL		LABOR		SUB-CONTR.		TOTAL
			UNIT PRICE	TOTAL MATL.	UNIT PRICE	TOTAL LABOR	UNIT PRICE	TOTAL SUB	
197	PLUMBING								
198	Fixtures								
199	Misc.								
200	Water Line								
201	Sewer								
202	HVAC								
203	Dryer Vent								
204	Hood Vent								
205	Exhaust vent								
206	ELECTRICAL								
207	Lights								
208	Receptacles								
209	Switches-Single								
210	Switches–3 Way								
211	Switches–4 Way								
212	Range–One Unit								
213	Range–Surface								
214	Oven								
215	Dishwasher								
216	Trash Compactor								
217	Dryer								
218	Washer								
219	Freezer								
220	Furnace–Gas								
221	Furnace–Elec.								
222	A/C								
223	Heat Pump								
224	Attic Fan								
225	Bath Fan								
226	Smoke Detector								
227	Water Htr/Elec.								
228	Flood Lights								
229	Door Bell								

CODE NO.	DESCRIPTION	QTY.	MATERIAL		LABOR		SUB-CONTR.		TOTAL
			UNIT PRICE	TOTAL MATL.	UNIT PRICE	TOTAL LABOR	UNIT PRICE	TOTAL SUB	
230	Vent-a-Hood								
231	Switched Recept.								
232	150 Amp Service								
233	200 Amp Service								
234	Disposal								
235	Refrigerator								
236	Permit								
237	Ground Fault Inter.								
238	Fixtures								
239	FIREPLACE								
240	Log Lighter								
241	INSULATION								
242	Walls								
243	Ceiling								
244	Floor								
245	WALLBOARD								
246	Finish								
247	Stipple								
248	STONE								
249	Interior								
250	Exterior								
251	TRIM–INTERIOR								
252	Doors								
253	Bifold								
254	Base								
255	Casing								
256	Shoe								
257	Window Stool								
258	Window Stop								
259	Window Mull								
260	1x5 Jamb Matl.								
261	Crown Mold								
262	Bed Mold								

CODE NO.	DESCRIPTION	QTY.	MATERIAL		LABOR		SUB-CONTR.		TOTAL
			UNIT PRICE	TOTAL MATL.	UNIT PRICE	TOTAL LABOR	UNIT PRICE	TOTAL SUB	
263	Picture Mold								
264	Paneling								
265	OS Corner Mold								
266	IS Corner Mold								
267	Cap Mold								
268	False Beam Matl.								
269	STAIRS								
270	Cap								
271	Rail								
272	Baluster								
273	Post								
274	Riser								
275	Tread								
276	Skirtboard								
277	Bracing								
278	LOCKS								
279	Exterior								
280	Passage								
281	Closet								
282	Bedroom								
283	Bath								
284	Dummy								
285	Pocket Door								
286	Bolt Single								
287	Bolt Double								
288	Flush Bolts								
289	Sash Locks								
290	TRIM–MISC.								
291	Door Bumpers								
292	Wedge Shingles								
293	Attic Stairs								
294	Scuttle Hole								
295	1x12 Shelving								

CODE NO.	DESCRIPTION	QTY.	MATERIAL		LABOR		SUB-CONTR.		TOTAL
			UNIT PRICE	TOTAL MATL.	UNIT PRICE	TOTAL LABOR	UNIT PRICE	TOTAL SUB	
296	Shelf & Rod Br.								
297	Rod Socket Sets								
298	FINISH NAILS								
299	3D								
300	4D								
301	6D								
302	8D								
303	Closet Rods								
304	Sash Handles								
305	SEPTIC TANK								
306	Dry Well								
307	BACKFILL								
308	DRIVES & WALKS								
309	Form Boards								
310	Rewire								
311	Rerods								
312	Expansion Joints								
313	Concrete								
314	Asphalt								
315	Gravel								
316	LANDSCAPE								
317	PAINT & STAIN								
318	House								
319	Garage								
320	Cabinets								
321	WALLPAPER								
322	TILE								
323	Wall								
324	Floor								
325	Misc.								
326	GARAGE DOORS								
327	GUTTERS								
328	Gutters								

CODE NO.	DESCRIPTION	QTY.	MATERIAL		LABOR		SUB-CONTR.		TOTAL
			UNIT PRICE	TOTAL MATL.	UNIT PRICE	TOTAL LABOR	UNIT PRICE	TOTAL SUB	
329	Downspouts								
330	Elbows								
331	Splash Blocks								
332	CABINETS								
333	Wall								
334	Base								
335	Vanities								
336	Laundry								
337	GLASS								
338	SHOWER DOORS								
339	MIRRORS								
340	ACCESSORIES								
341	Tissue Holder								
342	Towel Racks								
343	Soap Dish								
344	Toothbrush Holder								
345	Medicine Cabinet								
346	Shower Rods								
347	FLOOR COVERING—BATH								
348	Vinyl								
349	Carpet								
350	Hardwood								
351	Slate or Stone								
352	MISCELLANEOUS								
353	CLEAN-UP								
354	HANG ACCESSORIES								
355	FLOOR COVERING—OTHER								
356	Vinyl								
357	Carpet								
358	Hardwood								
359	Slate or stone								

CODE NO.	DESCRIPTION	QTY.	MATERIAL		LABOR		SUB-CONTR.		TOTAL
			UNIT PRICE	TOTAL MATL.	UNIT PRICE	TOTAL LABOR	UNIT PRICE	TOTAL SUB	
360	MISCELLANEOUS								
	SUB-TOTALS								
	GRAND TOTALS								

ITEM ESTIMATE WORKSHEET

VENDOR NAME	DESCRIPTION	MEASURING QTY.	MEASURING UNIT	CONVERSION FACTOR	ORDERING QTY.	ORDERING UNIT	PRICE EACH	COST	TAX	TOTAL COST	COST TYPE

EXPENSE CATEGORY	MATERIAL COST	LABOR COST	SUBCONTRACTOR COST	TOTAL COST

COST ESTIMATE CHECKLIST

CODE NO.	DESCRIPTION	QTY.	MATERIAL		LABOR		SUB-CONTR.		TOTAL
			UNIT PRICE	TOTAL MATL.	UNIT PRICE	TOTAL LABOR	UNIT PRICE	TOTAL SUB	

SECTION II: PROJECT MANAGEMENT

Pre-Construction

INTRODUCTION

The Project Management Section covers each of the trades normally encountered in residential construction. They will be covered in the order in which they normally occur in the construction process. The stages covered are:

- Pre-Construction
- Excavation
- Foundation, Waterproofing and Pest Control
- Framing
- Roofing and Gutters
- Plumbing
- HVAC (Heating, Ventilation and Air Conditioning)
- Electrical
- Masonry and Stucco
- Siding and Cornice
- Insulation and Soundproofing
- Drywall
- Trim and Stain
- Painting and Wallcovering
- Cabinetry and Countertops
- Flooring, Tile and Glazing
- Landscaping

NOTE: The multitude of combinations and options in a home are as infinite as the ways in which to get them done. The steps and checklists outlined on the following pages attempt to cover MOST of the possible steps needed to build MOST homes.

For this reason, there are bound to be a number of steps in this manual relating to features you may not have planned. For example, you may not have a basement or require stucco work.

Skip steps that do not apply to your project. Likewise, there may be special efforts required in your project that are not covered in this manual. Also, there may be a number of steps you will undertake in special or unconventional circumstances that will not be covered in this book. In many instances, the exact order of steps is not critical; use your common sense.

PREPARATION

Before you run out and start building, there are a number of preparation steps that you should complete. These are somewhat frustrating because they show no visible signs of progress and are often time consuming. There are a lot of forms to fill out and chores to do here. But you will be better off to get them all out of the way. For most of the steps listed in this section, order of completion is not critical; just get them done.

Give yourself ample time to complete these steps. Rome wasn't built in a day. If you are a first-time builder, it is typical to spend AT LEAST as much time planning your project as you spend executing it. That is, if you plan to have your home completed six months after breaking ground, you should spend AT LEAST six months in planning and preparation prior to breaking ground.

Once you break ground, there's no turning back and no time to stop, so you'll be relieved that everything has been thought out ahead of time. This section will cover the items that should be completed prior to breaking ground.

PRE-CONSTRUCTION STEPS

PC1 BEGIN construction project scrapbook. This is where you will begin gathering all sorts of information and ideas you may need later. Start with a large binder or a file cabinet. Break into sections such as:

- Kitchen ideas
- Bath ideas
- Floor plans
- Landscaping ideas
- Sub-contractor names and addresses
- Material catalogs and prices

Your "scrapbook" will probably evolve into a small library, a wealth of information used to familiarize yourself with the task ahead, and serve as a constant and valuable source of reference for ideas to use in the future.

PC2 DETERMINE size of home. Calculate the size of home you can afford to build. Refer to the HOUSE PLANS section in this book for details on this step.

PC3 EVALUATE alternate house plans. Consider traffic patterns, your lifestyle and personal tastes. Refer to the HOUSE PLANS section, presented earlier, for details on evaluating house plans.

PC4 SELECT house plan or have house plan drawn. If you use an architect, he will probably charge you a certain fee per square foot. Make sure you really like it before you go out and buy a dozen copies of the blueprints!

PC5 MAKE design changes. Unless you have an architect custom design your home, there will always be a few things you might want to change — kitchen and kitchen cabinets, master bath, a partition, a door, etc. This is the time to make changes. Refer to the material on making changes in the HOW TO BE A BUILDER and HOUSE PLANS sections.

PC6 PERFORM material and labor take-off. This will be a time-consuming, but important, step. Refer to the COST ESTIMATING section for details on this step. Get bids to home in on true costs.

PC7 CUT costs. After you have determined estimated cost, you may need to pull the cost down. Refer to the SAVING MONEY section for details on reducing costs without reducing quality.

PC8 UPDATE material and labor take-off. Based on changes you may have made, update and recalculate your estimated costs based on bids.

PC9 ARRANGE temporary housing. If you own a home and must sell it in order to build, or your current home is too far from your future construction site, consider renting an apartment or home close to your site. If possible, select a place between your site and your office (if you have one). This will greatly facilitate site visits. Since it will take approximately six months to build even the smallest house (unless you are using a pre-fabricated "kit"), you should get at least a six-month lease with a month-to-month option thereafter, or a one-year lease. For first-time, part-time builders, count on ten months to a year before move-in. Delays caused by weather, sub absenteeism, material delays and other problems always seem to add months to the effort. Consider that during the course of the project, you will be paying rent, construction interest and miscellaneous expenses, as well as additional travel costs. Plan extra money to handle this.

PC10 FORM a separate corporation if you want to set your "enterprise" off from your personal affairs. This may give you a better standing among members of the building trade if they feel that they're dealing with a company, instead of an individual. Be advised that your lender may not take kindly to this.

PC11 APPLY for and obtain a business license if required. This may be a legal requirement to conduct business as a professional builder in the county where your site is located. Check with your local authorities for advice.

PC12 ORDER business cards. These will be helpful in opening doors with banks, suppliers and subs. List yourself as president for extra clout.

PC13 OBTAIN free and clear title to land. This must be done before applying for a construction loan. Bankers want to make sure that you have something at stake in this project, too. It is strongly recommended that you only build on land that you own outright.

PC14 APPLY for construction loan. In proper terms, you should be applying for a "construction and permanent loan". This saves you one loan closing since the construction loan turns into a permanent loan when construction is completed.

PC15 ESTABLISH project checking account. This will be used as the single source of project funds to minimize reconciliation problems. Write all checks from this account and keep an accurate balance.

PC16 CLOSE construction loan. This allows you access to funds up to your loan amount. You will pay interest only on money drawn from your reserve. You will not be paying interest on money you have not yet used. Remember, though, that money is paid out as work is completed, based on the judgment of bank officials. Hence, you will need a certain amount of money to begin work (excavation and perhaps some concrete work). Do not begin any physical site work until this is done. Many financial institutions will not even loan you money if you have already started construction prior to contacting them.

PC17 OPEN builder accounts with material suppliers. This will involve filling out forms and waiting for mail replies notifying you of your account number. Read and be familiar with the payment and return policies of each supplier.

PC18 OBTAIN purchase order forms. Look for bound, pre-numbered ones with a carbon copy. You will use these forms for all purchases. Pay only those invoices that reference one of your purchase order numbers. (Make sure to advise suppliers that you are using a purchase order system.)

PC19 OBTAIN building permit. This involves filling out building permit applications with your county planning and zoning department. Build a friendly relationship with ALL county officials. You may need to count on them later.

PC20 OBTAIN builder's risk policy. Your construction site is a liability. You, laborers, sub-contractors or neighborhood children could get hurt. Materials may get damaged or stolen. An inexpensive insurance policy is a must. Your financial institution and/or your county officials can point you in the right direction. You should also check with your home and/or auto insurance company for a quote.

PC21 OBTAIN worker's compensation policy. This is normally charged out as a percentage of the cost of your project. There may be a minimum size policy you can purchase.

PC22 ACQUIRE minimum tools. Certain items are a must. Consider locating some of these items at a pawn shop.

- Good ankle height leather construction boots, preferably with steel-tipped toes. Keep these in your trunk through construction.
- Fiberglass hard hat. Preferably yellow or orange. Scratch your name inside.
- Six foot level. Your level will be a frequently used tool throughout the project. Try to get a used one.
- Strong flashlight
- Roll of heavy-duty cotton twine and blue chalk marker
- Good all-purpose 14 oz. framing hammer
- Good set of heavy-duty gloves
- Fifty or hundred foot steel tape
- Twenty-five foot tape measure
- First aid kit
- UL-approved 50-100 foot grounded extension cord and work lamp
- Garden hose
- Large broom or shop vacuum
- Trash can

If you do not own a pickup truck and can't borrow one, try to buy an inexpensive trailer that can be attached to the back of your car. You can sell it later after the project is over.

You can probably borrow a pickup truck from your subs from time to time.

PC23 VISIT numerous residential construction sites in various stages of completion. Observe the progress, storage of materials, drainage after heavy rainfall and other aspects of those sites.

PC24 DETERMINE need for an on-site storage shack. If you do a lot of the work, this could be helpful.

PC25 NOTIFY all subs/labor. Call up all subs and labor to tell them of the date you plan to break ground. This should be done approximately a week before you plan to break ground. Confirm that they still to plan to do the work and at the agreed-upon price. If you must get a backup sub, this is the time to do it — look on your sub list for "number two".

PC26 OBTAIN compliance bond, if necessary. This is primarily for your protection if you have a builder assist you during construction or build for you.

PC27 DETERMINE minimum requirements for Certificate of Occupancy. As soon as you meet these requirements, you can move into your home while you finish it, avoiding unnecessary rent. During final construction stages, concentrate on meeting these requirements. For example, you can do landscaping and certain other tasks later. Don't move in unless you have finished the rooms you plan to live in immediately.

PC28 CONDUCT spot survey of lot. Locate a good, reliable licensed surveyor. Have him furnish a signed survey report. This confirms that the planned project and excavation are within allowable boundaries. Ask your surveyor to help evaluate water drainage if you are uncertain.

PC29 MARK all lot boundaries and corners with 2' stakes and bright red tape.

PC30 POST construction signs. You should have at least one "DANGER" or "WARNING" sign. Have one sign for each street exposure if you have a corner lot. You may also want another sign which has your name, "company" and phone number on it. Your lender may have their own sign also.

PC31 NAIL building permit to a tree (that will not be torn down) or a post in the front of the lot visible from the street. You may want to provide a little rain protection for it. You cannot do any work on site until this permit is posted.

PC32 ARRANGE for rental toilet. This is often viewed as a luxury among builders. They rent by the month at about $40 and up including maintenance.

PC33 ARRANGE for a site telephone with the phone company. If the site is located far away from anything, this becomes more of a necessity, especially in cases of emergency. If you get one, have the phone company install it with a strong metal case with a lock. You will have to provide a sturdy 4x4 post or tree to hang it on. Make sure you don't have to pay if it gets stolen. It should be in a place where you can hear the phone ring if you are inside. Specify a loud bell.

Site Location and Excavation

DIGGING IN

Now it's time to really get mud on your new construction shoes! You are now entering that phase of construction where your decisions will be much harder to change. Take great care in locating and excavating your home site. A mistake here will be almost impossible to repair later. Site location consists of several phases:

- Locating the house on the lot.

- Excavating the area where the house is located.

- Marking the foundation lines with batter boards.

Site Location

Before locating the house on the lot, make sure to obtain a site plan from your surveyor. The site plan should indicate the dimensions of the lot, public and private easements and the setback requirements of your county's local building code. With this information in hand, you can insure that you place the house properly with no encroachment on another person's property or on public easements. You can also request that the surveyor place the house on the site plan and install corner stakes when surveying.

If you decide to locate the corner stakes, check the drainage of the property and look for any subsoil rocks or springs. After the house is located and the grading is properly done, the drainage of the lot should drain away from the house, but not onto any other property. If you change the natural drainage of the lot so that water now flows onto someone else's property, you can be held liable for any damage that results. You should know before excavation starts where the top of your foundation will be located. You may want to run a string at this height between the corner stakes to aid in excavating to the proper depth. Use a string level, leveling hoses or a builder's transit to ensure that the string is plumb and level.

Leveling hoses are simple but effective tools to find the absolute level of two distant objects. You can use simple garden hoses for this, but a much better version is available at most do-it-yourself stores for a very reasonable price (much cheaper than renting a builder's transit). Fill the hose with water and mount one end of the hose at the highest corner of the foundation. Raise or lower the other end of the hose (while adding more water) until both ends of the hose are completely full of water. Since water seeks its own level, the two hose ends will then be exactly level. Mark this elevation for string placement.

Once excavation commences, make sure that the depth of excavation will match your intended foundation height. You can measure from the string to ensure proper depth.

To lay out the corner stakes, start from an established reference line, such as the curb of the street. Most houses look best when located parallel to the street. However, you may violate this rule if you are concerned about other factors such as solar orientation. Just make sure to place the house well within the

Figure 3. Reference lines on a site plan

front, side and back setback limits. Establish the front line of the house first by measuring from your reference lines. Then locate the back corners of the house. Make sure that your stakes are reasonably square by measuring the diagonals of the square. (see illustration). The length of each diagonal should be the same. To obtain a 90° angle use the old geometric principle of the "golden triangle". The golden triangle has three sides in *multiples* of 3 ft., 4 ft. and 5 ft. and will form a 90° angle (see illustration).

Breaking Ground

This is perhaps one of the most exciting moments during your homebuilding project! This phase actually involves several tasks. You may use your grader four times during the project:

■ Clear site and excavate.

■ Backfill and smooth out basement floor area.

■ Cut the driveway, rough grade and haul away trash.

■ Finish grade

The excavation sub-contractor is one sub you will pay by the hour. This is usually tracked by the "hour" meter on the bulldozer. Don't let the machine idle while talking with the operator — shut it off. The rates can vary, so shop around. You may be able to get a better rate by hiring excavators to work on "off-hours", such as weekends.

Avoid clearing or excavating when the ground is wet or muddy; it will take more time, be less accurate and create a mess. Know your lot. Do you have large, heavy trees which need heavy-duty clearing equipment? Or could you use lighter equipment which rents for less?

Remember: The more "horsepower" the higher the hourly rate, but the more it can accomplish in less time. But never use overpowered equipment for the job or you'll end up paying too much. Negotiate hours with the sub. Does he include travel time to and from the site (drag time).

If you want to save money cutting the trees down yourself, go ahead. But cut them 4' from the ground; the bulldozer needs a good piece of the tree to pull the roots out of the ground. If you don't have a fireplace, consider selling the wood.

Batter Boards

Once the site is properly excavated, you need to lay out the batter boards. These boards provide a precise reference for the foundation subs to install foundation forms. If you have excavated for a full basement, you may be able to get your poured foundation sub to

Figure 4. Staking and laying out batter boards

install forms without the need for batter boards. This is one of the advantages of using a poured concrete foundation.

If you are using a block wall foundation or a slab foundation, batter boards will be necessary for the subs. Since the subs will be laying out the foundation to the dimensions of the batter boards, you must make sure that the layout is completely plumb and square! A mistake here can cause a great deal of frustration and expense to correct later. Crooked slabs are almost impossible to correct without re-pouring. So use a pound of prevention here.

EXCAVATION — Steps

EX1 CONDUCT excavation bidding process on all site preparation work.

EX2 LOCATE underground utilities (gas main, water line, electrical or telephone cables) if they cross your property. You may want to call a locater service or your local utilities for help in locating utility lines. Mark their location with color-coded flags and mark them on a copy of the plat. Don't place flags down more than two or three days in advance. Kids love to pull them up. Your excavator will need to know where the utility lines run. Damaging utilities can be time consuming and expensive.

EX3 DETERMINE where dwelling is to be situated exactly. Your surveyor can help you with this. Make sure to allow both for zoning setbacks and for any utility or highway easements. A landscape architect can help you determine exactly where the home should face from a passive solar and appearance aspect. Mark all corners of the house with stakes so the grader will know where to clear. The grader should dig an extra 3' beyond the corner stakes of the house. For consistency you should have the same setback as the adjacent homes if there are any.

EX4 MARK area to be cleared. Trees to be saved should be marked with red tape or ribbon. Allow clearance for necessary deliveries and several parked vehicles. Now is the time to clear an area for the driveway, patio and septic tank (if you plan to have one).

EX5 MARK where curb is to be cut (if it is to be cut). The standard curb cut is 14' wide. This allows for a slight flare on each side of the driveway area. In some cases, if you do not cut the curb, you will have a tough bump to deal with getting into your driveway. If it is to be cut later, you can remedy the problem by piling dirt or gravel up at the curb. You may need a variance if you plan to cut more than one curb area — as in the case of a circular driveway on a corner lot.

EX6 TAKE last picture of site area. This is the last chance you have to see it untouched.

EX7 CLEAR site area. Be present for this step. This is normally not something that is worthwhile for you to do because the grader can clear in an hour what would take you a week or more by hand. Cut down necessary trees and brush. Pull stumps out of the ground and remove as necessary. Make sure to go over the plan with the grader. If your plan is reversed, make sure the grader is aware of this fact. At this point you may wish to mark the foundation area with powdered lime or corner stakes. Do not try to save time by cutting down trees yourself; the grader needs the weight of the tree to pull the stump out of the ground.

EX8 EXCAVATE trash pit. Trash pit location should a minimum of 20' from the building or driveway. Make sure not to locate the pit near where you plan to add a swimming pool at a later date. A trash pit can save money normally spent on hauling a large amount of scrap off-site as well as a dumping fee at a landfill. Some builders don't like them because they attract termites that might eventually be attracted to your home. The area may settle over time as materials decompose. The pit is also a hazard for young children and adults during construction. In most areas it is unlawful to burn or bury trash.

EX9 INSPECT cleared site. Check for proper building dimensions, scarred trees and thoroughness. Have trash, roots, stumps and other debris been hauled away?

EX10 EXCAVATE foundation/basement area. You must be present when this step is being

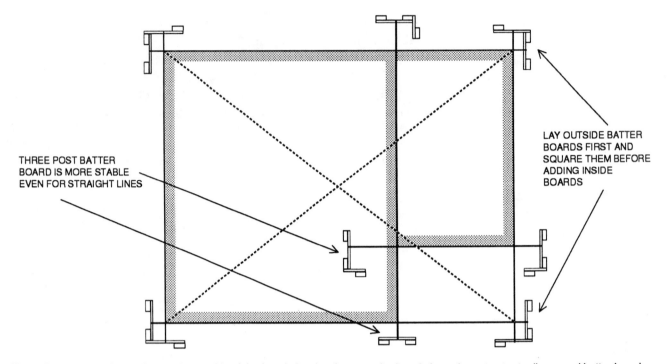

THREE POST BATTER BOARD IS MORE STABLE EVEN FOR STRAIGHT LINES

LAY OUTSIDE BATTER BOARDS FIRST AND SQUARE THEM BEFORE ADDING INSIDE BOARDS

Figure 5. Lay batter board lines to the outside of the foundation, leaving room for foundation sub-contractor to dig around batter boards and lines.

performed. To execute this step properly, you should have a transit set up. Take depth measures continuously. This will help you to keep the foundation grade level and at the proper depth. It is better to set the basement a little high than too low. This will help prevent water problems later. You are normally paying this person by the hour unless, of course, you have decided on a firm dollar bid. Make sure he works hard doing exactly what you have in mind. It would be handy to have a copy of the written contract with you. Have the excavator also clear the topsoil off the driveway and foundation area. This must

be done before the crushed stone is put down on it or the stone will just sink into the loose topsoil. Have the topsoil stacked in its own pile so that you can redistribute it on the lawn area after construction. Your yard will be much healthier with an extra layer of topsoil.

Make sure the operator digs down to firm soil and below the frost line, no matter how deep. Don't scrimp here! A poor footing can ruin your house. If you are not sure of the firmness of the soil, use a wider footing to provide more stability.

EX11 INSPECT site and excavated area. Refer to attached inspection sheet and contract specifications.

BATTER BOARD — Steps

EX12 LAY OUT outer four corners of house with stakes and square up using a transit or the "golden triangle". Make sure tops of stakes are level with the proposed top of foundation. Check this with a builder's transit or leveling hoses. Re-measure distances and drive a small finishing nail or mark top of stake at exact corner of the building line.

CONTROL OR HIGH POINT

FOUNDATION WALL OUTLINE

Figure 6. Establishing depth of excavation

This will act as a reference for the batter boards.

EX13 DRIVE three 2x4 stakes of suitable length in a triangular pattern 4 feet outside the corner stake with the tops of the stakes 6-12 inches higher than the corner stake. Make sure to sharpen the end of the stake before using!

EX14 NAIL 1x4 or 1x6 boards horizontally between the three stakes so that the tops are all level with the tops of the corner stakes. You may want to clamp the horizontal boards initially until final height adjustments are complete.

EX15 PULL a string between opposite batter boards and adjust until the string is exactly over the nails in the corner stakes. Attach string with a finishing nail. Repeat with each batter board until the four outside corners are marked properly.

EX16 RE-CHECK the distance of each string — measuring from the intersections of the strings. Measure the diagonal distance of the corners of the strings — if the distance is the same, the corners are square. Check the height and level of each string. Make minor adjustments. Once the strings are positioned accurately, mark the top of the batter board or saw a kerf in the board where the lines touch the board so that they can be replaced if broken or moved.

EX17 LAY OUT all inside corners and remaining batter boards using the existing batter board strings as a reference. Re-check the measurements, height and diagonals of the strings as you add batter boards.

DRAINAGE — Steps

EX18 APPLY crusher run to driveway area. This will provide an excellent base for a paved drive and allows for easy site access for your subs and supply trucks when the ground is muddy.

EX19 SET UP a silt fence. Local ordinances will probably not allow mud run-off from your site to drain into the street or adjacent properties. A silt fence prevents mud from flowing

into the street and neighboring yards. Two foot stakes will support the fence. Staple the covering to the stakes with a stapler. Rolls of plastic, mesh or burlap are available at material suppliers for this purpose, or you may choose to use bales of hay. These bales can be reused later when landscaping.

EX20 PAY excavator. Have him sign a receipt. Pay only for work done up to this point. Give him an idea of when you will be needing him for the backfill work.

Backfill

EX21 PLACE supports on interior side of foundation wall to support wall during backfill. Don't backfill until the house is framed in to provide additional support for the foundation walls.

EX22 INSPECT backfill area. Refer to related checklist in this section.

EX23 BACKFILL foundation. Remind excavator not to puncture waterproofing poly with large roots or branches in dirt.

EX24 CUT driveway area.

EX25 COVER septic tank and septic tank line.

EX26 COVER trash pit. Area should be compacted with heavy equipment and covered with at least two feet of dirt.

EX27 PERFORM final grade. Topsoil should be spread over top surface. If you have truckloads of topsoil hauled in, you may want to

Figure 7. Finish grade sloped for drainage

get a free soil pH test done by the county extension service. This could save you money in buying expensive fertilizers to compensate for inferior soil.

EX28 CONDUCT final inspection. Check all excavation and grading work.

EX29 PAY excavator (final). Have them sign an affadavit.

EXCAVATION - Sample Specifications

■ Excavator to perform all necessary excavation and grading as indicated below and on the attached drawing(s) and provide all necessary equipment to complete the job.

■ Bid to include all equipment and equipment drag time for two trips.

■ Bid to include necessary chain saw work.

■ Trees to be saved will be marked with red ribbon. Trees to be saved are to remain unscarred and otherwise undamaged.

■ Foundation to be dug to depth indicated at foundation corners. Foundation hole is to be 3' wider than foundation for ease of access. Foundation base not to be dug too deeply in order to pour footings and basement floor on stable base.

■ Foundation floor to be dug smooth within 2" of level.

■ Excavate trash pit (10' x 12') at specified location as depicted on attached drawing.

■ Driveway area to be cleared of topsoil and cut to proper level. All topsoil to be piled where specified.

■ All excess dirt to be hauled away by excavator.

■ All stumps and trees to be dug up and hauled away. Hardwoods to be cut up to fit fireplace and piled on site where directed.

■ Grade level shall be established by the builder, who will also furnish a survey of the lot showing the location of the dwelling and all underground utilities.

■ Finish grade to slope away from home where pos-

sible.

■ Backfill foundation walls after waterproofing, gravel and drain tile have been installed and inspected.

■ Builder to be notified prior to clearing and excavation. Builder must be on site at start of operation.

EXCAVATION - Inspection

Clearing

☐ Underground utilities left undisturbed.

☐ All area to be cleared is thoroughly cleared and other areas left as they were originally.

☐ All felled trees removed or buried. All remaining trees are standing and have no scars from excavation. Firewood cut and stacked if requested.

Excavation

☐ All area to be excavated is excavated including necessary work space:

- Foundation area (extra 3' at perimeter)
- Porch and stoop areas
- Fireplace slab
- Crawl space cut and graded with proper slope to insure dry crawl space.

☐ Trash pit dug according to plan if specified.

☐ All excavations done to proper depth with bottoms relatively smooth. Should be within 1" of level.

Checklist Prior to Digging and Clearing

☐ All underground utilities marked.

☐ All trees and natural areas properly marked off.

☐ Planned clearing area will allow access to site by cement and other large supply trucks. Room to park several vehicles.

☐ All survey stakes in ground.

Checklist Prior to Backfill

☐ Any needed repairs to foundation wall complete.

☐ Form ties broken off and tie holes covered with

tar (poured wall only).

☐ All foundation waterproofing completed and correct. This includes parging, sprayed tar, poly, etc.

☐ Joint between footing and foundation sealed properly and watertight.

☐ Footing drain tile and gravel installed according to plan.

☐ All necessary run-off drain tile in place and marked with stakes to prevent burial during backfill.

☐ All garbage and scrap wood out of trench and fill area.

☐ Backfill supports in place and secure.

☐ Backfill dirt contains no sharp edges to puncture waterproofing.

Checklist After Backfill

☐ All backfill area completely filled in.

☐ Lot smoothed out to a rough grade.

☐ Necessary dirt hauled in and spread.

Checklist After Final Grade Completed

☐ Two to three percent slope or better away from dwelling.

☐ Berms in proper place, of proper height and form.

☐ Water meter elevation correct.

☐ Final grade smooth. Topsoil replaced on top if requested.

☐ No damage to curb, walkways, driveway, base of home, water meter, gutter downspots, HVAC, splash blocks and/or trees.

EXCAVATION - Glossary

BACKFILL—Process of placing soil up against foundation after all necessary foundation treatments have been performed. In many instances, foundation wall must have temporary interior bracing or house framed in to support weight of dirt until it has had time to settle.

BATTER BOARD—A pair of horizontal boards nailed to vertical posts set at the corners of an excavation area used to indicate the desired level of excavation. Also used for fastening taut strings to indicate outlines of the foundation walls.

BERM—Built-up mound of dirt for drainage and landscaping.

BUILDER'S LEVEL—A surveying tool consisting of an optical siting scope and a measuring stick. It is used to check the level of batter boards and foundation.

BULKHEAD—Vertical drop in footing when changing from one depth to another.

DRAG TIME—Time required to haul heavy excavation equipment to and from the site.

FILL DIRT—Loose dirt. Normally dirt brought in from another location to fill a void. Sturdier than topsoil used under slabs, drives, and sidewalks.

FINISH GRADE—Final process of leveling and smoothing topsoil into final position prior to landscaping.

FOOTING DITCH—Trough area dug to accommodate concrete or footing forms.

FROSTLINE—The depth to which frost penetrates the soil. Footings should always be poured below this line to prevent cracking.

GRADING—Process of shaping the surface of a lot to give it the desired contours. See FINISH GRADE.

KERF—Vertical notch or cut made in a batter board where a string is fastened tightly.

PLUMB—The condition when something is exactly vertical to the ground, such as the wall of a house.

PLUMB BOB—A weight attached to a string used to indicate a plumb (vertical) condition.

ROUGH GRADE—First grading effort used to level terrain to approximate shape for drainage and landscaping.

SETTLING—Movement of unstable dirt over time. Fill dirt normally settles downward as it is compacted by its own weight or a structure above it.

SILT FENCE—A barrier constructed of burlap, plastic or bales of hay used to prevent the washing away of mud and silt from a cleared lot onto street or adjacent lots.

STAKING—To lay out the position of a home, the batter boards, excavation lines and depth(s).

TOPSOIL—Two or three inch layer of rich, loose soil. This must be removed from areas to be cleared or excavated and replaced in other areas later. Not for load bearing areas.

TRANSIT—Similiar to a builder's level except that the instrument can be adjusted vertically. Used for testing walls for plumb and laying out batter board, and establishing degree of a slope.

Foundation

The foundation will be one of the most critical stages of construction. Foundation work has one chance to be right — the consequences of poor craftsmanship are permanent. Additionally, this effort will involve individuals from more than one company, which can complicate the job. Hire the best.

This phase of construction requires coordination between a small army of sub-contractors and all of them must work with you over a relatively short period of time. The following list briefly describes the sequence of events:

(1) Footing subs dig footings.

(2) Exterminator treats soil in and around footings to prevent termites.

(3) County inspector checks footings before pouring.

(4) Footings are poured.

(5) Foundation walls are laid or poured (basement construction).

(6) Plumber and HVAC subs lay water, sewer and gas pipes before slab floor is poured (slab construction only).

(7) Slab is inspected.

(8) Slab is poured by concrete finishers.

(9) Basement wall is waterproofed.

(10) Basement wall drainage system is installed.

As you can see, foundation work can be an exercise in scheduling and diplomacy. Make sure to contact all involved parties well in advance of the pour and plan around rain delays. If possible, cover the foundation area with poly well in advance to prevent rain from ruining your well laid plans. This poly can be used during the pour as the vapor barrier under the slab, if left undamaged.

PEST CONTROL

Below ground, all slab and footing areas must be permanently poisoned prior to laying any gravel, poly or concrete. Poison must be allowed to soak in after application without rain. Rain will reduce or nullify the effectiveness of the pest control treatment. Your pest control treatment can be taken care of in one or two visits depending upon how thorough you want to be. Some builders have a second treatment applied around the base of the home after all work is done. This is just more insurance, especially if you are building for yourself.

THE CONCRETE SUBS

You will likely deal with several different parties when working with concrete for foundations, slabs and driveways:

■ A full service foundation company

■ A sub-contractor to dig and pour footings

■ Labor to lay concrete block walls

■ Concrete finishers to finish concrete slab, patios, walkways and driveways

■ Concrete supplier

Full Service Foundation Company

This subcontractor can be one of the best bargains you will encounter in your project. This sub replaces most of the other foundation subs listed above and may not cost a penny more. A full service foundation company can:

■ Lay out the entire foundation for you, including installing batter boards. Only the corners of the foundation need to be marked with stakes. The foundation sub will do the rest.

■ Lay out, dig and pour the footings.

■ Pour all basement walls.

■ Handle all scheduling of inspectors and concrete deliveries.

■ Waterproof (tar, gravel, and drain pipe).

Generally, poured foundations are slightly more expensive than other types; but this cost can be offset by savings in time, labor, hassle and interest paid on your construction loan. However, this sub is only cost effective to use if you plan a full basement.

The Footings Sub

The footings sub will normally charge you by the lineal foot of footings required. He will provide either steel or wood forms, but may ask you to supply some of the form material. Form work can cost approximately one-third of the total footing job. In many areas of the country with stable soil, the footings subs can pour directly into the footings trench with no forms required.

Concrete Block Masons

If you do plan to have a basement made of concrete block you'll need this sub. Concrete block masons will likely be a different group than those laying your brick veneer (if you have any). They will charge for labor by the unit (block) laid.

Concrete Finishers

The concrete finisher may be the footing sub, but not necessarily. He will charge by the square footage finished. Costs will also vary in the type of finishes you want. Slick, rough, smooth, trowel finish or pea gravel are a few of the surfaces that this sub can produce. Don't use a crew that has less than three men — this is a tough job. Finishing must be done fast and even faster in hot weather. Concrete can set in half an hour. The finishers will finish the slab and then come back to do drives and walkways later.

Concrete Supplier

The concrete supplier will charge by the cubic yard of concrete used. A standard cement truck can hold 8-10 cubic yards. The supplier may charge you a flat rate just to make the trip, so pour and finish as much of the concrete work at a time as you can to minimize his trips.

CONCRETE STRUCTURES

The concrete structures that you will use will vary somewhat depending upon whether or not you have a basement. If you plan to have a basement, you will have footings, foundation walls and a foundation floor. If you plan to have no basement, you will have a slab with a footing built into the edge. These structures are described briefly below.

FOOTINGS are what your home rests on. A footing is a solid, sub-grade rectangle of concrete around the perimeter of the dwelling. Its width and thickness will vary depending on the local building code, soil and weight of materials supported. Footings are normally twice as wide as the wall they support. Additional footings are provided for fireplaces and column supports.

CONCRETE BLOCKS will be used if you have a basement and you decide not to pour the walls. Concrete blocks are normally cast hollow units measuring 7 5/8" wide, 7 5/8" high and 15 5/8" long. These are often referred to as 8" x 8" x 16" units because when laid with 3/8" mortar joints, they will occupy a space 16" long and 8" high. Concrete masonry units come in a wide variety of shapes and sizes. Your local building code may have certain guidelines in the use of concrete units.

STEEL REINFORCEMENT is used to strengthen concrete slabs, walls and footings and help them resist the effects of shrinkage and temperature change. Reinforcing comes in two major forms: bars and mesh. Reinforcing bars used for residential construction are normally about 3/8" in diameter. Reinforcing wire, normally with a 6" grid and 1/4" wire, is adequate to do the job. For monolithic slabs, mesh is used more than bar steel. Steel reinforcement should be laid before cement is poured, and secured so that no movement will occur during the pouring process. Normally the steel is located two-thirds of the way up from the bottom of a slab and in the center of poured concrete walls. Your concrete sub and concrete supplier will have primary responsibility for proper reinforcement.

Foundation Walls

Foundation walls are made of either concrete blocks or poured concrete.

Concrete Block: This method is normally a little less expensive than a poured wall. However, concrete block walls must be leveled by hand. The concrete block wall must be coated with two ¼" layers of portland cement below grade level.

Poured Wall: This method, which is growing in popularity, costs a bit more but yields a wall three times as strong as a block wall and more impervious to water. If you are planning to have a brick veneer exterior, you must tell the form sub to provide for a brick ledge in the forms. This is what your brick wall will rest on.

Foundation Floors

Foundation floors are poured after the footings and walls have been properly cured. Coarse, washed gravel is normally used as an underlayment. The reinforcing is raised to the proper level with rocks or other items. The concrete is normally poured to a depth of 4". The floor should be finished as close to level as possible with a slight slope toward the drains.

Monolithic Slab: This is a combination of footings and foundation floor poured all at once. If fill dirt is used below slab, extra reinforcing bars should be used. The dirt should be well compacted with machinery prior to pouring.

Driveways: Driveway slabs are generally 4" thick and should be allowed to cure for 2-3 days before any vehicles are allowed to drive on it. Driveways are not usually installed until trimwork starts.

Sidewalks and Patios: These are simple structures which should only be poured after the surface ground has had ample time to settle. This is usually done when the driveway is poured.

Concrete Joints

One of the most common reasons for concrete cracking, aside from unstable soil and tree roots, is cracking due to expansion and contraction. Expansion and contraction are best controlled by using two types of joints:

Isolation (Expansion Control) Joints: These joints are placed between concrete structures in order to keep one structure's expansion from affecting adjacent structures. Common places used are between:

- Driveway and garage slab
- Driveway and roadway
- Driveway and sidewalk
- Slabs and foundation wall

Control (Contraction) Joints: These joints are placed within concrete units, such as driveways (normally every 15'), sidewalks (normally every 5' or closer), and patios (normally every 12').

Construction joints: A third type are temporary joints marking the end of a concrete pour due to delays in concrete supply. If you are lucky, you won't need any of these. Your concrete formsman and/or finisher should be placed responsible for setting all expansion joints, and finishers are responsible for all control joints.

WEATHER CONSIDERATIONS

RAINY WEATHER can adversely affect almost any concrete work. Heavy rain can affect poured concrete surfaces and slow the drying process. Schedule your concrete pouring for periods of forecasted dry weather. Have rolls of heavy plastic available if the weather forecast is wrong.

COLD WEATHER is a challenge. The main problem to prevent here is freezing. Concrete work in temperatures below 40° Fahrenheit becomes difficult. Several methods to protect work include heating water and heating aggregate, covered with tarpaulins over hot pipes. Frozen sub-grade must be heated to ensure that it will not freeze during the curing process. Mix the heated aggregate and water before adding the concrete. Consider using high-early-strength concrete to reduce the time required to protect the concrete from freezing. Once concrete has been poured, if freezing weather is likely, the concrete should be protected either by special heated enclosures or insulation such as batts or blankets.

HOT WEATHER is also a challenge. The main problem to prevent here is rapid drying which induces cracking and reduction in concrete strength. Regardless of the external temperature, concrete should not be allowed to exceed 85° Fahrenheit. This can be achieved by using a combination of the following methods:

■ Cool the aggregate with water before mixing.

■ Mix concrete with cold water. Ice can be used in extreme cases.

■ Provide sources of shade for materials.

■ Work at night or very early in the morning.

■ Protect drying concrete from sun and winds, which accelerate the drying process. Wet straw or tarpaulins can be used.

Concrete trucks normally hold about 9 cubic yards. Make sure to schedule trucks to provide a constant supply of concrete.

WATERPROOFING

Waterproofing normally applies to foundation wall treatments and drainage tile used to maintain proper foundation water drainage. This is critical to ensure that you will have a DRY basement in the many years to come.

Wall Treatment

Wall treatments are applied below the finished grade (below ground level). Normally, this treatment consists of hot tar, asphalt or bituminous material applied to the exterior surface. A layer of 6 mil (millimeter) poly (polyethylene) is then applied to the tar while still tacky. This is an added protection against water seepage. If masonry block walls are used, two ¼" coats of portland cement are applied to the masonry blocks, extending 6" above the unfinished grade level. The first coating is roughened up before drying, allowing the second coat to adhere properly. Masonry blocks and the first coating of portland cement are dampened before applying coats of portland cement. The second coating should be kept damp for at least 48 hours. The joint between the footing and wall should be filled with portland cement before applying the tar coating. This is called parging and further protects against underground water and moisture.

New waterproofing compounds are available on the market that are superior to asphalt and carry a 10 year warranty if applied correctly. This compound has the ability to bridge cracks in masonry and block and

will not degrade with age. It is considerably more expensive than asphalt; however, since wet basements top the list of major homeowner complaints, the extra expense seems well worth it. Ask your waterproofing contractor if he is trained to apply this compound.

Drain Pipe

Four-inch perforated drain pipe (plastic preferred over tile) is placed around the perimeter of the foundation with #57 gravel below and 8" to 12" of #57 gravel above. The pipe should be sloped at least 1" every 20 feet. Pipe sections should be spaced ¼" apart with a strip of tar paper (roofing paper) over each joint. The drain pipe will only serve its purpose if it drains off somewhere. You should make it so that the drain slopes to one corner. If you like, have a run-off pipe installed to carry the water farther away.

PEST CONTROL — Steps

PS1 CONDUCT standard bidding process and select pest control sub. Use a company that has been around for at least ten years since you may want to get annual pest control and a warranty. In some cases builders are not charged for the pre-treating service. The pest control sub looks for a contract with the homebuyer.

PS2 NOTIFY pest control sub of when to show up for the pre-treat.

PS3 APPLY poison to all footing, slab ground and surrounding area. Since it is hard to test the effectiveness and coverage of treatment, it is advised that someone be present to oversee this critical step. This treatment should only be done if rain is unlikely for 48 hours.

After Construction

PS4 APPLY poison to ground-level perimeter of home. Again, it is advised to have someone oversee this step.

PS5 OBTAIN signed pest control warranty and file it away. Many lenders require a pest warranty at closing to insure proper protection.

PS6 PAY pest control sub and have him sign an affidavit.

CONCRETE — Steps

CN1 CONDUCT standard bidding process (concrete supplier). Bid will be measured in cubic feet. If you use a full service foundation sub, this will probably be unnecessary.

CN2 CONDUCT standard bidding process (formwork and finishing). If you use a full service foundation company, they will lay out the foundation, pour footings and walls and arrange for the concrete. Pricing can get pretty complicated, depending on the height and size of the walls.

CN3 CONDUCT standard bidding process (concrete block masonry).

FOOTINGS

CN4 INSPECT batter boards. This is quite critical since your entire project is based on the position of your batter boards and string. This is done with a transit.

CN5 DIG footings for foundation, A/C compressor, fireplaces and all support columns.

CN6 SET footing forms as necessary. Be very

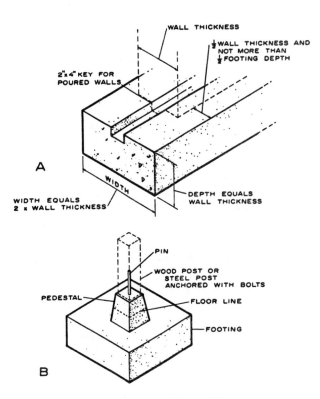

Figure 9. Concrete footing: A, Wall footing; B, Post footing

Figure 8. Establishing corners for excavation and footings

careful that the footing sub places footings so that walls will sit in the center of the footing. Subs can either use their own forms or use lumber at the site. If the sub asks you to provide forms material, have three times the foundation perimeter in 16 foot 2x4's.

CN7 INSPECT footing forms. Refer to related checklist in this section. Make sure that the side forms are sturdy as they will have to support lots of wet concrete. Make sure that the tops of the forms are level as they will be used as a guide in finishing the footing surface. Also make sure that the forms are parallel with each other. Footings are normally coated on the inside with some form of oil so that the concrete doesn't stick to them. Check for this. If you plan to have poured walls on your footings, have the forms sub supply the "key" forms which will be pressed into the footings after they are poured. In many areas, steel rods are inserted vertically in footings prior to pouring.

CN8 SCHEDULE and complete footing inspection. Obtain signed, written approval from local building inspector.

CN9 CALL your concrete supplier to schedule delivery of concrete if you are not using a full service finisher. This should be done at least 24 hours in advance. Make sure good weather is forecast for the next few days. Have rolls of 6 mil poly available in case of rain. Make sure to add calcium carbonate if freezing is a potential problem.

CN10 POUR footings. This should be done as quickly as possible once the footing trenches have been dug so that the soil does not get soft from rain and exposure.

CN11 INSTALL key forms in footings before setting has taken place. Your forms sub should do this. Budget finishers will just cut a groove in the footing with a 2x4.

CN12 FINISH footings as needed. This normally involves simply screeding the top and smoothing out the surface a bit.

CN13 REMOVE footing forms. If subs used your lumber, have them clean and stack it to be used later for bracing. Framers won't use this lumber because it will dull their saws.

CN14 INSPECT footings. Make sure that the footings are level and that there are no visible cracks.

CN15 PAY concrete supplier for footing concrete, unless you are using a full service finisher in which case you will make one payment after the walls have been poured and inspected.

Poured Wall

CN16 SET poured wall foundation and stoop arm forms. These are normally special units made out of steel held together with metal ties. Make stoop arms extra long to insure that the front porch will not settle or crack.

CN17 CALL concrete supplier in advance to schedule concrete. This step will usually be done by a full service foundation contractor.

CN18 INSPECT poured foundation wall and stoop

Figure 10. Forming for poured concrete walls

arm forms. Again, make sure they are level, parallel, sturdy and oiled.

CN19 POUR foundation walls and stoop arms. If more than one truckload is required, make sure to schedule deliveries so that a constant supply of concrete is available for pouring. It is unsatisfactory to have cement setting when wet cement will be poured over it. This can result in a fault crack in the foundation. Make sure that additional loads of concrete are on site or on the way to insure a continuous pour. If the weather is rainy, have a grader available in case you have to push the concrete truck up a muddy slope.

CN20 FINISH poured foundation walls. Again, the tops of the forms serve as screed guides. The surface is smoothed and lag bolts should be set into the surface. Make sure the bolts are at least 4" in the concrete and are standing straight up. Also make sure that the bolts are not in places that will interfere with any studs or door openings. Put wide washers on the sunken end of the lag bolts for greater holding strength. Many builders are omitting lag bolts and just using concrete nails to anchor sill plate to the foundation.

CN21 REMOVE poured foundation wall forms.

Figure 11. Stepped footings

This should only be done several days after the concrete has had time to set.

CN22 INSPECT poured foundation walls. Check for square, level and visible surface cracks.

CN23 BREAK off tie ends if metal footing forms are used.

CN24 PAY concrete supplier for poured foundation wall concrete.

Block Wall

CN25 ORDER concrete blocks and schedule block masons. Make sure the blocks are placed as near to the work area as possible. Block masons will charge extra if they have to move excessive amounts of block very far.

CN26 LAY concrete blocks. You may want to watch some of this in progress since it will be very hard to correct mistakes when the blocks have set. If you see globs of cement on blocks, wait till it dries to clean it off — it will come off in one piece. Compare against blueprints as the work proceeds.

CN27 FINISH concrete blocks. While mortar is still setting, the masons will tool the joints concave if you like. However, for subgrade work, it is better to have the mortar flush with the blockwork. If any of the block wall is to be exposed, have the block mason

stucco the block to provide a smooth, more attractive surface.

CN28 INSPECT concrete block work. Compare work with blueprints. Refer to your specifications and inspection guidelines.

CN29 PAY concrete block masons. Have them sign an affidavit.

CN30 CLEAN up after block masons. Stack or return extra block. Spread leftover sand in drive area. Bags of mortar mix should be protected from moisture.

Concrete Slab

CN31 SET slab forms for basement, front stoop, fireplace pad, garage, etc. Check this against blueprints as they are being erected. If the slab is the floor of the basement, the walls will act as the forms.

CN32 PACK slab sub-soil. Soil should be moistened slightly, then packed with a power tamper. This has got to be a solid surface.

CN33 INSTALL stub plumbing. If the slab is to be the floor of the house, schedule the plumber to set all water and sewer lines under slab area. Ask the plumber to install a foam collar around all sewer lines that protrude out of the slab. This makes final adjustments to the pipe easier during finish plumbing. If the pipe needs to be moved slightly, the foam

Figure 12. Combined slab and foundation (thickened edge slab)

Figure 13. Reinforced grade beam for concrete slab. Beam spans between concrete piers located below frostline.

can be chipped away instead of the concrete. Make sure any resulting gap is resealed with spray foam insulation.

CN34 SCHEDULE HVAC sub to run any gas lines that may run under the slab, such as gas fireplace starters.

CN35 INSPECT plumbing and gas lines against blueprint for proper location. Make sure that plumbing is not dislodged, moved or damaged in subsequent steps.

CN36 POUR and spread crushed stone (crusher run) evenly on slab or foundation floor and garage slab area.

CN37 INSTALL 6 mil poly vapor barrier. Can be omitted in garage slab.

CN38 LAY reinforcing wire as required. The rewire should lie either in the middle of the slab and garage slab or at a point two-thirds from the bottom. It can be supported by the gravel or rocks.

CN39 INSTALL rigid insulation around the perimeter of the slab to cut down on heat loss through the slab.

CN40 CALL concrete supplier to schedule delivery of concrete for slab. Confirm concrete type,

quantity, time of pour and site location. Finishers should also be contacted.

CN41 INSPECT slab forms. Compare them against the blueprints. Make sure that all necessary plumbing is in place! Check that forms are parallel, perpendicular and plumb as required. Forms should be sturdy and oiled to keep from sticking to concrete. See checklist.

CN42 POUR slab and garage slab. This should be done as quickly as possible. Call it off if rain looks likely. Have 6 mil poly protection available.

CN43 FINISH slab and garage slab. Finishers should put their smoothest finish on all slab work. This normally requires four steps:

- rough screed with a floater
- rough trowel
- power trowel
- finish trowel

CN44 INSPECT slab. Check for rough spots, cracks and high or low spots. High and low spots can be checked with a hose. See where the water collects and drains. Water should never completely cover a nickel laid flat. Make sure any backfill does not cover the brick ledge if one is present.

CN45 PAY concrete supplier for slab and garage slab concrete.

Figure 14. Full foundation wall for cold climates. Perimeter heat duct insulated to reduce loss.

DRIVEWAYS AND PATIOS

CN46 COMPACT driveway, walkway, patio and mailbox pad sub-soil. This must be a solid surface.

CN47 SET driveway, walkway, patio and mailbox forms. You should not pour less than a 3" thick driveway. If you did not lay down crushed stone previously, you may want to do it now. If your electrical or gas service crosses the driveway area, it must be installed before this step. Use scrap lumber for forms.

CN48 CALL your concrete supplier to schedule delivery of concrete. Confirm type and quantity of concrete, delivery time and site location. Schedule finishers.

CN49 INSPECT driveway, walkway, patio and mailbox forms. Pull a line level across forms to determine slope. Forms should be installed so that driveway will slope slightly away from house and toward an area with good drainage.

CN50 POUR driveway, walkway and patio areas.

Make sure finishers do not thin concrete for easier working.

CN51 FINISH driveway, walkway, patio and mailbox areas. Make sure that the finishers put isolation joints between the slab, driveway, patio and walkways. Expansion joints should be put about every 12' in the driveway and every 5' or less in the walkways. Driveway should be formed where it meets the street.

CN52 INSPECT driveway, walkway and patio areas.

CN53 ROPE off drive, walk, patio and mailbox areas so that people and pets don't make footprints. Put some red tape on the strings so that they can be seen.

CN54 PAY concrete supplier for driveway, walkway, patio, and mailbox pad concrete.

CN55 PAY concrete finishers and have them sign an affidavit.

CN56 PAY concrete finishers retainage.

Figure 15. Driveway turnaround

Figure 16. Masonry paved walks: A, brick; B, flagstone

Figure 17. Sidewalks on slopes: A, stairs; B, stepped ram

Figure 18. Driveway details: A, single slab driveway; B, ribbon-type driveway.

WATERPROOFING — Steps

WP1 CONDUCT standard bidding process. Invite your full service company to bid.

WP2 SEAL footing and wall intersection with portland cement. Skip if you have no basement.

WP3 APPLY ¼" portland cement to moistened masonry wall. Roughen surface and allow to dry 24 hours. Perform only if you have a masonry foundation.

WP4 APPLY second ¼" portland cement to moistened wall. Keep moist for 48 hours and allow to set. Perform only if you have a masonry foundation.

Figure 19. Damp-proofing for basement slab and wall

Figure 20. Crawl space damp-proofing

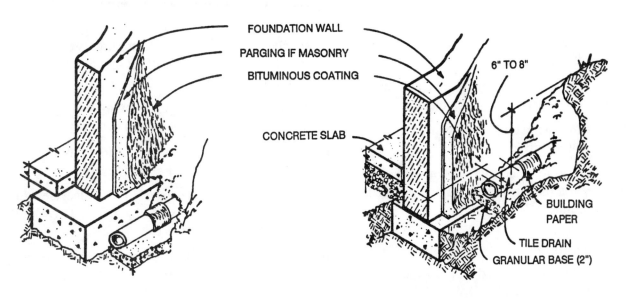

Figure 21. Drain tiles along side of footing

Drain tiles on top of footing

WP5 APPLY waterproofing compound to all below grade walls.

WP6 APPLY black 6 mil poly (4 mil is a bit too thin) to tarred surface while still tacky. Roll it out horizontally and overlap seams.

WP7 INSPECT waterproofing (tar/poly). No holes should be visible.

WP8 INSTALL 1" layer of gravel as bed for drain tile. Optional for crawl spaces may use even if you have no basement.

WP9 INSTALL 4" perforated plastic drain tile around entire foundation perimeter. Also install PVC run-off drain pipe.

WP10 INSPECT drain tile for proper drainage. Mark the ends with a stake to prevent them from being buried.

WP11 APPLY 8" to 12" of top gravel (#57) above drain tile. HINT: Surround water spigot area with any excess gravel to prevent muddy mess during construction. Spigot will be used quite often.

WP12 PAY waterproofing sub and have him sign an affidavit.

WP13 PAY waterproofing sub retainage.

CONCRETE - Sample Specifications

General

- All concrete, form and finish work is to conform to the local building code.
- Concrete will not be poured if precipitation is likely or unless otherwise instructed.
- All form, finishing and concrete work MUST be within ¼" within level.
- All payments to be made five working days after satisfactory completion of each major structure as seen fit by builder.

Concrete Supplier

- Concrete is to be air-entrained ASTM Type I (General Purpose), 3000 psi after 28 days.
- Concrete is to be delivered to site and poured into forms in accordance with generally accepted standards.
- Washed gravel and concrete silica sand to be used.
- Each concrete pour to be done without interruption. No more than one half hour between loads of concrete to prevent poor bondage and seams.
- Concrete to be poured near to final location to avoid excessive working. Concrete will not be thinned at the site for easier working.

Formwork

- Bid is to perform all formwork per attached drawings including footings for:
- Exterior walls
- Monolithic slab
- Poured walls
- Bulkheads
- Garage
- AC compressor slabs
- Patio
- Basement pier footings
- All footing forms to be of 2" or thicker wood or steel.
- All forms to be properly oiled or otherwise lubricated before being placed into service.
- All forms, washed gravel, reinforcing bars to be supplied by form sub-contractor unless otherwise specified in writing. All of these materials to be included in bid price.
- All forms will be sufficiently strong so as to resist bowing under weight of poured concrete.
- Form keys to be used at base of footings and for brick ledge.
- Expansion joints and expansion joint placement to be included in bid. Expansion joints: Driveway every 15 feet. Sidewalks every 5 feet.
- Pier footings and perimeter footings to be poured to exactly the same level.
- All concrete to be cured at the proper rate and kept moist for at least three days.

- Foundation and garage floor to be steel troweled smooth with no high or low points.

- Finished basement floor will slope toward drains.

- Garage floor, driveway and patios will slope away from dwelling for proper drainage.

- Concrete to be poured and finished in sections on hot days in order to avoid premature setting.

Concrete Block

- All courses to be running bond within ¼" level.

- Top course to be within ¼" level.

- Standard 12" block to be used on backfilled basement area.

- 4" cap block to finish all walls.

- Horizontal reinforcing to be used on every three courses.

- Trowel joints to be flush with block surface.

WATERPROOFING - Specifications

- Bid is to include all material and labor required to waterproof dwelling based on specifications described below.

- Two ¼" coats of portland cement to be applied smoothly and evenly. First coat to be applied to moistened masonry blocks and roughened before drying. Second coat to be kept moist for 48 hours to set (block wall only).

- Portland cement to be applied smoothly to intersection of footing and wall.

- Sharp points in portland cement coating to be removed prior to application of tar coating, as they will puncture 6 mil poly.

- Asphalt coat to be applied hot, covering entire sub-grade area. Coat to be a minimum of ¹⁄₆₄".

- 4" diameter perforated PVC drain pipe to be installed around entire perimeter of foundation. Tile sections to be separated ¼" with tar paper to cover all joints. Drain tile should have a minimum slope of 1" in 20'. Drain holes every 6" in pipe.

PEST CONTROL - Specifications

- Bid is to provide all materials, chemicals and labor to treat all footing and slab area.

- Base of home to be sprayed after all construction is complete.

- Termite treatment warranty to be provided.

CONCRETE - Inspection

Batter Boards

☐ All batter boards installed:
  - Exterior walls
  - Piers and support columns
  - Garage or carport
  - Fireplace slabs
  - Porches and entryway
  - Other required batter boards

☐ All batter boards installed properly:
  - Level
  - Square
  - Proper dimensions according to blueprints
  - All strings tight and secure
  - All string nails to be marked to prevent movement.

☐ All bulkheads well-formed and according to plan. Step down depth dimension correct.

Checklist Prior to Pouring Any Concrete

☐ All planned concrete and form work has been inspected by state and/or local officials if necessary prior to pouring.

☐ Forms laid out in proper dimensions according to plans. Length, height, depth, etc.

☐ Correct relationship to property lines, set-back lines, easements and site plan (front, back and all sides).

☐ No rain predicted for 6-8 hours minimum.

☐ Forms secure with proper bracing.

☐ Forms on proper elevation.

☐ No presence of ground water or mud.

☐ No soft spots in ground area affected.

☐ Ground adequately packed.

☐ Forms laid out according to specifications: parallel, perpendicular and plumb where indicated.

☐ All corners square.

☐ Necessary portions straight. No bowing. Wood forms should be nominal 2" thick.

☐ Spacers used where necessary to keep parallel forms proper distance apart.

☐ Expansion joints in place and level with top of surface. Approximately ½" wide.

☐ All plumbing underneath or in concrete is installed, complete, inspected and approved.

☐ Reinforcing bars bent around corners — no bars just intersecting at corners.

☐ Concrete supplier scheduled.

☐ Adequate finishers available to do finish work.

☐ Holes under forms filled with crushed stone.

☐ Proper concrete ordered.

☐ Forms tested for strength prior to pouring.

☐ Backfill stable and not in the way. Will not roll onto freshly finished cement or get in finisher's way.

☐ Garage, carport, patio, entrance and porch slabs angled to slope away from home.

☐ Any necessary plumbing has been inspected.

☐ Gravel, re-wire and 6 mil poly have been placed properly when and where required.

☐ All water and sewer lines installed and protected from abrasions during pouring of concrete.

☐ Finishers have been scheduled or are present.

☐ Crawl space, if any, has been cleared with a rake.

☐ Foam collars placed over all water and sewer pipes where they protrude out of the concrete slab.

General Checklist After Concrete and Blockwork

☐ Surface checked for level with string level, builder's level or transom.

☐ Corners square using a builder's square.

☐ No cracks, rough spots or other visible irregularities on surface.

☐ Sill bolts vertical and properly spaced (if used).

Foundation Wall (Concrete Block)

☐ Masonry joints properly tooled and even.

☐ Blocks have no major cracks or irregularities.

☐ Cap blocks installed level as top course.

☐ Room allowed for brick veneer above, if any is to be used.

☐ Joint between wall and footing properly parged (sloped away from wall) with mortar.

WATERPROOFING - Inspection

☐ Portland cement is relatively smooth and even with no sharp edges protruding.

☐ Portland cement completely covers intersection of wall and footings.

☐ Asphalt coating completely covers entire subgrade area, including intersection of wall and footings.

☐ Black 6 mil poly completely covers entire tar coating and adheres firmly to it. Look for any tears or punctures in poly which need to be patched before backfill. Remove large rocks and roots from backfill area so that poly will not be torn during backfill process later.

☐ Tarred area does not go above grade level or where stucco is to be placed.

☐ Poly secured to stay in place during backfill.

☐ No rain in basement.

☐ No wet spots on interior basement walls.

CONCRETE - Glossary

AGGREGATE—Irregular-shaped gravel suspended in cement.

CRAWL SPACE— Area below living area where no basement is used.

CRUSHER RUN—Crushed stone, normally up to 2" or 3" in size. Sharp edges. Used for drive and foundation support as a base. Very stable surface, as opposed to gravel, which is not very stable.

CURING—Process of maintaining proper moisture level and temperature (about 73° Fahrenheit) until the design strength is achieved. Curing methods include adding moisture (sprinkling with water, applying wet coverings such as burlap or straw) and retaining moisture (covering with waterproof materials such as polyurethane).

EXPANSION JOINT— A joint or gap between concrete structure to allow for expansion and contraction of the structures without cracking.

FLOATING— A process used after screeding to provide a smoother surface. The process normally involves embedding larger aggregate below the surface by vibrating, removing imperfections, high and low spots and compacting the surface concrete.

FOOTING—Lowest perimeter portion of a structure resting on firm soil or rock that supports the weight of the structure.

HYDRATION—The chemical process wherein portland cement becomes a bonding agent as water is slowly removed from the mixture. The rate of hydration determines the strength of the bond and hence the strength of the concrete. Hydration stops when all the water has been removed. Once hydration stops, it cannot be restarted.

LINE— A string pulled tight. Normally used to check or establish straightness.

LINTEL— A section of precast concrete placed over doors and windows.

PARGING—Thin coatings (¼") of mortar applied to the exterior face of concrete block where block wall and footing meet; serves as a waterproofing mechanism.

PLASTIC—Term interchangeable with "wet" as in "plastic cement".

POLY—Polyethylene. A heavy gauge plastic used for vapor barriers and material protection. The accepted thickness is 6 mil.

RE-BAR—Metal rods used to improve the strength of concrete structures.

SCREEDING—The process of running a straightedge over the top of forms to produce a smooth surface on wet (plastic) cement. The screeding proceeds in one direction, normally in a sawing motion.

STOOP ARMS—Section of foundation wall extending out perpendicular to exterior wall used to support a masonry or stone stoop.

TERMITE SHIELD— A shield, normally of galvanized sheet metal, placed between footing and foundation wall to prevent the passage of termites.

TROWELING—A process used after floating to provide an even smoother surface.

WIRE MESH—A heavy gauge steel mesh sold in rolls for providing reinforcing in concrete slabs.

Framing

Framing is one of the most visible signs of progress on the building project. Become close friends with your framing contractor. He will be involved with the project longer than any other contractor. His skills will have a large impact on the quality of your home and your ability to stay on schedule.

Take adequate time and choose your framer carefully. A good framer is worth his weight in 2x4's! A good framing crew should consist of at least three people in order to move lumber around efficiently. Check your carpenter's ability to read blueprints. He will be making many interpretations of these plans when framing. Your carpenter should have experience as the master carpenter on several jobs and not just as a helper.

When you feel comfortable with your carpenter's experience proceed by informing him of the quality of work you demand. Ask him to be sure to "crown" all material during construction. What is "crowning"? All lumber has a natural curve to it. Observe the concentric arcs when looking at the end of a board. When framing, the carpenter should be sure to turn all the lumber so that the natural curves of the lumber are in the same direction. When framing horizontal joists, this curve should bow up. The top of the curve is the "crown". Ask your carpenter to lay aside any badly warped or curved lumber to be sent back to the materials supplier or to be used for short framing pieces such as cripples or dead wood.

Use surfaced, kiln-dried lumber to reduce warping due to shrinkage. Warpage in framing pieces can also be reduced by using a higher grade of lumber and will result in a neater framing job and a happier framing sub. The additional cost is worth it unless you have an unusually careful carpenter willing to spend hours picking out bad lumber. Specify Douglas fir for the best job. Avoid mixing fir and pine lumber on the same job. Pine can be ¼" to ½" differ-

ent in size because of different shrinkage rates. Any lumber in contact with the foundation or concrete must be pressure treated pine or "celcure" as it is commonly called. This lumber provides moisture and termite protection between the foundation and the framing of the rest of the house.

PAYMENT OF FRAMING CONTRACTOR

The framing contractor does not usually provide any of his own materials for the job except perhaps nails. It is your responsibility to make sure that all necessary materials are on the site when needed. Carpenters usually charge by the square footage of the area framed plus extras or will appraise the job and supply a total bid price. This includes ALL space covered by a roof, not just heated space. This includes the garage area, enclosed porches, tool sheds, garden houses, etc. The framing charge usually includes setting the exterior doors and windows and installing the sheathing. Special items such as bay windows, stairs, curved stairs,

Figure 22. Wall framing used in platform construction

Figure 23. Wall framing used in balloon construction

chimney chases, recessed or tray ceilings usually require additional charges.

TYPES OF FRAMING

The two main types of framing used for residential construction are balloon framing and platform framing. For a more complete description of these two methods, refer to a good carpentry manual. Platform framing is the most widely used type and will be the type your carpenter is probably familiar with. In this book, only platform framing will be covered, as it is by far the most popular framing method.

Figure 24. Floor framing: (1) nailing bridging to joists; (2) nailing board subfloor to joists; (3) nailing header to joists; (4) toenailing header to sill.

Figure 25. "In-line" joist system. Alternate extension of joists over the center support with plywood gusset allows the use of smaller joist size.

SUB-FLOOR FRAMING

There are two types of floor framing: joist floors and floor trusses. Joist floors usually consist of 2x8's or 2x10's spaced 12", 16" or 24" on center with bridging in between. Bridging consists of diagonal bracing between joists to improve stability and to help transfer the load to adjacent joists. Joist floors are by far the most common type in use today, but floor trusses are becoming more popular due to several advantages over the conventional method. A floor truss, like a roof truss, consists of 2x4's with diagonal bracing in between, which makes the entire unit very strong for its weight.

Floor trusses have the following advantages over standard joists:

■ Because of their added rigidity, floor trusses can span longer distances without the need for beam support.

■ Wiring and heating ducts may be run within the floor truss, eliminating the need to box in heating ducts below ceiling level. This makes the jobs of the plumber, electrician, HVAC and telephone sub much easier. Make sure to point this out to these contractors when bargaining for rates.

■ Floor trusses provide better sound insulation between floors because there is less solid wood for sound to travel through.

■ Floor trusses warp less, squeak less and are generally stronger than comparable joist floors.

Figure 26.

- Crawl space ventilator and soil cover.

- Steel post for wood or steel girder: connection to beam.

- Wood post for wood girder:
A, Connection to girder B, base.

- Built up wood girder.

- Anchoring floor system to concrete or masonry walls:
A, With sill plate; B, without sill plate.

- Clearances for wood construction.

■ Even though floor trusses are a bit more expensive, their advantages can simplify a construction project and can save money in the long run. Your supplier for these units will be the same as for roof trusses.

FLOORING MATERIALS

The flooring design is another area where recent innovations have produced a simpler and superior product. Most standard flooring consists of a subfloor, usually of ½" or ⅝" CDX plywood, and a finish floor which can be ⅝" particleboard or another layer of plywood. The second layer is installed after drying in the structure. If this method is used, be sure to install a layer of asphalt felt (the type used in

Figure 27. End-wall framing for platform construction (junction of first-floor ceiling with upper-story floor framing).

roofing) or heavy craft construction paper between the two layers. This acts as a sound buffer and reduces floor squeaking. Often a two story house will use ½" flooring on the first floor and ⅝" on the second floor.

A potentially superior flooring method has been introduced by the American Plywood Association called the APA Sturdifloor a single-layer floor that saves labor and materials. This floor is constructed with one layer of Sturdifloor approved CDX plywood (usually tongue and groove) that is nailed and glued to the floor framing members. Tongue and groove (T & G) plywood has edges that interlock

along the two longest edges. This reduces the tendency for boards to flex separately when a load is applied directly to the joint. The act of gluing the plywood to the joists produces an extremely rigid floor and virtually eliminates floor squeaking. This method works extremely well in conjunction with floor trusses and produces a sturdy floor with a minimum of time, hassle and materials.

NOTE: Whatever method you use, make sure you purchase only approved plywood for this purpose. Plywood used for single layer construction will have an approved APA stamp on it. Ask your supplier about this type of plywood. All flooring plywood must be CDX grade. The "C" refers to the grade of plywood on one side, the "D" refers to the grade on the other side and the "X" refers to exterior grade. This grade of plywood is made with an exterior type glue that is waterproof and will stand up to prolonged exposure to the elements during construction. If you use a two layer floor with particle board as your second layer, do not leave this material exposed to the weather. It is not waterproof and will swell up like a sponge.

WALL FRAMING

Wall framing is a critical stage in construction. You must be sure that everything is in its right place so that surprises do not occur later. If you make any last minute changes to the plans, consult with your framer or architect to insure that you don't create new problems. Even a simple change of framing height from 8' to 9' can cause many design problems. Windows may not appear proportional. The length of the stairs "run" will change because more steps will be needed to reach the second floor. Your plan may not have the room for additional steps.

Supervision

During construction, make sure that the walls are spaced properly in relation to plumbing that may be cast in a concrete slab. By the time the plumber discovers a problem you might have a major reconstruction project ahead. DON'T FORGET: If you plan to install one-piece fiberglass shower stalls, you must set them in place before putting up the walls! Some fiberglass stalls will not fit through bathroom door openings.

Figure 28. Vertical application of plywood or structural insulating board sheathing

Make sure to check periodically to be sure that all the carpenter's walls are square. It is easier to get this wrong than you think. Stairs and fireplaces are other sources of potential problems. Check them carefully. Many older carpenters have the habit of installing bridging between studs to prevent warpage. Discourage this practice, as it is an unnecessary waste of lumber and can make insulation more difficult to install and less effective. Also, energy-minded individuals should consider using 2x6 instead of 2x4 stud walls, which allows space for more insulation. This applies to the exterior walls only, of course.

Your carpenter will be required by building code to brace the corners of the structure for added rigidity. This can be accomplished by using a sheet of plywood in the corners, a diagonal wood brace cut into the studs, or a metal strap brace made for that purpose. Although more tedious, diagonal bracing or metal strapping is advantageous because it is cheaper and does not interfere with the insulating ability of sheathing. Plywood is not a good insulator.

As the house is "dried-in", make sure to cover openings in the walls and ceiling as soon as possible to protect the interior from rain. Place poly over all openings until the windows and doors arrive. Once the windows and doors are installed, lock them with the locksets or by nailing them shut with finishing nails.

Stud Spacing

The vast majority of houses in the United States are built with 2 x 4's spaced 16" on center (apart, or O.C.). Framing studs are a genuine classification of framing lumber. Stud grade is more expensive than standard framing lumber. Studs are more uniform and straight with fewer cracks. You should not frame walls with utility grade 2x4's. They will be more uneven, making drywall application a nightmare. Utility grade lumber also may not be capable of supporting the proper load. To save costs, however, you can use standard #3 fir for the top and bottom plates and jacks, since they do not support any load. The plates only serve to hold the studs together.

A recent trend is to deviate from the normal 16" framing for cost and energy reasons. Many houses are now constructed with 2x6's to allow more room for insulation. This construction change can increase a wall's insulation factor from R-13 to R-19, a significant energy conservation measure. When this method is used, studs are spaced 24" apart. This simplifies construction and reduces the number of studs used by 20-30%. This method is not without its problems however. The biggest problem is that most doors and windows are designed to be set in walls of 2x4 depth. Buying special doors and windows or

Figure 29. Application of plywood roof sheathing

Figure 30.   Construction of a 26-foot W truss: A, bevel-heel gusset; B, peak gusset; C, upper chord intermediate gusset; D, splice of lower chord; E, lower chord intermediate gusset.

having custom setting done can cost a considerable sum and can negate many of the cost savings. However, many doors and windows today adjust to accommodate either wall size. Generally, 2x6 stud construction is slightly more expensive than conventional construction, but it does provide a significant energy savings. Make sure your carpenter is familiar with the inherent problems of this type of construction before deciding to use it.

Many of the cost savings of 2x6 construction can be preserved without any of the headaches by going to 2x4 construction spaced 24" on center. This method is approved by all national building codes for single story construction and some local municipalities allow it on two story construction, or at least on the second floor. Check your local building codes to be sure. Spacing studs 24" on center saves time and materials and allows more space for insulation since fewer studs are used. Ask your carpenter if he is comfortable with this method of construction. Look for window units that will match the 2' framing width if you want to insert winoows between the studs.

ROOF FRAMING

The two basic types of roof framing consist of stick-built roofs and roof trusses. As with floor trusses, roof trusses have the advantage of being very sturdy for their size and weight. In most house designs, roof trusses require no load-bearing walls between the exterior walls. This gives you more flexibility in designing the interior of your home. Roof trusses are also generally cheaper than stick-built roofs because of significant labor savings in construction. Their only major disadvantage is the lack of attic space as a result of the cross member supports. This can be alleviated somewhat by ordering "space saving" trusses that have the inner cross members angled to provide more attic space. This is called a "W" truss. Stick-built roofs are more appropriate for high pitches or odd shaped or contemporary roof lines.

Your carpenter will install the roof sheathing, which usually consists of ½" CDX plywood or pressed chipboard (also known as flake board and oriented strand board E— less expensive) especially made for this purpose. Request that plywood clips be used in

Figure 31. Headers for window and door openings

Figure 32. Application of gypsum lath

Figure 33. Horizontal application of 2-by-8-foot structural insulating board or gypsum sheathing

between each sheet of roofing material. These clips are small "H"-shaped aluminum clips designed to hold the ends and sides of the plywood sheets together for added rigidity. This will help prevent warpage and "wavy" roof surfaces.

Due to the popularity of asphalt and fiberglass roofing shingles, this manual relates specifically to roof framing where these two types of roofing are used. Normal roof decking is not used with cedar shake, slate or tile roofs. If you are planning to have such a roof, consult with your framing and roofing subs. When installing the roof sheathing, the carpenter should be aware of the type of roof ventilation to be used. The most convenient and efficient type to use is continuous eave and ridge vents. The carpenter should leave a 1" gap in the plywood at the roof ridge for installation of the ridge vent, if used.

SHEATHING

Sheathing comes in several different types. Asphalt-soaked fiber sheathing is the most common and the cheapest but it has the least insulating value. The next in line would probably be "blue foam" insulation. It is a good compromise of value and insulation ability. Foil-backed urethane is by far the best insulator but also the most expensive. If you plan to stucco, exterior gypsum board is most often used. Talk to your local supplier to see what types are available in your area and their insulation ability. When installing the sheathing, your carpenter should take care not to rip or puncture the sheathing. If he does, ask him to replace the defective piece. Pay him only after all defective pieces have been replaced. He should use special nails that have a plate on the shaft that holds the sheathing to the stud without puncturing the sheathing.

DOORS AND WINDOWS

After the roof and sheathing have been installed, the framing contractor will be ready to install the doors and windows and "dry in" the structure. The proper installation of doors and windows is probably the source of more irritation and hot tempers than anything. A poorly hung door isn't worth much except as an argument starter at the end of a hard day's work. The advent of pre-hung doors has made the job quite a bit easier, but still not foolproof. With your level, check to make sure each door is completely square and that there is an even gap between door and frame from top to bottom. Make sure the door has plenty of room to swell in damp weather (if it is wood) and still open freely. Measure under the door to make sure there is plenty of room for subflooring, carpet pad and carpet without the door rubbing over the carpet when it is installed. The same amount of care should be taken with the windows to guarantee that they will slide freely within their frames. An ounce of prevention is worth a pound of pounding!

WASTE DISPOSAL

Few projects generate more scrap than frame construction. If your area allows burning, this may be your best option. Stack scrap lumber in convenient piles far away from the house and burn only on non-windy days. Consult with your local fire marshall to determine if the weather is conducive to burning. Monitor the fire constantly and keep a water hose available at all times. Don't burn plastic or other petroleum products. These items leave non-degradable byproducts that will stay in your yard practically forever. Keep paint cans, and aerosol cans out of the fire. These items can become explosive weapons when heated.

In winter, don't burn waste until the project is completed. You will usually find the sub-contractors burning your scrap (and sometimes non-scraps!) in order to keep warm on the job site. Also, make sure the scraps you are burning are not usable. Many small pieces of lumber can be used as blocking and other items. Cornice subs use 2x4's 8" and longer to run cornice framing. Electricians use 4-6" 2x4's for blocking around outlets and switch boxes. Plumbers use 2x4's 6" and up to brace pipes, tubs, and other fixtures.

Stack all usable scrap in a neat, accessible pile protected from the elements. This way your subs can't help but notice the material. This will keep them from wasting lumber by cutting up new, larger pieces.

OTHER TRADES

Your framing sub must be familiar with the workings of the plumbing, HVAC, and pre-fab fireplace subs so that he can anticipate for them where ductwork, pipes and heating equipment must be placed. Make sure his copy of the blueprints indicates the location of furnace and ducting.

FRAMING — Steps

FR1 CONDUCT standard material bidding process. Find the best package deal on good quality studs, sheathing, press-board, plywood, interior doors (pre-hung or otherwise), exterior doors and windows. Find out their return policy on damaged and surplus material and whether their price includes delivery.

FR2 CONDUCT framing labor bidding process. Ask to see their work and get recommendations. A good crew should have at least three people. Any less and the framing probably won't go as quickly as you would like it. Consider a speed/quality incentive tied to payment.

FR3 DISCUSS all aspects of framing with the crew. This includes all special angles, openings, clearances and other particulars. Also make sure that the electrical service has been ordered. Discuss special order materials such as flitch plates or glue-lam beams and order them as soon as possible.

FR4 ORDER special materials ahead of time to prevent delays later. This includes custom doors, windows, beams and skylights. This is also a good time to make sure your temporary electric pole works — you will need it for the power saws.

FR5 ORDER and receive first load of framing lumber. Have a flat platform ready to lay it on near the foundation. "Line out" framing walls with chalk lines on the foundation to act as a framing guide. Check chalk lines for accurate dimensions and squareness.

FR6 INSTALL sill felt, sill caulk, or both.

FR7 ATTACH pre-treated sill plate to lag bolts embedded in the foundation.

FR8 INSTALL steel or wood support columns in basement.

FR9 SUPERVISE framing process. Check framing dimensions to be sure flooring and wall measurements are in the right place. This is an ongoing process. Check with framer in the morning each day to discuss progress and problems. Check for needed materials. Don't leave excess materials on site — they have a tendency to disappear. Ask framers to cover lumber with plastic if rain is likely. Ask them to put nails and other valuable supplies in their truck to prevent theft.

Check wall plates with a level. Also run a span board between two parallel walls and check with a level to insure that walls are all at the same exact height.

FR10 FRAME first floor joists and install subfloor. Place these as close together as you can afford. If you can afford 2x10's instead of 2x8's, this will help give your floor a more solid feel. Tongue and groove plywood is a popular sub-floor. Make sure to use exterior grade plywood since it will be exposed to the weather during framing. At bay windows, joists will extend out beyond the wall.

FR11 FRAME stairs to basement (if any). In many respects a home is built around staircases. This is a critical step.

FR12 POSITION all large items that must be inserted before framing walls prior to setting doorways and inner partitions. These include bathtubs, modular shower units, HVAC units and oversized appliances. Beware of installing oversized appliances that will not fit through the door when you move or when they have to be replaced.

Figure 34. Framing for bathtub.

FR13 FRAME exterior walls/partitions (first floor). Keep track of all window and door opening measurements. Constantly check squareness.

FR14 PLUMB and line first floor. This is critical to a quality job in drywall and trim. This involves setting the top plates for all first floor walls with lapped joints while someone is checking to make sure that all the angles are plumb and perpendicular. This involves straightening the walls exactly — fine tuning. Walls are braced one by one. Start from one exterior corner and go in a circular direction around the exterior perimeter of the house, adjusting and finishing each wall.

FR15 FRAME second floor joists and subfloor.

FR16 POSITION all large second floor units prior to setting doorways and partitions. Again, these include bathtubs, modular shower units and other large items.

FR17 FRAME 2nd floor exterior walls/partitions.

FR18 PLUMB and line second floor. Refer to plumbing/lining first floor.

FR19 INSTALL second floor ceiling joists if roof is stick built. Have your window and door supplier visit the site to check actual dimensions of all openings.

FR20 FRAME roof. If you want a space between your window trim and cornice, add a second plate on the top of the second floor wall. Depending upon the size and complexity of your roof, you may either use pre-fab trusses, or stick build your roof. Chances are, if your home is over 2200 sq. ft. or has an 8/12 or steeper roof, your framers will probably end up stick building it.

FR21 INSTALL roof deck. Plywood sheathing will be applied in 4' x 8' sheets in a horizontal fashion. Each course of plywood should be staggered one-half width from the one below it. Your framers should use ply clips to hold the sheets together between rafters.

FR22 PAY first framing payment (about 45% of total cost). Check for missed items such as framing for attic stairs, fir downs for kitchen cabinets, framing for house fan, hearth framing, stud supports around tubs, etc.

FR23 INSTALL lapped tar paper. This protects your roofing deck and entire structure from rain. At this point, the structure is "dried in" and a major race against the elements is over.

FR24 FRAME chimney chases, if you have them. Ask framer to cover top of chase with plywood or rain caps to protect against rain.

FR25 INSTALL prefab fireplaces. Install a fireplace with at least a 42" opening and 24" depth. Anything smaller will have problems taking full-sized firewood. Prefab fireplaces are usually installed by the supplier or a separate sub. Since plans seldom indicate the specific type of fireplace, make sure framer is aware of the brand and requirements of your particular fireplace. Store your gas log lighter key in a safe place to avoid losing it.

FR26 FRAME dormers and skylights.

FR27 FRAME tray ceilings, skylight shafts and bay windows if you have them. Skylight shafts should flare out as they come into the room. This allows more light to enter.

FR28 INSTALL sheathing on all exterior walls.

FR29 INSPECT sheathing. Watch for punctures and gaps in the insulation that can be fixed with duct tape.

FR30 REMOVE temporary bracing supports. Bracing supports installed prior to backfill and those used during the framing process are removed and used as scrap.

FR31 INSTALL exterior windows and doors. The siding and cornice sub may do this operation. If you are using pre-hung doors, this becomes an easier process. A pre-hung door comes with its own door frame, but without door knobs and locks. After installing door knobs and locks, the house can be locked up to prevent theft and vandalism. Just make sure to give your subs temporary keys. If your siding and cornice sub installs your windows, this is covered under another step.

FR32 APPLY dead wood. "Dead wood" consists of short pieces of lumber installed in areas that need backing on which to nail drywall. These include: tops and sides of windows where curtain hardware will be attached, small areas around stairs, locations of electrical boxes and bracing for ceiling lights or fans.

FR33 INSTALL roof ventilators. This should only be done on the back of the roof.

FR34 FRAME DECKS using pressure-treated lumber to prevent rotting and termite infestation.

FR35 INSPECT framing. You should have been checking on the framing process all along, so there should be no big surprises at this point. This is the LAST chance to get things fixed before you make your last payment to the framing crew.

FR36 SCHEDULE and have your loan officer visit the site to approve rough framing draw.

FR37 CORRECT any problems with framing job. This is an ongoing process that should occur throughout the framing process. The earlier a problem is detected, the easier and cheaper it is to fix. Look for bowed wood that will making drywall attachment difficult. Correct these by shimming or by cutting a slice partway through the stud. At this point, you have one last bargaining tool before making the next payment to the framing crew.

FR38 PAY framing labor. Retain a percentage of pay until all work is completed and final inspection is approved. Remember to deduct any necessary worker's compensation.

FR39 PAY framing labor retainage. Get a signed affidavit when final payment is made.

FRAMING - Sample Specifications

- All materials to be crowned (circular grain goes in the same direction). Where possible, all wall studs have crown pointing the same direction.

- All walls and joists to be framed as specified in the blueprints.

- All joists to be framed 16" OC.

- All vertical wall studs to be framed 16" OC.

- All measurements to be within ¼" and plumb, perpendicular and level.

- Cross bridging to be used at all joist midspans to increase strength and stability of floor.

- All lumber in contact with concrete must be pressure treated.

- Double joists to be used under load-bearing partitions and bathtubs unless truss floors are used.

- Floor joists not to interfere with tub, sink and shower drains.

- Four-inch overlap on lap joists supported over girders.

- All cuts necessary for HVAC and plumbing work to be braced.

- Hip roof to be 10/12 pitch and gable roof to be 12/12 pitch.

- No cuts to be made in laminated beams.

- All chimney chases framed with a cricket installed to allow drainage of excess water.

- Worker's compensation insurance to be provided by builder.

Framing extras include:

- Bay windows

- Stacked bay windows

- Staircases

- Prefab fireplace opening and chase

- Skylights

- Basement stud walls

SHEATHING

- Sheathing to be installed vertically along studs.

- Sheathing nailed every foot along studs.

- All gaps over ¼" to be taped.

- Skin on sheathing not to be broken by nail heads, hammer or other means.

- Sheathing nails to be used exclusively.

FRAMING - Inspection

Framing inspection will be an ongoing process. Errors must be detected as soon as they are made for easy correction.

☐ All work done according to master blueprints.

☐ No framing deviations exceed standard ¼" leeway for error.

☐ Vertical walls are plumb.

☐ Opposite walls of rooms are parallel.

☐ Horizontal members such as joists, headers and sub-floors are level.

☐ Window and door openings are proper dimensions and are square. Rough openings are 2" wider than opening dimension.

☐ Adequate room at all door openings for trim to be attached. Opening is not flush against a corner.

☐ No loose or un-reinforced boards or structures.

☐ Purlins in all basement walls and load-bearing walls.

☐ Corner bracing used in all wall corners.

☐ No room framed before installing large fixtures or appliances that are larger than door openings.

☐ All framing is being done to within 1" of on center (O.C.) spacing requested.

☐ Wall corner angles are square. This is especially critical in kitchens (where cabinets and counter tops are expressly designed for 90° angles).

☐ Check that vertical studs in stud walls are even and unwarped. This can be done by pulling a string along each stud wall. The string should just touch all studs at the same time.

☐ All joists, vertical studs and rafters are crowned. This means that the natural bow of the wood is running in the same direction for all adjacent members.

☐ No excessive scrap.

☐ Adequate lumber is available for framers. Have them notify you if shortages are about to occur.

☐ Site measurements match the blueprints. If something is to change, it should be recorded on the blueprints in red.

Sub-floor

☐ Specified plywood or other sub-flooring used. Proper spacing and nailing of sheets. Tongue and groove plywood where specified.

☐ No weak or crushed plywood in floor. Bottom two sheets in a plywood load often are broken when sliding load off truck. Make sure it is not used in the floor.

☐ All sill studs are exterior grade and pressure treated.

☐ All sub-flooring glued to studs with construction adhesive and nailed adequately. Check from underneath.

☐ Bracing between floor joists as specified.

Stairs

☐ No squeaks or other noise from treads or risers.

☐ Treads deep enough for high-heeled shoes to fit on comfortably.

☐ Proper bracing in walls to support rails later.

☐ All risers same height.

☐ All treads same width or as specified.

☐ All framing complete for trimwork to begin.

☐ Attic staircase works properly.

Fireplace

☐ Fireplace area headers in proper position for pre-fab or masonry work.

☐ Framing for raised mantel installed.

☐ Flue framed with clearances according to building code.

☐ Proper height for raised hearth if used.

Roofing Deck

☐ Plywood sheets staggered from row to row.

☐ Plywood sheets nailed every 8" along rafters or trusses.

☐ Ply clips used on all plywood between supports.

☐ Proper exterior grade of plywood used.

☐ Plywood sheets and roofing felt cut properly for ridge and roof vents.

Deck or Porch

☐ Deck has galvanized joist hangers on joist ends.

☐ Pressure-treated lumber used on outdoor decks.

☐ Galvanized decking nails or screws used.

Miscellaneous Framing

☐ Tray ceiling areas framed as specified.

☐ Tray ceiling angles even.

☐ Skylight openings and skylights according to specifications.

☐ Skylights sealed and flashed.

☐ Access door to crawl space and wall storage areas installed according to specifications.

☐ Pull-down attic staircase installed and operable.

Sheathing

☐ Proper sheathing installed.

☐ Sheathing applied vertically.

☐ Sheathing nails used.

☐ No punctures or other damage to sheathing.

☐ Perimeter of sheets nailed adequately to prevent sheathing from blowing off in wind.

☐ Sheathing joints tight and taped where necessary.

FRAMING - Glossary

BAY WINDOW— Any window that projects out from the walls of the structure.

BEAM— A long piece of lumber or metal used to support a load placed at right angles to the beam — usually floor joists.

BOARD FOOT— A unit of measurement equal to a 1" thick piece of wood one foot square. Thickness x Length x Width equals board feet.

BRACE— Diagonally framed member used to temporarily hold wall in place during framing.

BRIDGING— Diagonal metal or wood cross braces installed between joists to prevent twisting and to spread the load to adjoining joists.

BUTT JOINT— Junction of the ends of two framing members such as on a sill. Normally a square cut joint.

CASEMENT WINDOW— A window that swings out to the side on hinges.

CORNER BRACES— Diagonal bracing in the corners of a structure used to improve rigidity.

CRICKET— A sloped area at the intersection of a vertical surface and the roof, such as a chimney. Used to channel off water that might otherwise get trapped behind the vertical structure.

CRIPPLE— A short stud used as bracing under windows and other structural framing.

DEAD LOAD— The total weight of walls, floors and roof bearing on the structure.

DEAD WOOD— Wood used as backing for drywall.

DRESSED SIZE— Dimensions of lumber after planing smooth.

DRIED IN— Term describing the framed structure after the roof deck and protective tar paper have been installed.

FACE NAILING— Nailing applied perpendicular to the members. Also known as direct nailing.

FIRRING— Long strips of wood attached to walls or ceilings to allow attachment of drywall or ceiling tiles. Firring out refers to adding firring strips to a wall to bring it out further into a room. Firring down refers to using firring strips to lower a ceiling.

GABLE— The vertical section under the sloped part of a roof.

GRAIN— The direction of the fibers in the wood. Edge grain wood has been sawed parallel to the growth rings. Flat grain lumber is sawed perpendicular to the growth rings. Studs are flat grain lumber.

GUSSET— A piece of metal or wood used in trusses to connect bracing members together.

HEADER— One or two pieces of lumber installed over doors and windows to support the load above the opening.

JAMB— Exterior frame of a door.

JOIST— A long piece of lumber used to support the load of a floor or ceiling. Joists are always positioned on edge.

KERF— The area of a board removed by the saw when cutting.

LAMINATED BEAM— A very strong beam created from several smaller pieces of wood that have been glued together under heat and pressure.

LINEAL FOOT— A measure of lumber based on the actual length of the piece.

LOAD BEARING WALL— Any wall that supports the weight of other structural members.

MASTIC— Any pasty material used as a cement or protective coating. Usually comes in caulking tubes or 5 gallon cans.

MITER JOINT— Joint of two members each cut at a 45° angle.

NOMINAL SIZE— Original size of lumber when cut.

ON CENTER (O.C.)— Distance from the middle of one stud to the middle of the next. Normally refers to wall or joist framing of 12", 16" or 18" O.C.

PARTITION— An interior wall in a framed structure dividing two spaces.

PLATE— A horizontal member used to anchor studs to the floor or ceiling. A sill plate anchors floor joists to a masonry wall.

PIERS— Concrete supports for a floor beam.

PURLIN— A horizontal board the supports a roof rafter or stud to prevent bowing of the member by weight.

RAFTER— A long piece of lumber used in roof framing that supports the roof sheathing and shingles.

RIPPING— Cutting lumber parallel to the grain.

SILL CAULK— Mastic placed between top of foundation wall and sill studs to make an airtight seal.

SPAN— The distance between two supporting members of a joist or beam. The longest unsupported distance along a joist.

STUD— Standard 2 x 4 lumber normally cut to 8 or 10-foot nominal lengths used for framing walls.

TOE NAILING— Nailing at an angle (normally 45°) to bind two or more members. Normally used in nailing studs to plates.

TONGUE and GROOVE— Boards that join on edge with a groove on one unit and a corresponding tongue on the other to interlock. Certain plywoods and hardwood flooring are tongue and grooved.

TRAY CEILING— Raised area in a ceiling. Looks like a small vaulted ceiling.

Roofing and Gutters

ROOFING

Roofing is measured, estimated and bid based on squares (units of 100 square feet roof coverage). Common roofing compositions include asphalt, fiberglass and cedar shakes, although special roofs are also composed of tile, slate and other more expensive materials. Fiberglass is a popular choice due to its favorable combination of appearance, price and durability. Roofing warranties are most often a minimum of 20 years. This pertains to material only.

Asphalt and fiberglass shingles, the most common and inexpensive forms, are of two basic types:

■ Strip

■ Individual

STRIP SHINGLES are normally 12" tall and 36" wide with two or three tabs to make the units look like several individual shingles when installed. Weights vary from 160 lb. (per square) on the cheap side up to 280 lb. on the high end. The heavier they are, the more sound and long-lived will be the roof. Lighter shingles also have a tendency to get blown around in heavy wind. Strip shingles normally come in packages of 80 strips. About three packages cover one square of roof. When installed, about 5" of the shingle's height remains exposed, hence a 7" top lap. There are some fiberglass shingles out on the market that resemble slate roofing — from a distance. You just have to look around.

INDIVIDUAL SHINGLES are individual sheets normally measuring 16" x 16" or 12" x 16". Weights vary from 160 lbs. to 330 lbs. Be advised, your roofing sub will probably charge you more to install these than asphalt or fiberglass, and they are not nearly as popular as strip shingles. So make sure you really want them.

ROOFING SUBS should quote you a price with and without material. The steeper your roof pitch, the steeper his price per square installed. Prices start to get steep after about 10/12, which represents the 10 feet of rise for every 12 feet of run (horizontal). Hence, 12/12 is a 45 degree angle. Appeal is growing for steeper and steeper pitches. Make sure the roofing sub has plenty of worker's compensation insurance or deduct heavily from his fee if you have to add him to your policy. He's one fellow with a very high risk of injury. If you plan to supply the shingles, make sure they are at the site a day or so early.

NOTE: Since asphalt and fiberglass shingles are by far the most common used, the STEPS on the following pages relate specifically to them. If you use roofing materials other than these two, refer to a handbook and detailed construction methods. Due to the high asphalt content in asphalt and fiberglass shingles, it is highly recommended to apply them in 50° Fahrenheit or warmer weather as they are highly susceptible to cracking in cold weather.

GUTTERS

Gutters are used to channel rain water to downspouts and then to planned drainage paths. In some cases, gutters are used more for appearance than functionality. Typically, gutters are made of galvanized iron or aluminum. The number of downspouts will vary. Your gutter sub-contractor will help you in determining the number and placement of your downspouts and gutters. If you can, use underground drain pipes instead of simple splash blocks. Care must be taken that they are not completely buried during the backfill stage. A heavy gauge PVC black tubing should be used. The primary gutter materials are:

ALUMINUM— These are good, but you must specify "paint grip" aluminum or the paint will not stick.

VINYL— This maintenance free alternative is fast becoming a favorite.

Gutter subs normally charge by lineal feet of gutters and downspouts installed. They may charge you a certain amount for any more than four corners. They will also charge you extra for installing gutter screens and drain pipe.

Get your gutters up as soon as possible to start good drainage and to keep mud from splashing on the side of the house. Gutters shouldn't go on until the cornice is primed and painted and the exterior walls finished (because of downspouts).

ROOFING - Steps

RF1 SELECT shingle style, material and color.

RF2 PERFORM standard bidding process for material and labor.

RF3 ORDER shingles and roofing felt (tar paper). This is done only if you have decided to use your roofer for labor only. Check with him to make sure he knows of the brand and how to install them.

RF4 INSTALL 3" metal drip edge on eave nailed 10" on center. Roofing paper will go directly on top of this drip edge (optional).

RF5 INSTALL roofing felt. This should be done immediately after the roofing deck has been installed and inspected. Your framer will install the tar paper as the last thing before finishing the job. This step protects the entire structure from immediate water damage. Until this step is performed, the project should proceed as quickly as possible.

RF6 INSTALL 3" metal drip edge on rake. This drip edge goes over the roofing paper. Also install aluminum flashing at walls and valleys (optional).

A

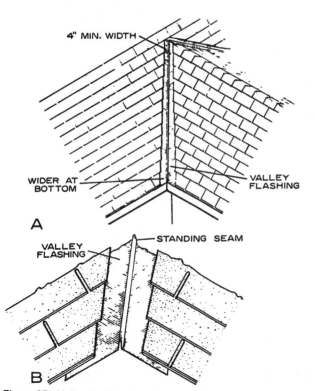

Figure 35. Valley flashing: A, valley; B, standing seam.

B

Figure 36. Roof and wall intersection: A, wood siding wall; B, brick wall.

RF7 INSTALL roofing shingles. Roofs over 30" wide should be shingled starting in the middle. Shorter roofs can be shingled starting at either rake. Starter strips, normally 9" wide, are either continuous rolls of shingle material that start at the eave or doubled shingle strips. Shingles are laid from the eave, over-

Figure 37. Application of asphalt shingles: A, normal method with strip shingles; B, metal edging at gable end.

lapping courses up to the highest ridge. Don't install shingles on very cold days, if you have a choice.

RF8 INSPECT roofing. Refer to contract specifications and inspection checklist for guidelines. You will have to get up on the roof to check most of this.

RF9 PAY roofing sub-contractor. Get him to sign an affidavit. Deduct for worker's compensation if applicable.

RF10 PAY roofing sub retainage.

GUTTERS - Steps

GU1 SELECT gutter type and color.

GU2 PERFORM standard bidding process.

GU3 INSTALL underground drain pipe. Flexible plastic pipe is the type used most often. Make sure it is covered properly.

GU4 INSTALL gutters and downspouts.

GU5 INSTALL splashblocks and/or other water channeling devices.

GU6 INSPECT gutters. Refer to inspection guidelines, related checklist, contract specifications and your building code.

GU7 INSTALL copper awnings and dormer tops.

GU8 PAY gutter sub-contractor. Have him sign an affidavit.

GU9 PAY gutter sub retainage.

ROOFING - Sample Specifications

■ Bid is to perform complete roofing job per attached drawings and modifications.

■ Bid to include all materials and labor and ten year warranty against leakage.

■ Apply 240 lb. 30-year fiberglass shingles (Make/Style/Color) to roof using galvanized roofing nails.

■ Install two thermostatically controlled roof vents on rear of roof as indicated on attached drawings.

■ Install continuous ridge vent per drawing specifications.

■ Roofing felt to be applied and stapled to deck as indicated below: no. 15 asphalt saturated felt over entire plywood deck.

■ All roofing felt to have a vertical overlap of 6".

■ Install 3" galvanized eave and rake drip edges nailed 10" O.C.

■ All work and materials are to conform to or exceed requirements of the local building code and be satisfactory to contractor.

■ Roofer to notify builder immediately of any condition which is or may be a violation of the building code.

■ Nails are to be threaded and corrosion resistant. Either aluminum or hot-dipped galvanized roofing nails to be used depending upon shingle manufacturer recommendations.

■ Nails to be driven flush with shingles and installed per roofing specs.

Figure 38.   Gutters and downspouts: A, half-round gutter; B, formed gutter; C, round downspout; D, rectangular downspout.

Figure 40.   Gutter installation: A, formed metal gutter; B, wood gutter.

Figure 39.   Downspout installation: A, downspout with splash block; B, drain to storm sewer.

- Soil stacks to cover all vents. All vents to be sealed to shingle surface with plastic asphalt cement.

- Flashing to be installed at chimney, all roof valleys, soil and vent stacks and skylights.

GUTTERS - Specifications

- Bid is to provide and install seamless, paint-grip aluminum gutters around entire lower perimeter of dwelling as specified in attached drawings.

- 5" gutter troughs and 3" corrugated downspouts to be used exclusively.

- Gutter troughs are to be supported by galvanized steel spikes and ferrules spaced not more than 5 feet apart.

- Downspouts to be fastened to wall every 6 vertical feet.

- Gutter troughs are to be sloped toward downspouts 1 (one) inch for every 12 lineal feet. Gutters should be installed for minimum visibility.

ROOFING - Inspection

☐ Shingle lines inspected for straightness with string drawn taught. Tips of shingles line up with string.

☐ Even shingle pattern and uniform shingle color from both close up and afar (at least 80 feet away).

☐ Shingles extend over edge of roofing deck by at least 3".

☐ All roofing nails are galvanized and nailed flush with all shingles (random inspection).

☐ No shingle cracks visible through random inspection.

☐ Hips and valleys are smooth and uniform.

☐ Roofing conforms to contract specifications and local building codes in all respects.

☐ Water cannot collect anywhere on the roof.

☐ Shingles fit tightly around all stack vents and skylights. Areas are well sealed with an asphalt roofing compound that blends with the shingles.

☐ Drip edges have been installed on eave and rakes.

☐ No nail heads are visible while standing up on the roof.

☐ All shingles lie flat (no buckling).

☐ No visible lumps in roofing due to poor decking or truss work.

☐ Edges of roof trimmed smooth and evenly.

☐ All vents and roof flashing painted proper color with exterior grade paint.

☐ All garbage on roof removed.

☐ Shingle tabs have been glued down if this was specified. (Used only in very windy areas or where very lightweight shingles are used.)

GUTTERS - Inspection

☐ Proper materials used as specified. Aluminum, vinyl, etc.

☐ Proper trough and downspout sizes used.

☐ Downspouts secured to exterior walls.

☐ Adequate number of gutter nails used to support gutters securely.

☐ Water drains well to and through troughs when water from a garden hose or rain water is applied.

☐ No leaks in miters and elbows while water is running.

☐ Water does not collect anywhere in troughs and is completely drained within one minute.

ROOFING AND GUTTERS — Glossary

ASPHALT— Base ingredient of asphalt shingles and roofing paper (felt composition saturated in asphalt base).

BULL— A covering for a wide soil stack so that rain will not enter.

COURSE— A horizontal row of shingles.

COVERAGE— The maximum number of shingles that overlap in any one spot. This determines the degree of weather performance a roof has.

DOWNSPOUT— Vertical member used to bring water from trough to ground level.

DRIP EDGE— Metal flashing normally 3" wide which goes on the eave and rakes to provide a precise point for water to drip from so that the cornice does not rot.

EAVE— Lowest point on a roof that overhangs edge of house.

ELBOW— Trough corner extending outward from roof.

EXPOSURE— The vertical length of exposed shingle (portion not lapped by the shingle above).

FELT— Typical shingle underlayment. Also known as roofing felt or tar paper. See ASPHALT.

FERRULE— Aluminum sleeve used in attaching trough to gutter spike.

FLASHING— Galvanized sheet metal used as a lining around joints between shingles and chimneys, exhaust and ventilation vents and other protrusions in the roof deck. Flashing helps prevent water from seeping under the shingles.

HEAD LAP— Length (inches) of the amount of overlap between shingles (measured vertically).

INSIDE MITER— Trough corner extending toward roof.

PITCH— Slope of roof, measured in 12' lengths. Example: A 10/12 pitch indicates that the roof rises 10 feet for every 12 feet of run.

RAKE— The angled edge of a roof located at the end of a roof that extends past gable.

RIDGE— Intersection of any two roofing planes where water drains away from the intersection. Special shingles are applied to ridges.

RIDGE VENT— Opening at the point where roof decking normally intersects along the highest point on a roof where air is allowed to flow from the attic. A small cap covers this opening to prevent rain from entering. When these are long, they are normally known as continuous ridge vents.

SCREEN— Metallic or vinyl grid used to keep troughs free of leaves and other debris. Some screens are hinged.

SHINGLE— Uniform unit used in the coverage of a roofing deck. Shingles are manufactured from many materials including asphalt, fiberglass, wood shakes, tile and slate. Sizes normally vary from 12" x 36" to 12 ¼" x 36 ¼" with many sizes in between.

SHINGLE BUTT— The lower, exposed side of a shingle.

SIDE LAP— Length (inches) of the amount of overlap between two horizontally adjoining shingles.

SOIL STACK— Corrosion resistant collar placed over vent pipes coming out of the roof deck.

SPIKE— A long nail used to attach the trough to the roof. Used in conjunction with ferrule. (See FERRULE.)

SPLASHBLOCK— Special concrete form used to direct water from downspout and away from dwelling.

SQUARE— Roofing material required to roof 100 square feet of roof surface.

STACK— Also known as vent stack. A ventilation pipe coming out of the roofing deck.

STARTER STRIP— A continuous strip of asphalt roofing used as the first course, applied to hang over the eave.

UNDERLAYMENT— Any paper or felt composition used to separate the roofing deck from the shingles. Underlayments such as asphalt felt (tar paper) are common.

VALLEY— Intersection of any two roofing planes where water drains at the intersection.

Plumbing

Plumbing work can be started as soon as the house has been "dried-in". Getting the plumbing right is essential — it is very difficult to change plumbing decisions later.

Plumbing is composed of three interrelated systems:

- The water supply
- The sewer system
- The (wet) vent system

THE WATER SUPPLY

Unless you have opted for an individual water supply (such as a well), you will tap into a public water supply. Unless you plan to live in your home many years (eight or more), the cost of drilling a well cannot be justified on cost alone. Remember, your water bill includes sewer service, too. You'll still pay for that (unless you opt for a septic tank or cesspool). If your local water supply is 80 psi or greater, you will need to install a pressure reduction valve at the main water service pipe. High water pressure can AND WILL take its toll on most pipes and fixtures in a short period of time.

Copper has been the material of choice of plumbers for water pipes for many years, but new materials available today have numerous advantages over copper. CPVC pipe is a plastic used for hot and cold supplies as well as its cousin PVC, which is only rated for cold water and sewer installations. CPVC offers several advantages over copper, including ease and speed of installation and some cost savings. Some people complain of a slight aftertaste in the water for the first year or so.

Polybutylene is a new semi-flexible material that has taken the plumbing world by storm in recent years. It offers many advantages over copper and CPVC. It is totally inert and imparts no taste to the water. Its flexible nature allows it to be installed with a minimum of joints, which are the most expensive material in water systems. Polybutylene is also virtually freeze proof; a characteristic that can be appreciated by anyone who has had his pipes freeze in cold weather. It is very quiet in operation and reduces the effect of water hammer. Polybutylene joints are installed by one of two methods: crimping or grabber fittings. Crimp joints are the most cost effective, but the grabber joints are ridiculously easy to install. You simply insert the pipe into the fitting and push; that's it.

Polybutylene pipe is by far the least expensive method of installing plumbing, but you may have trouble finding plumbers willing to work with it. Plumbers are slow to accept new innovations and may not pass the full savings of the installation to you. Many plumbers fail to realize the full cost savings available to them because they tend to install many more joints than are necessary. The flexibility of polybutylene allows it to be wrapped and molded around obstructions, eliminating the need for many joints. Check with your local plumbing inspector for plumbers familiar with this new material. It is well worth the research.

THE SEWER SYSTEM

The sewer system collects all used water and waste and disposes of it properly. Unless you opted for a private sewer (septic tank), you will connect to the public sewer system. In most cases, building codes will not allow you to build a private sewer if a public one is available. When designing the house, keep in mind that sewer systems are powered by gravity. Hence, your lowest sink, toilet or drain must be higher than the sewer line. The sewer line must have at least ¼" drop per foot in order to operate properly. This may mean raising your foundation if necessary to accommodate proper drainage.

With sewer pipe materials, technology has created a new problem. PVC pipe is now the most common material used because of its ease of installation; however, plastic pipes transmit the noise of flushing and water draining much more than the old cast iron pipes. Install cast iron sewer pipe if possible to reduce this noise. If you use PVC pipe, take care to position the pipes in walls that are isolated from bedrooms or you will constantly hear water noises. It is critical to discuss with your plumber where the sewer pipe will run if you have a basement. Many finished basements have been ruined by post framing around poorly placed sewer pipes that breaks up the future living space.

The (Wet) Vent System

Also known as the vertical wet venting system, this permits your plumbing system to "breathe". This system protects against siphonage and backpressure. All drains are attached to one of several vents in a network. These vents are seen as pipes sticking out the back side of your roof.

PLUMBING SUBS

Plumbers will normally bid and charge you a fixed price per fixture to install all three systems described above. You are likely to pay extra for jacuzzis, whirlpools and the like. The price of all fixtures (tubs, sinks, disposals) should be obtained from your sub. Fixtures above builder grade will usually cost more. If you use many custom fixtures, or if your house plan positions bathrooms and the kitchen close together to conserve plumbing material, consider asking for a bid based on actual material and labor costs. This can save you a considerable amount of money. If you purchase fancy fixtures, have the plumber deduct the standard fixture charge for the ones you have purchased.

After you have received the estimate, ask for the cash price. Ask your plumber how many hours it will take him to do the job. You will pay the plumber 40 percent after passing the rough-in inspection and 60 percent after passing the final inspection. If your plumbing code does not require individual shut-off valves on each fixture, do not use them on each fixture if you want to save a little money.

BUILDING CODES

Most likely, your local building code will impose a number of requirements on your plumbing system. This helps protect you from paying for an inadequate system. Your local building code will cover plumbing materials and allowable uses of each, water supply and sewer capacities, joints, drainage, valves, testing, etc. READ THIS AND KNOW IT WELL. Although you should rely on your plumbing sub for advice, know your plumbing cold!

ABOUT SEPTIC TANKS

If you are considering going this route:

■ CONFIRM that septic tanks are permissible. Contact local inspectors and consult your local building code.

■ CONDUCT a percolation test to determine how quickly the soil absorbs water. Certain minimum standards will be imposed on your system. It is necessary to hire a qualified engineer to perform this test.

■ ESTIMATE your minimum septic tank capacity requirements.

■ REFER to your local building code for additional guidelines and requirements on a private sewer system.

PLUMBING - Steps

Rough-In
PL1 DETERMINE type and quantity of plumbing fixtures (styles and colors). This includes:

- Sinks (kitchen, baths, utility, wet bar, etc.)
- Bathtubs (Consider one-piece fiberglass units with built-in walls requiring no tile. If you go this route get a heavy gauge unit.)
- Shower fixtures
- Toilets and toilet seats
- Water spigots (exterior)
- Water heater
- Garbage disposal
- Septic tank
- Sauna or steamroom
- Water softener
- Refrigerator ice maker
- Any other plumbing-related appliance

PL2 CONDUCT standard bidding process. Shop prices carefully; subs who bid on your job may vary greatly on their bid price, depending on what materials they use and their method of calculating their fee. This is where you will decide what kind of pipe to use.

PL3 WALK THROUGH site with plumber to discuss placement of plumbing and any special fixtures needed. For instance, if you have a brick exterior, the plumber must extend faucets to allow for the thickness of brick veneer.

PL4 ORDER special plumbing fixtures. This needs to be done well in advance because supply houses seldom stock large quantities of special fixtures. These will take some time to get in.

PL5 APPLY for water connection and sewer tap. You will probably have to pay a sewer tap fee. Ask the plumber for an adjustment piece that will allow you to connect a garden hose to the water main. Record the number stamped on the water meter.

PL6 INSTALL stub plumbing. This applies to instances where plumbing is cast in concrete foundations. This must be done after batter boards and strings are set and before the concrete slab is poured. The plumber will want to know where the sewer line is located.

PL7 PLACE all large plumbing fixtures such as large tubs, fiberglass shower stalls and hot tubs before wall framing begins. These fixtures will not fit through normal stud or door openings. For security, you may want to chain expensive fixtures to the studs or pipes.

PL8 MARK location of all plumbing fixtures including sinks, tubs, showers, toilets, outside spigots, wetbars, icemakers, utility tubs, washers and water heater. Make sure the plumber knows if you have a regular vanity or pedestal sink. Mark the end of tubs where drain will be located. Mark areas in wall and ceiling where pipes must not be located, such as locations for recessed lights or medicine cabinets.

PL9 INSTALL rough-in plumbing. This involves the laying of hot (left) and cold (right) water lines, sewer and vent pipe. Pipe running along studs should run within holes drilled (not notched) in the studs. All pipe supports should be in place. Your plumber should use FHA straps to protect pipe from being pierced by drywall subs where ever cut-outs

Figure 41. Plumbing stacks: A, 4-inch cast-iron stack; B, 3-inch pipe for vent.

Figure 42. Drilled holes in joists

are made. FHA straps are metal plates designed to protect the pipe from puncturing by nails. Exterior spigots should not be placed near the point where water mains or other pipes go through the exterior wall, as this will invite water into the home if the spigot freezes or leaks. Make sure plumber extends the spigot if brick veneer is used. The plumber will conduct a water pipe test using air pressure to insure against leaks.

PL10 INSTALL water meter and spigot. This has to be done early because masons will need a good source of water.

PL11 INSTALL sewer line. Mark locations of other pipes (water or gas) so diggers will avoid puncturing them.

PL12 SCHEDULE plumbing inspector.

PL13 INSTALL septic tank and line, if applicable.

PL14 CONDUCT rough-in plumbing inspection. Note: This is a VERY important step. No plumbing should be covered until your county inspector has issued an inspection certificate. Plan to go through the inspection with him so you will understand any problems and get a good interpretation of your sub's workmanship.

PL15 CORRECT any problems found during the inspection. Remember, you have the county's force behind you. You also have the specifications. Since your plumber has not been paid, you have plenty of leverage.

PL16 PAY plumbing sub for rough-in. Get him to sign a receipt or equivalent.

FINISH

PL17 INSTALL finish plumbing. This involves installation of all fixtures selected earlier. Sinks, faucets, toilets and shower heads are installed.

PL18 TAP into water supply. This is where your plumbing gets a real test. You will have to open all the faucets to allow air to bleed out of the system. The water will probably look dirty for a few minutes but don't be alarmed. The system needs to be flushed of excess debris and solvents.

PL19 CONDUCT finish plumbing inspection. Call your inspector several days prior to the inspection. Make every effort to perform this step with your local inspector to see what he is looking for so you will know exactly what, to have your sub correct if anything is in error.

PL20 CORRECT any problems found during the final inspection.

PL21 PAY plumbing sub for finish. Have him sign an affidavit.

PL22 PAY plumber retainage.

PLUMBING — Specifications

■ Bid is to perform complete plumbing job for dwelling as described on attached drawings.

■ Bid is to include all material and labor including all fixtures listed on the attached drawings.

■ All materials and workmanship shall meet or exceed all requirements of the local plumbing code.

■ No plumbing, draining and venting to be covered, concealed or put into use until tested, inspected and approved by local inspectors.

■ All necessary licenses and permits to be obtained by plumber.

■ Plumbing inspection to be scheduled by plumber.

■ All plumbing lines shall be supported so as to insure proper alignment and prevent sagging.

■ Worker's compensation to be provided by plumber.

■ Floor drain pan to be installed under washer if located upstairs or for water heater in attic.

■ Plan for gas dryer.

■ Install approved pressure reduction valve at water service pipe.

■ Stub in basement, plumbing for one sink, tub and toilet.

■ Drain pans to be installed in all tile shower bases.

■ Install construction water spigot on water meter with locked valve.

- Install refrigerator icemaker and drain.

- Plumb water supply so as to completely eliminate water hammer.

- Water pipes to be of adequate dimension to supply all necessary fixtures simultaneously.

- Cut-off valves to be installed at all sinks and toilets, and at water heater.

Sewer System

- Hook into public water system.

- Install approved, listed and adequately sized backwater valve.

- Horizontal drainage to be uniformly sloped not less than 1" in 4' toward point of disposal.

- Drainage pipes to be adequate diameter to remove all water and waste in proper manner.

Wet Vent System

- Vent piping shall extend through the roof flashing and terminate vertically not less than 6" above the roof surface and not less than 1' from any vertical surface, 10' from and 3' above a window, door or air intake or less than 10' from a hot line.

- All vent piping to be on rear side of roof without visibility from front.

- All vent piping to conform to the local plumbing and building code.

PLUMBING — Inspection

Rough-In

☐ All supplies and drains specified are present and of proper material (PVC, CPVC, copper, cast iron, polybutylene).

☐ Sewer tap done.

☐ No pipes pierced by nails.

☐ Hot water fixture on left of spigot.

☐ No evidence of any leaks. This is particularly critical at all joints, elbows and FHA straps.

☐ All plumbing lines inside of stud walls. Must allow for a flush wall.

☐ FHA straps used to protect pipes from nails where necessary.

☐ All cut-out framing done by plumber repaired so as to meet local building code.

☐ Tub centered in bath properly and secured in place.

☐ Tub levelers are all in contact with tub. Tub does not move or rock.

☐ Toilet drain at least 12" to center from all adjacent walls to accommodate toilet fixture.

☐ Toilet drain at least 15" to center from tub to accommodate toilet fixture.

☐ Exterior spigot stub-outs high enough so that they will not be covered over by backfill. Minimum of 6".

☐ Icemaker line for refrigerator in place (¼" copper pipe).

☐ Roof stacks have been properly flashed with galvanized sheet metal.

☐ All wall-hung sinks have metal bridge support located with center at proper level.

☐ Water heater firmly set and connected.

☐ Attic water heater has a floor drain pan.

☐ Water main shut-off valve works properly.

☐ Water lines to washer installed.

☐ Rough-in inspection approved and signed by local building inspector.

Finish

☐ Tub faucets (hot and cold) operate properly. No drip. Drain operates well.

☐ Sink faucets (hot and cold) operate properly. No drip. Drain operates well.

☐ Toilets flush properly. Fill to proper line and action stops completely with no seepage.

☐ Kitchen sink faucets (hot and cold) operate properly. No drips. Drain operates well.

☐ Garbage disposal operates properly. Test as needed.

☐ Dishwasher operates properly (hot and cold). No

leaks. Drain operates well. Run through one entire cycle.

☐ No scratches, chips, dents or other signs of damage on any appliances.

☐ No evidence of water hammer in entire system. Turn each faucet on and off very quickly and listen for a knock.

☐ All water supplies: hot on the left and cold on the right.

☐ Turn on all sinks and flush all toilets at the same time and check for significant reduction in water flow. Some is to be expected.

☐ Cut-off valves on all sinks, toilets and water heaters.

☐ All exterior water spigots freeze-proof and operating properly.

☐ All roof and exterior wall penetrations tested waterproof.

☐ Pipe holes in poured walls sealed with hydraulic cement.

☐ Note: It is HIGHLY recommended that you obtain the assistance of your local inspector when performing your plumbing inspections. Your plumbing inspector is well trained for such tests.

PLUMBING — Glossary

AIR CHAMBER— Pipe appendage with trapped air added to a line to serve as a shock absorber to retard or eliminate air hammer.

BACKFLOW— The flow of water or other fluids or materials into the distributing source of potable water from any source other than its intended source.

BEND— Any change in direction of a line.

BIBB— Special cover used where lines are stubbed through an exterior wall.

BUILDING DRAIN—The common artery of the drainage system receiving the discharge from other drainage pipes inside the building conveying it to the sewer system outside the building.

BUILDING SEWER—That part of the drainage system extending from the building drain to a public or private sewer system.

BUILDING SUPPLY—The pipe carrying potable water from the water meter or other water source to points of distribution throughout the building and lot.

CAP— Hardware used to terminate any line.

CLEAN-OUT— A sealed opening in a pipe which can be screwed off to unclog the line if necessary.

CPVC— Chlorinated Poly Vinyl Chloride. A flexible form of water line recently introduced. No soldering involved. Plastic.

ELBOW— A section of line which is used to change directions. Normally at right angles.

FIXTURE— Any end point in a plumbing system used as a source of potable water. Fixtures normally include sinks, tubs, showers, spigots, sprinkler systems, washer connections and other related items.

LINE— Any section of plumbing whether it is copper, PVC, CPVC or cast iron.

POTABLE WATER— Water satisfactory for human consumption and domestic use, meeting the local health authority requirements.

PVC— Poly Vinyl Chloride. A form of plastic line used primarily for sewer and cold water supply.

SEPTIC TANK— A receptacle used for storage of water, retained solids and digesting organic matter through bacteria and discharging liquids into the soil (subsurface, disposal fields or seepage pits), as permitted by local health authorities.

SOIL STACK— A vent opening out to the roof, which allows the plumbing system to equalize with external air pressure and allows the sewer system to "breathe".

STOP VALVE— A shut-off valve allowing water to be cutoff at a particular point in the system.

TRAP— A device providing a liquid seal which prevents the backflow of air without materially affecting the flow of sewage or waste water. "S" shaped drain traps are required in most building codes.

VENT SYSTEM— A pipe or network of pipes providing a flow of air to or from a drainage system to protect trap seals from siphonage or back pressure.

HVAC

Heating, Ventilation and Air Conditioning is one of the big three trades in terms of cost and impact. Heating and air conditioning systems share the same ventilation and ductwork. Cold air for air conditioning is heavier than hot air, hence it normally takes a higher speed fan. For this reason, see if you can get a two speed fan — one speed for cold air in the summer and one for hot air in the winter. The fan unit, normally a "squirrel cage" type, looks just like its name implies. If you have a two story home, a large split level or a long ranch, consider a zoned (split) system. Zoned systems work on the premise that two smaller, dedicated systems operate more efficiently than one larger one. For large homes (2500 sq. ft. or more), this becomes a STRONG consideration. Heating is measured in BTU's (British Thermal Units) while cooling is normally measured in tons (no relationship to 2000 lbs.). Normally, it takes 30,000 BTU's of heat and one ton of AC for each 800 sq. feet of area.

The efficiency of heating and cooling systems varies widely. Select your systems carefully with this in mind. Contact your local power and gas companies for information regarding energy efficiency ratings used to compare systems on the market. When shopping for systems, check the efficiency rating, and be prepared to pay more for more efficient systems. Your power and gas company may also conduct, free of charge, an energy audit of the home you plan to build, and help suggest heating and cooling requirements. For efficiency reasons, your HVAC system should be located as close to the center of your home as possible, to minimize the length of ductwork required. Also, ductwork should have as few turns in it as possible. Air flow slows down every time a turn is made, decreasing the system's overall efficiency and effective output. Seven inch diameter round ductwork is fairly standard.

Air conditioning units operate by transferring heat from the air inside your home to the outside via a fluid called Freon. Several grades of Freon exist. Freon-16 is used in most AC units. Freon is measured by the pound (weight) — not volume. Make sure your system is fully charged before operating to avoid damage to the compressor.

Other Climate Control

At your option, your HVAC sub will also install other climate control devices. Electric air filters attach to your HVAC system air intake, eliminating up to 90 percent of airborne dust particles when cleaned regularly. Humidifiers, popular in dry areas, add moisture to the air. Special water supplies can be attached for automatic water dispensing. Dehumidifiers, popular in the Southeast and other humid areas, draw water out of the air. These units may be attached to a water drain for easy disposal of accumulated water.

HVAC SUBS

HVAC subs charge based on the size of your system (BTU's and tonnage). There is a tendency for subs to overestimate your heating and cooling requirements for three reasons:

- More cost, more profit

- Nobody ever complains about having too much heating and cooling

- Better safe than sorry

Have your HVAC sub submit a separate bid for the ductwork. Your HVAC sub will also install your natural gas line (if you use natural gas), and hook it up to the gas main. The gas company will install your gas meter. Shop carefully for your HVAC sub; a wrong decision here can cost you increased utility bills in the future.

Figure 43. Spaced joists for supply ducts

Figure 44. Cold-air return

Ductwork

The ductwork circulates conditioned air to specific points in the home and is split between air supplies that deliver conditioned air and air returns, which recirculate the air back to the HVAC system. Ducts will usually be constructed of sheetmetal or insulated fiberglass cut and shaped to fit at the site. Fiberglass ducts are rapidly gaining in popularity due to their ease of fabrication at the site. The duct itself is made of insulated fiberglass and can be cut with a knife. This extra insulation makes for a more efficient and quieter air system. Sheetmetal ducts are notorious for developing mysterious noises caused by expansion and air movement that may be difficult or impossible to eliminate.

Register Placement

Proper placement of supplies and returns is critical to making your total HVAC system efficient and economical to run. Most registers are placed near doors or under windows. This type of placement puts the conditioned air near the sources of greatest heat loss and promotes more even distribution of air.

SUPPLIES should be located primarily along the exterior walls of the home. This is known as a radial duct system. Where possible, hot air supplies should be positioned directly below windows and alongside exterior doors near the floor since heat rises. Cold air supplies should be located up high in rooms since cool air falls.

RETURNS should be located low for warm air returns since the cooled air drops. Cool air returns should be located high to remove the air as it warms up. It is a good idea to have two supplies (high and low) and two returns (high and low) in critical rooms in order to handle either season. Your HVAC sub will be able to help you with the proper quantity and placement of your supplies and returns. As a general rule, you will need at least one supply and one return for each room.

Thermostats

Many elaborate thermostats are available on the market today. Many automatically shut heating systems down or set them at a low level during "off" hours. In any event, do not put the thermostat within 6' of any air supply register or facing one on an opposite wall. NEVER place a thermostat in a room which has a fireplace. Consider placing a thermostat in the hallway.

Get the Most Out of Your Subs

If you are building in the winter, subs will normally be used to working in a cold, unheated house. This means subs may not show up or when they do, they might spend a lot of time just getting warm by a fire somewhere. If you get your heating system approved early, normally by passing a quick test, you can turn it on before the house is finished. This will also save you some money when other builders may have gone out and rented a space heater. Drywall and paint will dry faster and subs will really appreciate the additional comfort.

HVAC - Steps

HV1 CONDUCT energy audit of home to determine HVAC requirements. Your local gas and electric companies can be very helpful with this, sometimes providing computer printouts at little or no cost. You may only have to drop off a set of blueprints. Decide whether you will have a gas or electric dryer and determine where it will be situated.

HV2 SHOP for best combination of cost, size and efficiency in heating and cooling systems. The higher the efficiency, the higher the price.

HV3 CONDUCT bidding process on complete HVAC job. Have them give a separate bid for the ductwork.

HV4 FINALIZE HVAC design. Have a representative from the local gas company or an inspector look over your plan to make sure you aren't doing anything that could be a problem. Specify location of dryer exhaust vent.

HV5 ROUGH-IN heating and air conditioning system. Do not install any external fixtures such as compressors at this time. Compressors are a favorite theft item. If you frame floor joists 12" O.C. you may need to use floor registers.

HV6 INSPECT heating and air conditioning rough-in. This should be done with your county inspector. Call him in advance.

HV7 CORRECT all deficiencies noted in the rough-in inspection.

HV8 PAY HVAC sub for rough-in work. Have him sign a receipt.

Finish Work

HV9 INSTALL heating and air conditioning (finish work). This is where the thermostat and all other HVAC electrical work are hooked up. All registers are installed. The AC compressor is installed and charged with Freon. Discuss the placement of the AC compressor location with the HVAC sub. He may supply the concrete pad if you do not have one.

HV10 INSPECT heating and air conditioning final. Again, this should be done by your county inspector. Call him several days in advance so you can be present for the inspection. Some builders like to have their HVAC sub present, too. Make a note of any deficiencies. Be sure electrician has run service to the unit and that it is functional.

HV11 CORRECT all deficiencies noted in the final inspection.

HV12 CALL gas company to hook up gas lines.

HV13 DRAW gas line on plat diagram.

HV14 PAY HVAC sub for finish work. Get him to sign an affidavit.

HV15 PAY HVAC sub retainage after system is fully tested.

HVAC - Sample Specifications

■ Bid is to install heating, ventilation and air conditioning system (HVAC) as indicated on attached drawings.

■ Install zoned forced air gas (FAG) fired heating unit. With five (5) year warranty. One in basement and one in attic.

■ Install two AC compressors.

■ Install gas range hook-up.

■ Install 50-gallon gas water heater.

■ Install downdraft line for island cooktop.

■ Connect 1½" copper gas line to gas main, a minimum of 12" under ground.

■ Install sloped PVC tubing for AC drainage.

■ Install gas grill line and grill unit on patio.

■ Install one fireplace log lighter and gas line.

■ Install gas line to porch and mailbox gas lights.

■ All work and materials to meet or exceed requirements of the local building code.

■ Provide and install all necessary air filters.

■ Opening to furnace large enough to permit removal and replacement.

■ All Freon lines charged with Freon.

HVAC - Inspection

Rough-In

☐ All equipment UL-approved with warranties on file.

☐ Heating and air units installed in place and well anchored.

☐ Heating and air units are proper make, model and size.

☐ Zoned systems have proper units in proper locations.

☐ Air compressors firmly anchored to footings.

☐ All ductwork installed according to specifications.

☐ Proper number of returns and supplies have been installed.

☐ All ductwork meets local building codes.

☐ All ductwork joints sealed tightly and smoothly with duct tape.

☐ No return ducts in baths or kitchen.

☐ Bathrooms vent to outside if specified.

☐ All ductwork in walls flush with walls, not to interfere with drywall.

☐ All ductwork in ceiling tied off so as not to interfere with drywall or paneling.

☐ Attic furnace has a floor drain pan, if in attic.

☐ All heat exhaust vents isolated from wood or roofing by at least 1".

☐ No exhaust vents visible from the front of the home.

☐ Air conditioning condensate drain installed.

☐ All ductwork outlets framed properly to allow installation of vent covers.

☐ Vent hood or downdraft installed in kitchen according to plan.

☐ HVAC rough-in inspection approved and signed by local building inspectors

☐ Gas meter in place.

☐ Gas line connected to gas main.

Finish

☐ Line to gas range hooked up. Range installed.

☐ Line to gas dryer hooked up. Dryer vent installed properly.

☐ Line to gas grill hooked up. Gas grill installed.

☐ HVAC electrical hookup completed.

☐ Thermostats operate properly and are installed near center of house. Thermostats located away from heat sources (fireplaces and registers) and doors and windows to provide accurate operation.

☐ Manual/Auto switch on thermostat works properly.

☐ A/C condensate pipe drains properly. This will be difficult or impossible to test in cold weather. The pipe should at least have a slight downward slope to it. You cannot test A/C if temperature is below 68 degrees.

☐ Fan noise not excessive.

☐ Furnace, A/C and electronic air filters installed.

☐ Water line to humidifier installed and operating.

☐ Water line from dehumidifier installed and operating.

☐ All vent covers on all duct openings and installed in proper direction.

☐ All holes and openings to exterior sealed with exterior grade caulk.

☐ Downdraft vent for cooktop installed and operating.

☐ All HVAC equipment papers filed away (warranty, maintenance, etc.).

☐ Strong air flow out of all air supplies.

☐ Air returns function properly.

HVAC — Glossary

BTU— British Thermal Unit. A standard unit of hot or cold air output.

COMPRESSOR— Component of the central air-conditioning system which sits outside of dwelling.

DAMPER— A metal flap controlling the flow of conditioned air through ductwork.

ELBOW— Ductwork joint used to turn supply or return at any angle.

EXHAUST— Air saturated with carbon dioxide. The byproduct of natural gas combustion in a forced air gas system. This exhaust gas should be vented directly out the top of the roof. It is dangerous to breathe this gas.

FREON— A special liquid used by an air-conditioning compressor to move heat in or out of the dwelling. This fluid circulates in a closed system. This fluid is also used in refrigerators and freezers.

PLENUM— Chamber immediately outside of the HVAC unit where conditioned air feeds into all of the supplies.

REGISTER— Metal facing plate on wall where supply air is released into room and where air enters returns. Registers can be used to direct the flow of air.

RETURN— Ductwork leading back to the HVAC unit to be reconditioned.

SUPPLY— Ductwork leading from the HVAC unit to the registers.

TON— An industry standard measure to express a quantity of cold air produced by an air conditioning system.

Electrical

Electricians will perform all necessary wiring for all interior and exterior fixtures and appliances. Electricians will often charge a fixed price for providing and wiring each switch, outlet and fixture. Double switches will count as two switches and so on. You can save money by purchasing your own fixtures; the markup is incredible. Code will normally require at least one outlet per wall of each room and/or one for each specified number of running wall feet. The electrical code most often used and referred to is the National Electrical Code (NEC). But the one in your county should prevail. Your electrician needs to be a licensed master electrician in your county.

Your electrical sub will help you determine where switches and outlets should be placed. There are a few standards, such as minimum spacing of outlets and height of switches and outlets, which should be indicated in your local building code. Consider multiple switches for a single light (such as at the top and bottom of stairs), floodlight switches in the master bedroom and photo-electric cells for driveway and porch lights. Make sure to install Ground Fault Interrupters (GFI's) in all bathroom outlets. GFI's are ultra sensitive circuit breakers that provide an extra margin of safety in areas where the risk of shock is high. Hobby shop and garage areas are also good sites for these devices. Key areas for additional outlets:

- Plugs in breakfast areas
- Along kitchen counters
- Switched outlets in attic
- Foyer area

Wire gauges used for circuits will vary. Electric stoves, ovens, refrigerators, washers, dryers and air compressors are each normally on separate circuits and use heavier gauges of wire. Your local building code will describe load limits on each circuit and the appropriate wire types and gauges to use.

After your home is dried in, the electrical sub will "rough in" all the electrical wiring, fuse box and electrical HVAC connections. Make sure to have the HVAC and plumbing sub-contractors complete the rough-in before calling in the electrician. This will prevent any wiring from having to be cut or rerouted in order to make room for plumbing or ducting. It is much easier for the electrician to work around obstructions. If all ducting is in place, the electrician will also know precisely where the furnace will be located and will be able to wire for it properly.

Many house plans include a wiring diagram; but make sure to examine it carefully. These diagrams are usually done as an afterthought and are produced by the draftsman, not an electrician. It is best to walk through the house with the electrician and mark the locations of outlets and switches. A good electrician will make helpful suggestions on the location of fixtures.

Additional Wiring

While the electrical wiring is being installed, consider installing other necessary wiring for appliances such as phones, alarm systems, TV antennas, doorbells, intercoms and computers. Ask your electrician for bids on installing this other wiring, although his price may be quite high. This type of wiring makes an excellent do-it-yourself project if you are eager to get involved. Installing this wiring before drywall is installed is easy and saves considerable installation expense later.

STEPS - Electrical

Rough-In
EL1 DETERMINE electrical requirements. Unless your set of blueprints includes a wiring diagram, you will want to decide where to place lighting fixtures, outlets and switches.

Make sure no switches are blocked by an open door. You may want to consider furniture placement while you are doing this. Even if your blueprint has an electrical diagram, don't assume it is correct. Most of the time, they can be improved. You may wish to investigate the use of low voltage and fluorescent lighting. Remember that you cannot dim fluorescent lights.

EL2 SELECT electrical fixtures and appliances. Visit lighting distributor showrooms. Keep an eye out for attractive fluorescent lighting which will be a long-term energy saver (but cannot use a dimmer switch). Special orders should be done now due to delivery times. You should listen to the doorbell sound before purchasing.

EL3 DETERMINE if phone company charges to wire home for modular phone system. Find out what they charge for and how much. Even if you plan wireless phones, install phone jacks in several locations.

EL4 CONDUCT standard bidding process. Have subs give a price to install each outlet, switch and fixture. They will normally charge extra for wiring the service panel and special work. Use only a licensed electrician.

EL5 SCHEDULE to have phone company install modular phone wiring and jacks. If your phone company charges too much for this service, just have your electrician do the job or do it yourself. Also try to arrange to have your home phone number transferred to your new house later so that you can keep the same phone number.

EL6 APPLY for and obtain permission to hookup your temporary pole to public power system. You may need to place a deposit. Perform this early so that hook-up will take place by the time the framers are on site.

EL7 INSTALL temporary electric pole. Make sure the pole is within 100 feet of the center of the house foundation (preferably closer).

EL8 PERFORM rough-in electrical. This involves installing wiring through holes in wall studs and above ceiling joists. All the wiring for light switches and outlets will be run to the location of the service panel. To insure that your outlets and switches are placed where you want them, mark their locations with chalk or a marker. Otherwise, the electrician will place them wherever he desires. It is important to get lights, switches and outlets exactly where you plan to place furniture and fittings. Provide scrap 2x4's for blocking next to outlets.

EL9 INSTALL modular phone wiring and jacks and any other wiring desired. You may also wish to run speaker, cable TV, security and computer wiring throughout the house. It's much easier to do it now than later. Staple wires to studs where wire enters the room so the drywall crew will notice them. Many security system contractors will pre-wire your home for their security system at their cost if you decide to purchase their system.

EL10 SCHEDULE electrical inspection. The electrician will usually do this.

EL11 INSPECT rough-in electrical. The county inspector will sign off the wiring. Remember that this MUST be done before final drywall is in place.

EL12 CORRECT any problems noted during rough-in inspection.

EL13 PAY electrical sub for rough-in work. Get a receipt or use canceled check as a receipt.

EL14 INSTALL garage door(s). Typically this is not done by the electrician, but by a specialist. The garage door must be installed so that the opener can be hooked up by the electrician.

EL15 INSTALL electric garage door openers. Store remote control units in a safe place. Wire electrical connection.

Finish

EL16 PERFORM finish electrical work. This includes terminating all wiring appropriately (switches, outlets, etc.). Major electrical appliances such as refrigerators, washers, dryers, ovens, vent hoods, exhaust fans, garage door openers, doorbells and other appliances are installed at this time. The air compressor will also be wired.

EL17 CALL phone company to connect service.

EL18 INSPECT finish electrical. Again, your county inspector must be scheduled. Have your electrician present so he will know just what to fix if there is a problem. Store all appliance manuals and warranties in a safe place.

EL19 CORRECT electrical problems if any exist.

EL20 CALL electrical utility to connect service.

EL21 PAY electrical sub, final. Have him sign an affidavit.

EL22 PAY electrical sub retainage after power is turned on and all switches and outlets are tested.

ELECTRICAL - Sample Specifications

■ Bid is to perform complete electrical wiring per attached drawings.

■ Bid to include all supplies except lighting fixtures and appliances. Bid to include installation of light fixtures.

■ Bid to include furnishing temporary electric pole and temporary hook-up to power line.

■ Bid to include brass switch plates in living room, dining room and foyer.

■ Bid may include wiring and installation of the following items:
  • 200 amp service panel with circuit breakers
  • Light switches (1-way)
  • Light switches (2-way)
  • Furnace
  • Dishwasher
  • Garbage disposal
  • Microwave (built-in)
  • Door chime set
  • Door chime button(s) with lighted buttons
  • Bath vent fans
  • Bath heat lamp with timer switch
  • Jacuzzi pump motor with timer switch
  • Light fixtures (all rooms and exerior areas)
  • Three-prong (grounded) interior outlets
  • Three-prong (grounded) waterproof exterior outlets
  • Electric range
  • Double lamp exterior flood lights
  • Electric garage door openers with auto light switch
  • Washer
  • Dryer
  • Central air conditioning compressor
  • Climate control thermostats
  • Electric hot water heater
  • Hood fan
  • Central vacuum system
  • Intercom, radio units, speaker wires
  • Co-axial cable TV lines and computer cables
  • Sump pump
  • Electronic security system with sensors
  • Ceiling fans
  • Whole house attic fan with timer switch
  • Automatic closet switches
  • Humidifier/dehumidifier
  • Time-controlled heat lamps
  • Thermostatic roof vents
  • Phone lines in all rooms as shown
  • Time-controlled sprinkler system

■ All work and materials to meet or exceed all requirements of the National Electrical Code unless otherwise specified.

■ Natural earth ground to be used.

■ Dimmer switches to be installed on fixtures as shown on plan.

■ Rheostat to be installed on ceiling fans.

ELECTRICAL - Inspection

Rough-in

☐ Outlets and switch boxes offset to allow for Drywall and base molding.

☐ All outlets and switches placed at 42" height as indicated on plans. Outlets and switch unobstructed by doors.

☐ All special outlets, switch boxes and fixtures are in place where intended. Refer to your specifications and blueprints.

☐ Electrical boxes for chandeliers and ceiling fans are adequately braced to hold weight of fixture.

☐ All lines are grounded.

☐ All visible splices have approved splice cap securely fastened.

☐ Bath ventilator fans installed.

☐ Attic power ventilators installed.

Finish

☐ All outlets and fixture wires measure 117 V with circuit tester or voltmeter. Test between the ground and each socket.

☐ Dimmer switches installed where specified (dining room, den, foyer and master bath).

☐ Air conditioner cut-off switch is installed at A/C unit.

☐ No scratches, dents or other damage to electrical appliances and fixtures.

☐ Furnace completely connected and operational.

☐ All bath vents connected and operational. Should be on separate circuit from light switch.

☐ Electric range connected and operational.

☐ Electric pilot light starter on gas range connected and operational.

☐ Range hood, downdraft and light connected and operational.

☐ Built-in microwave connected and operational.

☐ Garbage disposal connected and operational.

☐ Trash compactor connected and operational.

☐ Dishwasher connected and operational.

☐ Refrigerator outlet operational.

☐ Door chimes (all sets) connected and operational.

☐ Power/thermostatic ventilators on roof connected and operational.

☐ Washer and dryer outlet operational.

☐ Garage opener installed and operational.

☐ Electronic security system connected and operational. All sensors need to be tested one at a time.

☐ Phone outlets work at all locations.

☐ Service panel installed properly with sufficient load carrying capacity. Breakers are labeled properly.

☐ Exterior lighting fixtures installed and operational.

☐ All recessed lighting, ceiling lighting, heat lamps and other lighting fixtures connected as specified and operational.

☐ All intercom/radio units connected and operational.

☐ Jacuzzi pump motor connected and operational. For safety reasons, switch should not be reachable from the tub.

☐ Central vacuum system connected and operational.

☐ All other specified appliances and fixtures connected and operational.

☐ All switch plate and outlet covers are installed as specified (in rooms to be wallpapered, these will be temporarily removed).

☐ Finish electrical inspection approved and signed by local building inspector.

ELECTRICAL — Glossary

AMPERAGE— The amount of current flow in a wire. Similar to the amount of water flowing in a pipe.

CAN— Recessed lighting fixture.

CIRCUIT BREAKER— A device to ensure that current overloads do not occur. A circuit breaker "breaks the circuit" when a dangerous overload or short circuit occurs.

CONDUIT— Metal pipe used to run wiring through when extra protection of wiring is needed or wiring is to be exposed.

EER— (Energy Efficiency Rating) A national rating required to be displayed on appliances measuring their efficient use of electrical power.

GEM BOX— A metal box installed in electrical rough-in that holds outlets, receptacles and other electrical units.

GFI— (Ground Fault Interrupter) An extra sensitive circuit breaker usually installed in outlets in bathrooms and exterior locations to provide additional protection against shock. Required now by most building codes.

HOT— A wire carrying current.

SERVICE PANEL— Junction where main electrical service to the home is split among the many circuits internal to the home. Circuit breakers should exist on each internal circuit.

THINWALL— Thin flexible conduit used between outlet boxes.

3 WAY SWITCH— Type of switch that allows control of a lighting fixture from two switch locations such as both ends of a hallway.

VOLTAGE— The "force" of electrical potential. Similar to the pressure of water in a pipe.

WATTAGE— The product of the amperage times the voltage. A good indicator of the amount of electrical power needed to run the particular appliance. The higher the wattage, the more electricity used per hour.

Masonry and Stucco

MASONRY

Masonry is the trade involved with the application of concrete blocks, clay or tile bricks and stone. Masonry is a true art; watch a bricklayer sometime and you will see why. A skilled bricklayer possesses a strong combination of good workmanship and efficiency — key ingredients to producing a strong, well built brick structure on schedule. Your brick mason and stone mason may be two different subs.

Concrete Blocks

Concrete blocks are normally used below ground as an alternative to a poured foundation. Although a poured foundation is 3 times stronger, concrete blocks are less expensive, while being of adequate strength. The standard size of a concrete block is 7 ⅝" x 7 ⅝" x 15 ⅝" and are normally laid with ⅜" flush mortar joints. Concrete blocks are applied on concrete footings.

Figure 45. Step down block wall

CONCRETE TO BE POURED MONOLITHICALLY

6" MIN. FOR VERTICAL STEP
a = horizontal step
c = vertical step
t = footing thickness
p = projection of footing
w = width of footing

- ALL FOOTINGS AND STEPS SHOULD BE LEVEL.
- STEP (b) SHOULD NOT EXCEED 3/4 OF STEP (a).

CLAY BRICKS

Often called brick veneer, brick facing is normally comprised of brick 3 ⅝" x 7 ⅝" x 2 ¼" set in a ⅜" mortar joint. For estimating purposes, brick veneer, laid in running bond (a typical pattern), requires seven bricks per square foot of wall. This does not apply for such items as chimneys or fancy brickwork. Your mason charges for laying units of 1000 bricks (one skid). Additional expenses may be charged for multistory or fancy brickwork where scaffolding and/or additional skill and labor is required. Bricks are anchored to walls with galvanized metal wall ties. Once bricks are laid, brick walls are self supporting.

24" MAX. SPACING OF REINFORCEMENT
4" MIN. THICKNESS
12" MAX. UNLESS VENEER IS BONDED TO 4" PORTION
NOT LESS THAN DIMENSION "A"
REINFORCING REQUIRED WHEN "A" EXCEEDS 4"

Figure 46. Brick veneer wall

STUCCO

Once popular and widely used throughout Western Europe, stucco has come back in style to bring back that old flair. Stucco is really just mortar applied over a metal lath or screen used for support and adhesion.

STUCCO
STUCCO LATH
SHEATHING PAPER
METAL SCREED
1" (NOMINAL)

NOTE: Base screed shown on concrete slab construction without sheathing screeds or other foundations or on sheathing are similar.

Figure 47. Typical stucco base screed

DURABILITY. Some builders complain of maintenance problems (cracking) of traditional stucco after ten years or so of service. If stucco is applied properly with proper expansion joints, it should provide decades of sound performance. Expansion joints should be placed approximately every 300 square feet. Some stucco cracking should be expected.

INSULATION. Stucco is not the best insulator. As such, you should go with heavier batt insulation in your exterior walls. Higher grade sheathing is also in order.

NEW IMPROVED. Several brands of artificial stucco are on the market. Although they boast of higher insulating qualities and lower maintenance, they are also more expensive. Some say it pays off in use of cheaper insulation and lower utilities. It is also easier to do fancier trim work like lintels, quoins and other work because it uses Styrofoam cutouts as a base.

COSTS. Stucco is charged by the installed square yard. Normally, area is not deducted for doors and windows except for the garage door. Rationale is that it is at least as much trouble to work around an opening as it is to cover the area. Extras will probably include :

■ Smooth finish

■ Decorative corner work (quoins)

■ Decorative window and door work (keystones and bands)

■ Corner bead — all edges

Stucco can be applied rough, smooth or anywhere in between. Subs will charge you more for a smooth finish because it takes longer and imperfections show up easier. If you use a dyed stucco, it may not require painting.

For the Best Stucco Job

■ Don't attempt to stucco foil or polyethylene backed sheathing due to poor adherence. Use either styrofoam (5/8" to 2") or exterior gypsum (1/2"). Check to see what sheathing your stucco sub recommends.

■ Avoid mixing pigments with stucco mortar. This can lead to uneven drying and coloration. Paint the stucco after it is dry.

■ To avoid cracking, be liberal with expansion joints. They are hardly noticeable and do not detract from overall appearance.

■ Don't attempt to apply stucco if there is ANY chance of rain in the forecast.

About Fireplaces

If you go with a custom masonry fireplace, the critical thing to get is a proper draft. If your fireplace doesn't "breathe" properly, you will always have smoke in your home during its use. If it "breathes" too well, you may not get too much effect from the fireplace. This is not a big problem with pre-fabricated fireplace units since they are pre-designed to operate properly. Below are a few options you may want to consider regardless of what type fireplace you have:

Fresh air vent— Allows the fire to get its combustion air from outside your home so that it doesn't rob all your warm air.

ASH DUMP— Makes fireplace cleaning a lot easier.

LOG LIGHTER— Easier log starting.

RAISED HEARTH—Easier access to working on the fire.

BLOWER— May provide more room heating.

HEAT RECIRCULATOR— May also be able to provide more heating.

One important safety issue is the flue. Avoid burning pine whenever possible, especially if you are using a prefab fireplace. The resin buildup in the flue can cause problems later (fire hazard). If you plan to have a stucco home, consider a prefab fireplace. A masonry fireplace can look out of place unless covered over with stucco, which isn't very cost effective!

MASONRY/STONE - Steps

MA1 DETERMINE brick/stone pattern, color and coverage and joint tooling.

MA2 DETERMINE stucco pattern, color and coverage.

MA3 PERFORM standard bidding process. Contact material suppliers, local brick companies, masonry unions and other subs for the names of good masons. Do not select a mason until you have seen his work. Ask the suppliers if there is a penalty for returning unused bricks.

MA4 PERFORM standard bidding process for stucco subs. You really need to see their work, too.

MA5 APPLY flashing above all windows and doors if not already installed by roofer.

MA6 ORDER brick, stone, and angle irons.

MA7 LAY brick/stone veneer exterior, chimney, fireplace and hearth. This is the time to have the mason throw in a brick mailbox if you want one. Remember to provide a "postal approved" metal mailbox insert.

MA8 FINISH bricks and mortar.

MA9 INSPECT brickwork. Refer to specification, local code and checklist on following page.

MA10 CORRECT any brick/stone work requiring attention.

MA11 PAY mason. If you have extra bricks which either can't be returned or are not worth returning, turn them into a brick walkway or patio later.

MA12 CLEAN up excess bricks and dried mortar. Spread any extra sand in the driveway and sidewalk area. Masons charge too much by the hour to have them do this work.

MA13 INSTALL base for decorative stucco. This includes keys, bands and other trimwork. Use exterior grade lumber or Styrofoam if using synthetic stucco.

MA14 PREPARE stucco test area. This should be at least a 3' by 6' sheet of plywood covered with test stucco to make sure you agree with the actual color and texture. Make sub finish mailbox if desired. If you wish to protect the stoops from stucco, cover them with sand.

MA15 APPLY stucco lath and decorative formwork to sheathing.

MA16 APPLY first coat of stucco. The color of the first coat does not matter.

MA17 APPLY second coat of stucco. You need to wait a few days for the first coat to dry completely. Place a thick mat of straw at base of house to prevent mud from staining stucco. While the scaffolding is set up, have the painter work on cornice and second story windows.

MA18 INSPECT stucco work.

MA19 CORRECT any stucco work requiring attention.

MA20 PAY stucco subs.

MA21 PAY mason's retainage.

MA22 PAY stucco sub's retainage.

MASONRY — Specifications

■ Brick veneer coverage to be as indicated on attached drawings.

■ All brick, sand and mortar mix to be furnished by builder.

■ All necessary scaffolding to be supplied and erected by mason.

■ Brick entrance steps to be laid as indicated in attached drawings.

■ Brick patio to be laid as indicated in attached drawings.

■ All excess bricks to remain stacked on site.

■ Wrought iron railings to be installed on entrance steps as indicated in attached drawings. Wrought iron to be anchored into surface with sufficient bolts.

■ Bricks are to be moistened before laying to provide superior bonding.

■ Window, door, fascia and other special brick patterns are to be done as indicated in attached detail drawings.

■ Moistened brick is to be laid in running bond with 3/8" mortar joints.

■ Mortar is to be medium gray in color; Type "C" mortar is to be used throughout job.

- Mortar joints are to be tooled concave.

- Steel lintels are to be installed above all door and window openings.

- Masonry walls are to be reasonably free of mortar stains as determined by builder. Mortar stains are to be removed with a solution of one part commercial muriatic acid and nine parts water to sections of 15 square feet of moistened brick and then washed with water immediately. Door and window frames are to be protected from the cleaning solution.

- Flashing to be installed at the head and sill of all window openings.

- Flashing to be installed above foundation sill and below all masonry work.

- Bid to include all necessary touch-up work.

STUCCO — Specifications

- Bid is to provide all material, labor and tools to install lath and stucco per attached drawings.

- Stucco to be finished smooth, sand texture. (Specify color.)

- All trim areas to be 2" wide unless otherwise specified.

- Quoins to have beveled edges; alternating 12" and 8" wide.

- Two coats of stucco to be applied; pigment in second coat.

- Stucco work to come with a twenty year warranty for material and labor against defects, chipping and cracks.

- Expansion joints to be as indicated on blueprint or as agreed upon.

MASONRY & STUCCO — Inspection

- [ ] Brick and stone style and color are as specified.

- [ ] Mortar color and tooling are as specified.

- [ ] All wall sections plumb, checking with plumb bob and string. No course should be out of line more than ⅛". Overhang distance between top course and bottom course should not exceed ⅛".

- [ ] Flashing installed above all windows, exterior doors and foundation sill.

- [ ] No significant mortar stains visible from up close.

- [ ] Stoops and patio steps drain properly.

- [ ] No loose brick or stones.

- [ ] All quoins smooth, even and as specified.

- [ ] Touch-up brickwork finished.

- [ ] All wrought iron railing is complete per drawings and is sturdy.

STUCCO

- [ ] Stucco coverage, colors and materials are as specified.

- [ ] Stucco is finished as specified.

- [ ] Stucco finish is even with no adverse patterns in surface. Surface level with no dips or bumps. Sight down surface from corners.

- [ ] Stucco is applied to proper depth.

- [ ] All decorative stucco work such as quoins, keys and special trim are in place, complete as specified and well finished with sharp edges and corners.

- [ ] Adequate number of expansion joints (one approximately every 300 square feet). Expansion symmetrical between window openings.

- [ ] Openings for exterior outlets and fixtures not covered up.

- [ ] No large cracks.

MASONRY and STUCCO- Glossary

ACID— Cleaning agent used to clean brick.

BAND— Decorative trim around windows and doors and horizontal relief; normally 2x4 or 2x6.

BEAD— Any corner or edge that must be finished off with stucco.

BRICK VENEER—Exterior wall covered with brick.

CORBEL—Extending a course or courses of bricks beyond the face of a wall. No course should extend more than 2" beyond the course below it. Total corbeling projection should not exceed wall thickness.

COURSE— A horizontally laid set of bricks. A 32 course wall with ⅜" mortar joints stands 7 ' tall.

CUBE— A standard ordering unit for masonry block units (6 x 6 x 8).

JOINT— Mortar in between bricks or blocks.

KEY—Fancy decorative lintel above window made of brick, normally placed on various angles for a flared effect. Also known as a keystone.

LATH—A grid of some sort (normally metal or fiberglass) applied to exterior sheathing as a base for stucco.

LINTEL— A structural member placed above doors and window openings to support the weight of the bricks above the opening.

QUOIN—Fancy edging on outside corners made of brick veneer or stucco.

ROW LOCK— Intersecting bricks which overlap on outside corners.

SOLIDS— Solid bricks used for fireplace hearths, stoops, patios or driveways.

STOOP IRON—Corrugated iron sheeting used as a base for the tip of a brick or stone stoop. This is to eliminate the need for completely filling the stoop area with fill dirt (which may settle) or concrete.

TRIG — A string support for guide lines to prevent sagging and wind disturbances on long expanses of wall.

WATER LINE—Decorative relief line around foundation approximately 3' from the ground.

WEEP HOLE— Small gap in brick wall, normally on garage, that allows water to drain.

WOOD MOLD— A brick making process in which bricks are actually molded instead of extruded. Fancy shapes are the result of this process.

Siding and Cornice

The siding and cornice sub will handle all siding application and cornice work (soffit, fascia, frieze and eave vents). This sub can also install windows and exterior doors, if needed. Usually, the siding sub will first install the sheathing, then the windows and doors. Finally, the siding will be installed flush to the window and door frames.

SIDING

Siding is the most economical exterior covering. The most popular materials include cedar, vinyl, aluminum and Masonite. There are advantages and disadvantages to each:

Type	Advantages	Disadvantages
Cedar	Natural appearance Moderate cost	High maintenance. May raise fire insurance premium. May warp or crack
Texture 111®	Inexpensive	Poor appearance
Masonite®	Inexpensive	High maintenance. Requires painting
Vinyl	Washes easily Low maintenance	Expensive
Aluminum	Washes easily Low maintenance	Expensive

WOOD SIDING provides some of the greatest variety in styles and textures as well as cost effectiveness. It can be installed horizontally, vertically, diagonally or a combination to provide a creative and varied exterior.

Some of the wood types available include pine, cedar, cypress and redwood. The full range of types and styles exceeds the scope of this book. Check with your local supplier for the styles available in your area.

Regardless of the type of wood siding you choose, the important properties required for quality are freedom from warpage, knots and imperfections. Wood siding is prone to shrinkage after installation due to drying. If painted right after installation, lap siding will continue to shrink and leave an unpainted strip of wood where the pieces overlap. Try to delay painting until the siding has an opportunity to stabilize.

Drying will also cause boards to warp and crack as they shrink. Always retain a portion of your siding sub's payment so that you can get him to return later to replace these defective pieces.

The introduction of several plywood siding types such as Texture 111® has simplified siding installation. These plywood sheets simulate several styles of wood siding such as board and batten, but are much easier to install and do not shrink. Labor costs to install are also much lower than traditional wood siding.

Wood siding is prone to leakage around windows and doors, especially on contemporary designs that have many angled walls. Therefore, it is important that your siding sub or painter caulk all butt joints. Specify a tinted caulk that matches the final color of the siding.

Ask the siding sub to hand-pick the best siding pieces for the front and back of the house. These areas bordering decks and porches are the most visible; where visitors will be looking straight at the wood pieces.

MASONITE® SIDING has many of the aesthetic qualities of wood with the added advantage of more uniform and stable material. Masonite® is usually free of imperfections and will not shrink. It also has the added advantage of being preprimed, which may eliminate one paint coat. Most traditional styles that

Figure 48. Inlet ventilators: A, small insert ventilator; B, slot ventilator.

use siding have gone to Masonite®; however, the introduction of new textures that simulate wood have made Masonite® more popular for rustic and contemporary designs as well.

The nail holes in Masonite® are much more visible than in wood, so watch your sub carefully during installation. Specify that the nails to be used are galvanized and countersunk.

VINYL AND ALUMINUM SIDING is usually installed by a sub-contractor who supplies labor and materials for the job. Although expensive, these siding types will last for many years with little or no maintenance. Many come with a 20 year unconditional guarantee.

CORNICE

The cornice is the finishing applied to the overhang of the roof called the eave. The overhang of the roof serves a decorative function as well as protecting the siding from water stains and leakage. Generally, the greater the overhang, the more expensive the look of the house.

Figure 49. Eave protection for snow and ice dams. Lay smooth surface 45-pound roll roofing on roof sheathing over the eaves extending upward well above the inside line of the wall.

Figure 50. Wide bow cornice (without lookouts).

The cornice will installed by your siding or trim sub. If you plan to use fancy trim around your cornice such as dentil molding, you may want to trust the job to your trim sub. He is more used to working with decorative trim.

The two types of cornices most commonly used are the open cornice and the box cornice. The open cornice is the simplest type and is more appropriate for contemporary styles. The open cornice looks just as it sounds. The rafter overhang is left unfinished and open and requires care in the choice of roof sheathing, since it will be visible from below. The box cornice has the overhang boxed in with plywood and is finished off with a variety of trim types and styles. This style is more commonly used on traditional styling and has the added advantage of providing a place to install eave ventilation, which will improve the energy efficiency of the house.

The style and quality of the cornice can have a big effect on the appearance of your house, so take care in the design. If you use a draftsman or an architect, ask him to provide a cornice detail drawing so that its design will be clear to the cornice sub. This will also help you in estimating materials for the job.

Cornice work is installed before brick or stucco; so if you have that type of finish, be sure that the cornice sub builds the cornice out (usually with 1x6 or 2x6) so that the cornice sits out beyond the brick or stucco. Once installed, the cornice should be primed with exterior paint as soon as possible. For convenience you may wish to have your painters prime the cornice material prior to installation.

SIDING AND CORNICE - Steps

SC1 SELECT siding material, color, style and coverage.

SC2 CONDUCT standard bidding process. Most often the siding and cornice will be bid as a package deal.

SC3 ORDER windows and doors. Before ordering, have the window supplier walk through the site to check openings. All window and door brands differ in their real dimensions. The supplier can help to provide more exact dimension information. Mark the proper dimensions on the openings if adjustments need to be made by the framing or siding sub.

SC4 INSTALL windows and doors. Inspect windows and doors for bad millwork BEFORE installing. Have wood shims available to ad-just openings properly. If installing brick veneer, nail a 2x4 under exterior door thresholds for additional support until brick is installed. Inspect window and door positioning. They should be plumb and secure. Galvanized finish nails should be used, with the heads of the nails set below the surface of the trim. Install locks and hardware on doors and windows.

SC5 INSTALL flashing above windows, exterior door openings and around bottom perimeter of house.

SC6 INSTALL siding.

SC7 INSTALL siding trim around corners, windows and doors.

SC8 CAULK all areas where siding butts against trim or another piece of siding.

SC9 INSPECT siding. Refer to related checklist and specifications.

SC10 PAY sub for siding work. Make sure to retain a portion of payment for call backs.

SC11 INSTALL cornice. This involves installing the cornice, fascia, frieze, soffit and eave vents. If you have a traditional front, you may want to use a dentil molding. Stucco fronts normally use an exterior grade of crown molding ranging from 3" to 6" thick. Frieze bed mold runs in size from 4" to 12" and should be made of clear wood. Soffit should be made of an "AB" grade of ½" plywood.

SC12 INSPECT cornice work.

SC13 CORRECT any problems noted with cornice work.

SC14 PAY for cornice work.

SC15 CORRECT any problems noted with siding after it has had time to shrink.

SC16 ARRANGE for painter to paint and caulk trim.

SC17 PAY siding retainage.

SC18 PAY cornice retainage.

SIDING and CORNICE — Specifications

Siding

■ Exterior galvanized finish nails to be used exclusively.

■ All nails are to be flush or counter sunk.

■ All laps of siding to be parallel.

■ Joints to be staggered between courses.

■ All work and materials are to conform to the local building code.

■ All siding edges to be terminated in a finished manner and caulked.

■ All openings and trim caulked and flashed.

Cornice

■ All soffit and fascia joints to be trimmed smooth and fit tight.

■ All fascia to be straight and true.

■ Soffit vents to be installed.

■ All soffit, fascia, frieze and trim material to be paint grade fir or equivalent.

SIDING and CORNICE — Glossary

BED MOLDING— The trim piece (molding) that covers the intersection of the vertical wall and any overhanging horizontal surface, such as the soffit. In a series of moldings, the lowest one.

CORNICE— When used on the outside of the house, the trimwork that finishes off the intersection of the roof and siding. The cornice may be flush with the siding or may overhang the siding by as much as 2'.

CROWN MOLDING— The trim piece that tops off the trim on a vertical structure. Usually refers to the more ornamental pieces of cornice trim. Can also refer to the ornamental trim applied between the fascia and the roof.

EAVES— The portion of the roof that extends beyond the outside walls of the house. The main function of an overhanging eave is to provide visual separation of the roof and wall and to shelter the siding and windows from rain.

FASCIA— The vertical board on a cornice that covers the end of the rafter or the board that connects the top of the siding to the bottom of the soffit

FRIEZE— A vertical piece of wood used with or without molding to top off the intersection of the siding and the cornice. Frieze boards may be anywhere from 4" to 12" wide.

GABLE— The vertical part of the exterior wall that extends from the eaves upward to the peak or ridge of the roof. The gable may be covered with the same siding material as the exterior wall or may be trimmed with gable trim material.

LOOKOUT— The horizontal board (usually a 2x4 or 1x4) that connects the ends of the rafters to the siding. This board becomes the base for nailing on the soffit covering.

SOFFIT— The underside of the cornice or any part of the rood that overhangs the siding.

Insulation and Soundproofing

INSULATION

With the cost of most energy forms on the rise, insulation is gaining importance. The insulative property of a material is measured as an R Factor. The thickness of a material has little to do with its R rating. Don't buy thick insulation, buy high R-rated insulation. Insulation normally comes as fiberglass or cellulose. Either can be blown into most void areas, while fiberglass also comes in batts.

Insulation requirements vary across the country. Contact your local power company and they will assist you with recommended R ratings for ceilings, floors, walls, attics, etc. Observe that their recommendations may exceed your minimum local code requirements. Don't worry. You can pay for insulation now or pay for energy later. R factor requirements are not necessarily the same for all walls. Exposures which receive heavy sunlight or wind should be more heavily insulated. This is another job that you can do yourself. If you choose to insulate yourself, ask a supplier for a copy of the manufacturer's recommended installation instructions. Use gloves and an air filter over your nose.

Sheathing

Sheathing is a lightweight, rigid panel nailed to the outer side of the exterior walls. Several different types of sheathing are now available; each with different properties and costs. Foil covered sheathing has several advantages including higher insulation values, a finish more resistant to abrasion during installation and greater airtightness. It's also one of the most expensive types. Sheathing can add considerably to the insulative value of your house, so research your insulation needs carefully before deciding which type to use.

Fiberglass Batts

These are rolled sections of fiberglass bonded to a sheet of heavy duty kraft paper. Fiberglass, as well as most other forms of insulation, lose its effectiveness when wet, moist, compressed or otherwise not installed in accordance with the manufacturer's instructions. Batts should fit snugly between studs and joists with no gaps. Many subs staple them in place.

Figure 51. Application of insulation: A, wall section with blanket type; B, wall section with "press-fit" insulation; C, ceiling with full insulation.

Blown Materials

Blown-in materials are very popular as attic insulation because of ease of installation and the ability to fill in around odd shaped areas and framing. It is usually not suitable as wall insulation, however, because of its tendency to settle. Fiberglass, rock wool and cellulose can be blown in (as a loose material). This type of insulation is normally applied with depths ranging from 6" to 12". Cellulose is the best bargain, but is susceptible to rodents and moisture. Beware of cellulose that does not conform to local fire treatment standards. Rock wool is a good compromise between quality and cost. Blown insulation makes a good do-it-yourself project. You can usually rent the blowers from the insulation supplier.

Insulation Subs

Insulation subs should give you a price for material and labor. Insulation will normally be charged by the square foot for batts and by the cubic foot for blown-in insulation. Investigate whether you qualify for any energy credit.

SOUNDPROOFING

This is a refined touch. Consider soundproofing bathrooms and the HVAC area to quiet down the system. Rooms where you plan to have stereo systems are also good candidates. Soundproofing material comes in 4x8 sheets and can be applied between the drywall and studs.

INSULATION - Steps

IN1 DETERMINE insulation requirements. Your local energy company can help give you guidelines and suggestions.

IN2 PERFORM standard bidding process.

IN3 INSTALL wall insulation.

IN4 INSTALL soundproofing. This is a nice touch to deaden noise. Use in bathroom walls to deaden sound.

IN5 INSTALL floor insulation. Floor insulation will be installed on crawl space and basement foundations. Metal wires cut to the length of joist spacing are used to hold the insulation in place.

IN6 INSTALL attic insulation. This normally consists of batts or blown-in insulation. If blown-in, attic insulation will be installed after drywall has been nailed into place on the ceiling. Plug up all HVAC vent openings with leftover insulation. This keeps drywall dust out of the HVAC vents during the dusty drywall installation and sanding process.

IN7 INSPECT insulation. A kraft paper or poly vapor barrier should be installed on the warm side of the insulation. All areas around plumbing, electrical fixtures, doors and windows should be stuffed with insulation to prevent air infiltration.

IN8 CORRECT insulation work as needed.

IN9 PAY insulation sub and have him sign an affidavit.

IN10 PAY insulation sub retainage.

Figure 52. Precautions to be taken in insulating around openings

INSULATION - Sample Specifications

■ Bid is to provide and install insulation as indicated below:

Location	R Factor	Type
Walls	R13	Fiberglass batts
Ceiling	R19	Blown rock wool

■ Bid is to include labor and materials for wall and ceiling insulation.

■ All insulation is to include a vapor barrier on the warm side of the insulation, free of rips and reasonably sealed against air infiltration.

■ All joints and gaps around door frames, window frames and electrical outlets to be packed with fiberglass insulation.

■ All insulation used will be of thickness sufficient to meet R values specified after insulation has settled.

INSULATION - Inspection

☐ All specified insulation has been installed per specifications. Check labels on insulation.

☐ All insulation is installed tightly with no air gaps.

☐ No punctures have been made in vapor barrier.

☐ Insulation adheres firmly to all adjoining surfaces.

☐ No eave vents have been covered by insulation.

☐ Vapor barrier installed on warm side of wall.

☐ Ductwork insulated in basement.

☐ Plumbing in basement insulated.

☐ All gaps around doors and windows stuffed with insulation.

☐ Gap between wall and floor caulked completely.

☐ All openings to the outside for plumbing, wiring and gas lines sealed with spray foam insulation.

☐ All gaps in siding around windows and corners caulked thoroughly.

☐ All fireplaces properly insulated.

Drywall

DRYWALL

Drywall is composed of gypsum sandwiched between two layers of heavy gauge paper. This material, normally used for interior walls, comes in 4' x 8', 4' x 10' and 4' x 12' sizes. When planning your home, it may be helpful to plan around these dimensions to some extent to minimize waste.

Drywall comes in two common thicknesses: 3/8" and 5/8". Five-eighths inch is the thickness most often used because it does not warp as easily, especially where studs are 24" on center (O.C.). Drywall sheets have the long edges tapered and the short edges full thickness. This is to allow room for the drywall mud and tape. Sheets should be installed so that the full edges butt against studs. After drywall is applied to studs, the joints between sheets of drywall are smoothed using special drywall tape. Moisture affects drywall adversely, so always store it in a dry place until used.

Drywall installation normally involves the following steps:

- Apply drywall to studs with either nails or screws, and glue.
- Apply fill coat of joint compound and drywall tape.
- Sand all joints smooth (if necessary).
- Apply joint compound (second coat).
- Sand all joints smooth (if necessary).
- Apply finish coat of joint compound (third coat).
- Sand all joints smooth.

Application should not be done in extreme heat or cold. Ceilings are treated just as walls, unless you decide to stipple them. Stipple is a coarse-textured compound which eliminates the need for repeated sanding and joint compound application. This is a time and money saver.

Drywall Subs

Your drywall sub is a key player in the final, visible quality of most surfaces in the interior. Drywall subcontractors normally bid and charge for drywall work by the square foot, although they install it by the sheet. Drywall subs charge extra for special projects such as:

- tray ceilings
- vaulted ceilings
- open foyers
- curved walls and openings
- high ceilings
- unstippled ceilings
- water-resistant drywall

Of all your sub-contractors, quality here is important. Drywall is one of the most visible parts of your home. Get the best drywall sub you can afford. Below are signs of a good drywall sub:

- Finishing coats are very thin and feathered.
- No need to sand first two coats because they are so smooth.
- Pieces are cut in place to assure proper fit.

Your drywall sub can quickly tell you the quality of the framing job. Knots, warped lumber and out-of-square walls will make the drywall sub's job more difficult. If the problems are major, have the framer fix them before continuing. Your drywall sub can't fix these underlying problems effectively.

Warning: Your drywall sub may use stilts to reach ceilings and high walls. Stilts are dangerous, but many times virtually unavoidable. Some states will not award worker's compensation to subs injured while using stilts. If this is true in your state, have your sub sign a waiver of liability to protect you from such accidents. Scaffolding should be used for stairway work. If stilts are used, the floor should be cleared of scrap wood and trash to avoid tripping.

DRYWALL - Steps

DR1 PERFORM drywall bidding process (refer to standard bidding process). Refer to drywall contract specifications for ideas. You may wish to ask painters for names of good drywall subs; they know good finishing work — they paint over it for a living!

DR2 ORDER and receive drywall materials if not supplied by drywall sub.

NOTE: Before drywall is installed, mark the location of all studs on the floor with a builder's pencil. This will make it easier for the trim sub to locate studs when nailing trim to the wall.

DR3 HANG drywall on all walls. Outside corners must be protected with metal edging. Inside corners must also be taped.

Figure 53.   Application of gypsum board finish: A, vertical application; B, horizontal application.

DR4 FINISH drywall. Drywall must be finished in a series of steps as outlined below:

- Spackle all nail dimples.
- Sand nail dimples smooth.
- Apply tape to smoothed nailed joints.
- Spackle tape joints (fill coat).
- Sand tape joints (as needed).
- Spackle tape joints (second coat).
- Sand tape joints (as needed).
- Spackle tape joints (finish coat).
- Sand tape joints (third time).

DR5 INSPECT drywall. Refer to specifications and inspection guidelines. To do this properly, turn out all lights and look at the wall while shining a light on it from an angle. Slight shadows will appear if there are imperfections on the surface. Mark them with a pencil so the drywall sub will know where to fix walls. Don't use a pen, as it will leave a mark that will show through paint.

DR6 TOUCH up and repair imperfect drywall areas. There are always a few. Place large drywall scraps in basement if you want to finish the basement later.

DR7 PAY drywall sub. Get him to sign an affidavit.

DR8 PAY drywall sub retainage. You may want to wait until the first coat of paint has been applied so that you can get a good look at the finished product.

DRYWALL - Sample Specifications

- Bid is to provide all material, labor and equipment to perform complete job per specifications of attached plans. This includes:
  - Drywall, tape and drywall compound
  - Metal corner bead
  - All nails
  - Sandpaper
  - Ladders and scaffolding

- Apply ⅝" gypsum board (drywall), double nailed at top. Four nails per stud.

- All joints to be taped with 3 separate coats of joint compound each sanded smooth.

- All outside corners to be reinforced with metal corner bead.

- All inside corners to be reinforced with joint tape.

- All necessary electrical outlet, switch and fixture cutouts to be made.

- All necessary HVAC ductwork cutouts to be made.

- All ceilings to be stippled as specified.

- All ceiling sheets to be glued and screwed in place.

- Wall adhesive to be applied to all studs prior to applying drywall.

- Moisture resistant gypsum to be used along all wall areas around shower stalls and bathtubs.

- Use drywall stilts at your own risk.

DRYWALL - Inspection

Before Taping

☐ No more than a ⅜" gap between sheets.

☐ Nails driven in pairs (2" apart). Nail heads dimpled below the surface of the drywall.

☐ Nails not hit so hard as to break the surface paper. All joints shall be double nailed or glued.

Figure 54.   Finishing gypsum dry wall: A, nail set with crowned hammer; B, cementing and taping joint; C, taping at inside corners; D, alternate finish at ceiling.

☐ No nail heads exposed to interfere with drywall.

☐ No sheet warpage, bowing or damage. Sheets are easier to replace before taping.

☐ Rough cuts around door and window openings cut close so that trim will fit properly.

☐ Waterproof drywall, or wonderboard, installed in shower stalls and around bathtubs. No taping is necessary here.

☐ Metal bead installed flush on all outside corners.

During Finishing

☐ Three separate coats of mud are applied to all joints. Stippling will hide any imperfections. Each successive coat should leave a wider track and a smoother finish.

After Finishing

☐ Look down the length of installed drywall; there is no warpage or bumps. If found, circle the area with a pencil (ink may show through when painted). Have the drywall sub-contractor fix all marked areas before final payment.

☐ All joints feathered smooth. No noticeable bumps, either by sight or touch.

☐ All electrical wiring remains exposed including bath and kitchen vent fans, garage door opener switches and doorbell in garage.

☐ Proper ceilings smooth and stippled as specified.

☐ Clean cuts around register openings, switches and outlets so that covers will cover exposed area.

☐ Nap of paper not raised or roughened by excessive or improper sanding.

☐ All touch-up work completed and satisfactory.

☐ No exposed corner bead.

Note: Some drywall imperfections will not appear until the first coat of paint has been applied. This is the first time you will see the wall as a single, uniform color. If you can, wait until this point to pay retainage.

DRYWALL — Glossary

BAZOOKA— Term for a automated drywall application tool that tapes, applies mud and feathers in one pass. Gets its name because it looks like a bazooka. Expensive to buy or rent — only used on large scale operations.

DRYWALL — Term used to describe sheets of gypsum.

FEATHERING— Successive coats of drywall compound applied to joints. Each successive pass should widen the compound joint.

FLOAT— To spread drywall compound smooth.

GYPSUM BOARD— Same as DRYWALL.

HANG— To hang drywall is to nail it in place.

MUD— Slang for spackle, or drywall compound. Used to seal joints and hide nail head dimples.

SPACKLE — Soft putty-like compound used for drywall patching and touch-up that does not shrink as much as regular joint compound. Allows painting immediately after application.

STIPPLE— Rough and textured coatings applied to ceilings. This process makes it easier to finish ceilings since they do not have to be taped and sanded as many times as the walls.

TAPE— Paper used to cover the joints between sheets of gypsum. Tape joints are then sealed with mud (spackle).

Trim

Good trim requires some of the most precise work to be found in a home. If you are not very experienced in this type of work, you may not want to tackle this job. Interior trim sub-contractors usually will do the following:

- Set interior/exterior doors and door sills
- Set windows and window sills
- Install base, crown, chair rail, picture and other molding
- Install paneling, raised paneling and wainscoting
- Install stairway trim
- Install fireplace and main entry door mantels
- Install closet shelves and hanger rods
- Install any other special trim
- Install door and window hardware, door stops, etc.

Trim subs charge for work in many ways:

- By the opening (for doors, windows and entryways).
- By the cut. The more cuts involved, the greater the cost.
- By the hour or day.
- By the job.

It is advised to get the bid for the job. Have them give you a bottom line figure — let them do the figuring. Go with the bottom line price and quality you are most comfortable with.

Exterior trim (fascia and cornice work) is covered under a separate section since it is usually done by the siding and cornice sub.

Decorative trim is one of the most visible items in your house and can make the difference between an ordinary interior and one that stands out. The workmanship of your trim sub will be very visible and hard to repair if not done properly. Make sure your trim sub is very quality conscious and watch his work closely. If you want to keep a close eye on his work, volunteer to assist him in doing the trimwork.

The critical part of door installation is in making sure that the door is set level and square so that doorknob hardware will work properly and the door will operate without binding. Special care should also be taken with bifold and sliding track doors. Improper installation is hard to fix and results in binding.

Weatherstripping is essential in all exterior doors. This has become a specialty trade in itself. As such, your trim sub may not necessarily be the one who does this small, but critical job.

Trimwork has become somewhat easier with the advent of preset doors and window trim kits. To save money, consider using pre hung hollow core interior doors. These doors install easily and look as good as or better than custom hung doors.

In choosing your trim material, you must first decide whether you plan to paint or stain the trim. You may be able to use lesser grades of millwork or Masonite® doors if they will be painted. Finger joint trim consisting of scraps glued together is fine if you plan to paint. Masonite panel doors are becoming very popular and are inexpensive. If you plan to stain, you must use solid wood trim and birch paneled wood doors; but the fine appearance and low maintenance of stained trim may be worth the expense.

Protect trim from abuse prior to installation to avoid dents, cracks, scratches and excessive waste. Lay trim on the floor in neat stacks. Don't purchase trim from different suppliers — the different pieces may not match.

When installing base molding, consider whether trim will go around wall registers or merely be interrupted

Figure 55. Interior door parts: A, door jambs and stops; B, two-piece jamb; C, three piece jamb; D, colonial casing; E, ranch casing.

Figure 57. Door clearances

Figure 56. Door Details: A, installation of strike plate; B, location of stops.

Figure 58. Installation of door hardware: A, hinge; B, mortise lock; C, bored lock set.

Figure 59. Doorframe and trim: A, installation; B, miter joint for casing; C, butt joint for casing.

by the register. The first example is more expensive but yields a nicer appearance. If you use a tall base molding, you can build your registers and receptacles into the base molding.

Modern houses are making use of decorative trim extensively, such as paneling and wainscoting. Ask your trim sub for suggestions of decorative approaches. It is amazing what can be done with a minimum of materials.

TRIM - Steps

TR1 DETERMINE trim requirements. Millwork samples can help. Mark all walls that get different trim treatments.

TR2 SELECT molding, window frames and door frames.

TR3 INSTALL windows. Windows and exterior doors should be installed as soon after framing as possible. Don't have windows and doors delivered until just before installation. Remind the trim sub to use the best trim pieces around the openings in the most visible locations.

TR4 CONDUCT standard bidding process.

TR5 INSTALL interior doors. If pre-hung doors, install and adjust door stops and doors.

TR6 INSTALL window casing and aprons.

TR7 INSTALL trim around cased openings.

TR8 INSTALL staircase molding. Treads, risers, railings, newels, baluster, goosenecks, etc.

TR9 INSTALL crown molding. This includes special-made inside and outside corners if specified. This is installed first so that the ladder legs will not scratch the base molding.

TR10 INSTALL base and base cap molding. Where the final floor level will be higher than the subfloor (when hardwood is installed) the base should be installed a little higher.

TR11 INSTALL chair rail molding.

TR12 INSTALL picture molding.

TR13 INSTALL, sand and stain paneling.

TR14 CLEAN all sliding door tracks.

TR15 INSTALL thresholds and weather stripping on exterior doors and windows.

Figure 60.   Base molding: A, square-edge base; B, narrow ranch base; C, wide ranch base; D, installation; E, cope.

Figure 61.   Ceiling moldings: A, installation (inside corner); B, crown molding.

Figure 63.   Main stair detail with combination of treads and risers

Figure 62.   Enclosed stairway details: A, with full stringer; B, with notched stringer.

Figure 64.   Basement stairs: A, carriage details; B, ledger for carriage; C, kicker plate.

Figure 65.   Details of open main stairway

TR16 INSTALL shoe molding after flooring is installed. Painting the shoe molding before installation will reduce time and touch-up work.

TR17 INSTALL door knobs, deadbolts, door stops and window hardware. Rekey locks if necessary. Consider keying all the locks to just one key. Install a deadbolt-type lock on sliding glass doors for improved security.

TR18 INSPECT trim work. Refer to your specifications and the checklist that follows.

TR19 CORRECT any imperfect trim and stain work.

TR20 PAY trim sub.

TRIM - Sample Specifications

■ All materials except tools, to be furnished by builder.

■ Interior doors will be pre-hung.

■ Finish nails to be used exclusively and set below the surface, puttied and sanded over smooth.

Bid is to include the following:

■ Hang all interior doors. All doors to be right- and left-handed as indicated on attached drawings.

■ Install all door and window trim according to attached schedule.

■ Install base molding and base cap molding as specified. Raise base molding in areas of hardwood flooring.

■ Install apron and crown molding in living room, dining room and foyer area.

■ Install two-piece chair rail molding in dining room as specified.

■ Install 1" shoe molding in all rooms not carpeted.

■ Install den bookshelves as indicated on attached drawings.

■ Install staircase trim as indicated below:
- 12 oak treads
- 12 pine risers
- solid oak railing with involute

- gooseneck
- 36 spindles.

■ Build fireplace mantel as indicated on attached drawings.

■ Install door locks, door knobs, window hardware and dead bolts.

■ All trim paint grade unless otherwise stated.

■ Install all closet trim, shelves and closet rods.

TRIM - Inspection

Doors

☐ Proper doors installed. Correct style, size, type, etc.

☐ Doors open and close smoothly and quietly. Hinges do not bind or squeak. Doors should swing freely with no noise or friction against adjoining surfaces. Open doors at 30, 45 and 60 degree angles. Doors should remain where positioned. If not, remove center pin, bend it slightly with a hammer and replace it.

☐ Door knobs and latches align with latch insets. All deadbolt locks should align properly. Privacy locks installed on proper side of doors. Passage locks on proper doors.

☐ All exterior doors lock and unlock properly. Locks should function freely.

☐ All keys available. Have all locks keyed the same for ease of use.

☐ All doors open in proper direction. Door latch faces the proper direction.

☐ All doors are plumb against door jambs. With door slightly open, check for alignment and evenness of opening. Two screws in each strike plate. A pin in each door hinge.

☐ All door casing nails set below surface and filled with putty.

☐ Door knobs, door locks and dead bolts work properly without sticking.

☐ No hammer dents in door or door casing.

☐ Thresholds in place and properly adjusted.

☐ Weatherstripping in place if specified.

☐ Proper clearance from floor (about ½" above carpet level). Consider height of carpet and pad, tile, wood floor, etc.

☐ Door stops in proper places.

Windows

☐ Window frame secure in place with leveling wedges or chips.

☐ Windows installed with less than ½" gap between wall and frame.

☐ Windows open and close smoothly and easily. Windows should glide easily along tracks. Windows should close evenly and completely.

☐ Window sash locks installed and operating properly.

☐ No hammer dents in window or window casing.

☐ All window casing nails set below surface and sealed with putty.

☐ Weatherstripping in place if specified.

☐ Screens installed if specified.

☐ All window latches function properly.

☐ All window pulls in place and secure.

☐ No excessive damage to millwork.

Trim and Paneling

☐ All crown molding installed and finished as specified.

☐ All base molding installed and finished as specified.

☐ All chair rail molding installed and finished as specified.

☐ All wainscoting installed and finished as specified.

☐ Trim joints are caulked, sanded smooth and undetectable, both by sight and feel.

☐ Trim intersects with walls, ceilings and floors evenly with no gaps or other irregularities.

☐ All trim is void of major material defects.

☐ All finishing nails set below surface and sealed with wood putty.

☐ All den paneling and shelving installed and finished as specified.

☐ Fireplace mantel installed and finished as specified. Will support heavy load.

☐ Fireplace surround installed and finished as specified.

☐ All closet shelving and coat racks installed at proper height and level.

Staircase

☐ Proper treads used.

☐ Finished and curved treads installed correctly.

☐ All railings in place, secure, and angled parallel to stairs.

☐ Spindles and newel posts secure in place and properly finished.

☐ Balusters secure in place and properly finished.

☐ No squeaks in staircase steps or elsewhere on staircase.

TRIM — Glossary

APRON— Trim used at base of windows. Also used as base to build out crown molding.

BALUSTER— Vertical trim used in quantity to support staircase railings not supported by a wall.

BASE MOLDING— Molding applied at the intersection of the wall and floor.

CAP MOLDING— Trim applied to the top of base molding.

CASING— Molding of various widths used around door and window openings.

CASING NAILS— Used to apply finish trim and millwork. Nail head is small and is set below the surface of the wood to hide it.

CHAIR RAIL— Molding applied to the walls, normally at hip level.

CLEAR— Millwork with fine texture and no knots or other major imperfections.

CROWN MOLDING— Molding applied at the intersection of the ceiling and walls. Normally associated with more formal areas.

DEN PANELING— Paneling composed normally of sections of stain grade materials, joined with a number of vertical and/or horizontal strips of molding.

DENTIL MOLDING— A special type of crown molding with an even pattern of "teeth".

FILLER— Putty or other pasty material used to fill nail holes prior to painting or staining.

FINGER JOINT— Trim composed of many small scrap pieces by a joint resembling two sets of interlocking fingers. This trim is often used to reduce costs where such trim will be painted.

GOOSENECK— Section of staircase trim with a curve in it.

INVOLUTE— Curved portion of trim used to terminate a piece of staircase railing. Normally used on traditional homes.

MITER BOX— Special guide and saw used to cut trim lumber at precise angles.

MITER JOINT— A diagonal joint, normally 45° formed at the intersection of two pieces of molding.

MOLDING— Decorative strips of wood or other material applied to wall joints and surfaces as a decorative accent. Molding does not have any structural value.

PAINT GRADE— Millwork of quality intended for a painted finish. Not as fine as stain grade.

QUARTER ROUND— A small strip of molding whose cross-section is similar to a quarter of a circle. Used with or without base molding. May be applied elsewhere.

STAIN GRADE— Millwork of finest quality intended for a stain finish. Capable of receiving and absorbing stain easily.

TRAY MOLDING— Special type of crown molding where a large portion of the molding is applied to the ceiling as opposed to the wall.

WAINSCOTING— Paneling and trim applied from the floor to a height of about 3'. Used in dining areas to protect against marks from dining chairs. Popular decorative touch in modern homes.

Painting and Wallcovering

PAINT

If there is any job you can feel safe about doing yourself, it is painting and wallpapering. It may be worth several thousand dollars to you.

Paints can be purchased in standard colors or custom mixed. Custom mixed paints can't be returned, so be careful with color schemes and order quantities. Try to select a minimum of different colors to avoid having to store a lot of different colors. If you decide to paint yourself, purchase the highest quality paints you can find — but make sure to insist on the builder price. One-coat paints are a good choice. New drywall should always receive two coats but the one-coat paints guarantee the best coverage. Colors on small samples in a store will appear darker when they are applied to a room. If you plan to stipple ceilings, this should be done before any painting has begun. Although roller application is quick and yields good results, consider renting an electric paint sprayer. You may need to thin the paint if you go this route, and you will definitely need some form of eye and nose protection. Keep paint off areas to be stained or it will show up in the final work. When enamel thickens, thin it with paint thinner.

Painting Trim

Trim includes all molding and door/window trim. Although small in terms of absolute square feet, don't be surprised if this effort takes you as long or longer than painting walls. Trim paint (normally enamel-based) is thicker than wall paint. Be careful to use long, smooth strokes to avoid brush marks. For best results, use a high quality china bristle brush with tapered bristles.

Saving Time

You can save a significant amount of time if you use a power roller. These units keep adequate paint on the roller with a push of a button. Avoid using paint sprayers for interior walls except for the primer coat. Sprayers do not hide minor blemishes and drywall sanding marks like paint rollers do and will give disappointing results.

You can save a tremendous amount of time painting if you coordinate the paint, drywall and trim process between subs. Apply both coats of wall paint and the first coat of trim paint before the doors and trim are installed. This will allow you to roll paint the walls right up to the door openings without worrying about getting paint on the trim. Put one coat on the doors and trim before installation. These two steps will cut interior painting time in half. Make sure to coordinate this with your trim carpenter first. Many trim subs do not like to work with prepainted trim. It creates an irritating dust when sawed. Test masking tape to be sure that it does not pull off paint when removed.

STAIN

Stain grade moldings and handrails should be sanded with a very fine grit sandpaper before staining. Fill holes with a wood filler that accepts stain or color match filler to stain used. Use a good quality wiping stain and don't leave the stain on too long.

Wallcoverings

Wallpaper is an excellent do-it-yourself project. Most wallpaper outlet stores will be glad to show you the ins and outs of quality wallpaper selection and installation. Most wallpaper comes in double rolls of 32 feet per roll. Single rolls can be purchased at a premium. Wallpaper has a standard width of 24".

When purchasing wallpaper, make sure all rolls have the same run number. The same number tells you that wallpaper of a certain pattern was all made at the same time, and the colors will be exactly the same from roll to roll. Repeat pattern is a big factor in estimating the number of rolls that you will need. Repeat pattern is the width of the pattern before it starts over. On large repeat patterns, you will waste a lot of paper getting patterns to match up.

Wallpaper comes in unpasted and prepasted forms. Many wallpaper hangers still use a paint roller to roll on a wallpaper glue even on prepasted wallpaper. Wallpaper that will be used for baths should be either foil or vinyl due to the humid environment.

PAINTING — Steps

PT1 SELECT paint schemes. Minimize number of colors. Try not to rely only on paint samples since final colors may vary. Try a test mix on an entire wall if possible.

PT2 PERFORM standard bidding process. If you are planning or considering doing the painting yourself, this will help you to determine how much you will save by doing the job yourself. If you are not up to doing the entire job, consider hiring the painter for the exterior work only and doing the interior work yourself.

PT3 PURCHASE all painting materials if you plan to paint yourself. Materials needed will include:

- One or five gallon cans of ceiling and wall paint.
- Gallon or quart cans of trim paint
- Can opener
- Paint stir sticks
- Paint tray
- Trim guard
- Rolls of 1" wide masking tape that doesn't adhere to paint
- Tubes of trim caulk
- Caulk gun
- Single-edged razor blades and handle
- Six-foot step ladder
- Medium and fine-grained sandpaper
- Dropcloths
- Paint rags
- Paint roller (fine nap) or power roller (self feeding). Consider getting a professional type roller that has a 20" coverage to save time.

- Paint sprayer
- Good quality paint brushes
- Paint thinner

Exterior

PT4 PRIME and caulk all exterior surfaces: related trimwork, windows, doors, exterior corners and cornice. Exterior millwork should be primed immediately after installation.

PT5 PAINT exterior siding, trim, shutters and wrought iron railing. Iron railing should be painted with a rust-retarding paint. Painting two story fixtures can be simplified by coordinating with stucco, siding, or masonry subs. They will have scaffolding on site that can be used for painting.

PT6 PAINT all cornice work.

PT7 PAINT gutters if needed. NOTE: If the gutter seams require soldering, don't paint them until the soldering is finished.

Interior

PT8 PREPARE painting surfaces. This involves performing the following tasks:

- DUST off all drywall with a dry rag.
- APPLY trim caulk to joint between trim and wall. Smooth it with your finger. Wipe off excess. When dry, sand to a smooth joint. This is an important step which will help to yield professional quality results.
- REPAIR any dents in drywall or moldings with spackle or wood filler.
- Sand all repaired areas to a smooth finish.
- NOTE: If ceiling is to be stippled, you don't need to do a thing to it.
- NOTE: If you plan to paint stair spindles, do them before installing them. The painting process will be much easier.

PT9 PAINT prime coat: walls and trim. Just about any good painting job involves two coats of paint. Before you even start, make sure you have excellent lighting available in every room to be painted. Even if you intend to wallpaper, paint a primer coat so that it will be easier to remove the wallpaper if you ever want to later. If you have Masonite® interior doors, prime them also. Ceiling white makes a good neutral primer. Since there is nothing in the house that you can harm, you need not worry about dropcloths. You can either rent a commercial paint sprayer, purchase your own or use a roller. For a professional job, lightly sand the walls before the final coat after the primer has dried. Sand trim also.

PT10 PAINT or stipple ceilings. A paint roller with an extension arm makes this job easier. Wear goggles to keep paint splatters out of your eyes. If you have stippled ceilings, you won't be painting them.

PT11 PAINT walls. If you want your switch plates and outlet covers to match your wall color, install them before painting. Start with a small brush and paint around the ceiling, all windows and doors. Then cover the large areas with a roller. Do one wall at a time.

PT12 PAINT or stain trim. Start with the highest trim and work down. Allow the walls to dry first. It will be easier if you use a 1½" sash brush for doing windows and a 2" brush for all other trim. Some painters don't bother to cover all the little trim in multi-paned windows; they just scrape all the dried paint off with a razor blade. Stained trim should be coated with a varnish or other sealer.

PT13 REMOVE paint from windows with one-sided utility razor blades. Do this only when the paint has completely dried or the soft paint shavings will stick to the surface and make a mess.

PT14 INSPECT paint job for spots requiring touch-up. Make sure you are looking at the paint job either in good natural light or under a bright light.

PT15 TOUCH UP paint job.

PT16 CLEAN UP. Latex paints will come off with soap and warm water. Enamel, which you may have used on your trim, will require mineral spirits or Varsol for removal. Dry out the brushes and store them wrapped up in aluminum foil with the bristles in a smooth position. Place plastic wrap on the paint cans prior to storing them.

PT17 PAY painter (if applicable) and have him sign an affidavit.

PT18 PAY retainage after final inspection.

PAINTING — Specifications

Interior Painting

■ Bid is to include all material, labor and tools.

■ Primer coat and one finish coat to be applied to all walls including closet interiors.

■ Walls to be touch sanded after primer has dried.

■ Flat latex to be used on drywall; gloss enamel to be used on all trim work.

■ Ceiling white to be used on all ceilings.

■ All trim joints to be caulked and sanded before painting.

■ All paint to be applied evenly on all areas.

■ Window panes to be cleaned by painter.

■ Painting contractor to clean up after job.

■ Excess paint to be labeled and to remain on site when job is completed.

Exterior Painting

■ Five-year warranty exterior grade latex paint to be used on exterior walls and shutters.

■ All exterior trim and shutters to be primed with an exterior grade primer.

■ All trim area around windows, doors and corners to be caulked with exterior grade caulk before final coat. Caulk color to match paint color.

PAINTING - Inspection

☐ Proper paint colors used.

☐ All ceilings and walls appear uniform in color with no visible brush strokes.

☐ Trim painted with a smooth appearance. Gloss or semi-gloss enamel used as specified.

☐ All intersections (ceiling-wall, trim-wall, wall-floor) are sharp and clean. Clean, straight line between wall and trim colors.

☐ Window panes free of paint inside and out.

☐ Extra touch-up paint left at site.

☐ All exterior areas painted smoothly and evenly.

☐ No dried paint drops.

PAINTING - Glossary

ALKYD— A durable synthetic resin used in paints.

BASE COAT— First coat put on drywall. Normally a very light color. Should even be put on prior to wallpaper so that the paper can be easily removed.

ENAMEL— Oil base paint used in high soil areas such as trim and doors.

LATEX— Water soluble paint. Normally recommended because of ease of use for interior work.

SAGGING— Slow dripping of excessively heavy coats of paint.

SEMI-GLOSS— A paint or enamel with insufficient nonvolatile vehicle such that the dried coating has a luster but does not look glossy.

TOUCH SANDING— Very light sanding of prime paint coat.

Cabinetry and Countertops

CABINETS

Because of the cabinetry, the kitchen invariably turns out to be the most expensive room in the house. Cabinetry and countertops are used in both the kitchen and baths. Money spent on high quality cabinets can really add value to your home. Cabinetry can be prefabricated or custom built for your installation. Although custom cabinets are nice, the extra expense and time involved is rarely worth it. There is an abundance of high quality prefab cabinets available today.

When shopping for cabinets, pay attention to space-saving devices such as revolving corner units, drop down shelves and slide-out shelves. These options can significantly increase the usable space in your cabinets.

Kitchen Cabinets

Visit a few kitchen cabinet stores or kitchen design stores to become acquainted with the many functional types of cabinets that are available. Look at sample kitchen layouts to get ideas. Determine your material (wood, Formica, etc.), hinge and knob styles and finish. Also important, determine how much cabinet space you need. The amount of cabinet space is not as important as how well the space is used. Many American craftsman are turning out impressive reproductions of fine, expensive European models at a fraction of the price. The cabinetry should be an integral part of your kitchen design, complementing appliances, lighting and space. Remember, kitchens and baths sell houses.

Bathroom Cabinets and Vanities

Purchase all your cabinets from the same place if you can. Not only does this make your cabinet selections more uniform, but you can probably get a better price from your cabinet sub. Always look for bathroom cabinets with drawers for storing toiletries.

COUNTER TOPS AND VANITY TOPS

Counter tops are normally made of Formica. But other materials have become popular including Butcher Block, tile, Corian and marble (natural or cultured). Formica is by far the most popular and least expensive. Some companies sell bathroom vanities and countertops with the sink built into the countertop.

Counter tops typically should have a standard depth of 24" and may have a 3" or 4" splashblock against the wall. If you desire, add a few inches of additional depth to the countertop. This will leave more room to clean behind the sink. Countertops are priced and installed by the foot, while special charges may be incurred to cut openings for stoves, sinks and fancy edgework. If you get a separate company to do the

Figure 65. Kitchen cabinet dimensions

counter and vanity tops, which is most likely when cultured marble is used, installation is normally included in the price — but get this confirmed. Advantages to cultured marble tops is the lack of a seam between the top and the sink, no sink bowl to purchase and an easier job for the plumber.

Cabinet Sub

This sub will normally produce or supply all cabinetry and install them along with the counter tops. This includes making all the cuts for sinks, stoves, etc. Cabinet subs will normally bid the job at one price for material and labor.

CABINETRY - Steps

CB1 CONFIRM kitchen design. Make sure you have enough cabinets to store all pots, pans, utensils and food items.

CB2 SELECT cabinetry/counter top styles/colors.

CB3 COMPLETE diagram of cabinet layout for kitchen and baths. This is a critical step to perform prior to electrical and plumbing installation. Show locations of all plumbing connections on diagram: icemaker, dishwasher, and sink.

CB4 PERFORM standard bidding process. There are lots of independent cabinet makers who can copy expensive European cabinet designs.

CB5 PURCHASE or have constructed all cabinetry and counter top surfaces. If your counter tops come from a separate sub, coordinate the cabinetry and counter top sub. You can't install tops until vanities are in. Unless you know what you are doing, wait for the drywall to be hung before having the cabinet sub measure. This gives him more exact figures to work from and a place to mark on the wall. But do order your cabinets as soon as possible because they can be a source of big delays later.

Give your cabinet sub specs for all appliance dimensions and locations of all doors and windows. This will insure that the cabinets will install properly under the window sill. At a minimum, wait for framing to be finished. Walk through the structure with the cabinet sub, covering kitchen, baths and utility room. Countertops are typically 36" above the floor, kitchen desks 32" high with a minimum 24" knee space. When measuring, remember to account for ½" drywall on walls and widths of adjacent trim. Mark dimensions on the floor with builder's chalk or crayon.

CB6 STAIN and seal, paint or otherwise finish all cabinet woodwork. Stains will stain the grout and other nearby items, so cabinets must be stained before they are installed.

CB7 INSTALL bathroom vanities. These must be in place before your plumber can connect the sinks, drain pipes and faucets.

CB8 INSTALL kitchen wall cabinets. If you install base cabinets first, they get in your way while installing wall units.

CB9 INSTALL kitchen base cabinets. Also make necessary cutouts for sinks and cooktops. Show the cabinet sub where cutouts are to be made. Don't make any cutouts until the units have arrived.

CB10 INSTALL kitchen and bath counter tops, aprons and backsplashes.

CB11 INSTALL and adjust cabinetry hardware: pulls, hinges, etc.

CB12 INSTALL utility room cabinetry.

CB13 CAULK all wall/cabinetry joints as needed.

CB14 INSPECT all cabinetry and counter tops.

CB15 TOUCH up and repair any scratches and other marks on cabinetry and counter tops.

CB16 PAY cabinet sub. Have him sign an affidavit.

CABINETRY — Specifications

■ Bid is to provide and complete cabinetry and counter top installation as indicated on attached drawings.

■ All cabinets are to be installed by qualified craftsman.

- All cabinets are to be installed plumb and square and as indicated on attached drawings.

- All hardware such as hinges, pulls, bracing and supports to be included in bid.

- All necessary counter top cutouts and edging to be included in bid.

- All exposed corners on counter tops to be rounded.

- Install one double stainless steel sink (model/size).

- Special interior cabinet hardware includes:
  - Lazy susan
  - Broom rack
  - Pot racks
  - Sliding lid racks

VANITY TOPS — Specifications

- Bid is to manufacture and install the following cultured marble tops in ¾" solid color material. Sink bowls to be an integral part of top.

- Vanity A to be 24" deep, 55" wide, finished on left with backsplash; 19" oval sink cut with rounded edge with center of sink 22" from right side. Color is solid white. Spread faucet to be used.

- Vanity B to be 24" deep, 45" wide, finished on right with backsplash; 19" oval sink cut with rounded edge with center of sink 18" from left side. Color is solid almond. Standard faucet to be used.

CABINETRY - Inspection

- ☐ All cabinet doors open and close properly with no binding or squeaking. Doors open completely and remain in place half opened.

- ☐ All pulls and other hardware are securely fastened. Check for excessive play in hinges.

- ☐ All specified shelving is in place and level.

- ☐ All exposed cabinetry has an even and smooth finish.

- ☐ No nicks, scratches, scars or other damage/irregularity on any cabinetry and counter tops.

- ☐ Counter tops are level by placing water or marbles on surface. All joints are securely glued with no buckling or delamination.

- ☐ All drawers line up properly

- ☐ All mitered and flush joints tight.

- ☐ Cutouts for sinks and cooktops done properly and units fitted into place.

CABINETRY - Glossary

BACKSPLASH— A small strip (normally 3" or 4") placed against the wall and resting on the back of the countertop. This is normally used to protect the wall from water and stains.

BASE CABINET— A cabinet resting on the floor at waist level, supporting a counter top or an appliance.

CENTER SET— Standard holes for a standard faucet set.

CORIAN— An artificial material simulating marble manufactured by Corning.

LAMINATE— Any thin material, such as plastic or fine wood, glued to the exterior of the cabinet.

SELF-RIMMING— Term used to describe a type of sink that has a heavy rim around the edge that automatically seals the sink against the Formica top.

SPREAD SET— Faucet set that requires three holes to be cut wider than normal.

Flooring, Tile and Glazing

The most widely used floorings include:

- Carpet
- Hardwood (oak strip, plank and parquet)
- Vinyl floor covering
- Ceramic tile

CARPET

Carpet is measured, purchased and installed by the square yard and comes in rolls 12' wide. Do not try to install carpet yourself unless you have experience; it is not as easy as it appears. Carpet should be installed with a foam pad, which adds to the life of the carpet and makes the carpet feel more plush. A stretcher strip will be nailed around the perimeter of the room and the carpet will be stretched flush with the wall. Stretching the carpet prevents it from developing wrinkles. After two to three months, the carpet may need to be stretched again. Make sure your carpet company will agree to do this at no cost.

When pricing carpet, always get the installed price with the cost of the foam pad included. A thicker foam pad will make your carpet feel more luxurious but may cost extra. Do not install carpet until all worker traffic has ceased. Make sure that all bumps and trash have been cleaned from the floor before installation. Even the smallest bump will be noticeable through the carpet after installation.

HARDWOOD

Hardwood flooring is measured by the board foot (oak or other plank flooring) or by the square yard (parquet). Oak is laid in tongue and groove strips nailed to the sub-floor, stained and sealed. Parquet is normally installed as 6" squares with an asphalt adhesive. Parquet squares are available in stained and unstained styles. Avoid laying hardwood floors in humid weather because when the air dries out, gaps will appear between the boards. Buy the flooring a week or two before it is needed and store it in the rooms where it will be laid to let the moisture content stabilize. "Select and better" is the normal grade used in homes. It has a few knots in it. "Character grade" has more knots but is less expensive.

After installation you may want to sand the floor for an extra smooth finish. Pine flooring normally isn't sanded after installation. On all other wood floors, sanding should only be done with the grain, or sanding marks will show up. Use a professional-sized drum sander. An "edger" should be used to sand the edges. If you lay hardwood floors on a concrete slab, you need to seal the concrete and use a concrete adhesive. A better method will be to lay down runner strips and nail the floor to the strips. Wood strip floor installers usually work as a pair: one nailing strips in place while the other saws pieces to the proper length and sets them in place. If you can avoid it, do not lay wood floors on slabs.

VINYL

Vinyl floor covering is measured by the square yard and comes in a variety of styles and types. Padded vinyl rolls have become very popular because of their ease of installation and maintenance. Installation procedures vary depending on the material and manufacturer, so take care to follow the manufacturer's recommendations when installing. Warranties can be voided if the material is not installed properly.

When installing vinyl floors, consider laying an additional sub-floor of plywood over the area to be covered. This additional layer provides a smoother surface for the floor and brings the level of the floor up to the same level as any surrounding carpet.

TILE

Tile is measured and sold by the square foot although tile units can come in any size. Tile comes either glazed

Figure 66. Types of strip flooring: A, side and end-notched - 25/32-inch; B, thin flooring strips-matched; C, thin flooring strips-square-edged.

Figure 67. Wood block flooring: A, tongue-and-groove; B, square-edged-splined.

Figure 68. Nailing of flooring: A, nail angle; B, setting of nail.

or unglazed and can be installed over a wood sub-floor, although a special adhesive cement and latex grout must be used. Consider using a colored grout which can hide dirt. If you coat the tile grout with a protective coating, you may void the tile warranty.

Tile installation is a tedious and critical procedure. Make sure your tile sub is experienced and quality conscious. Improper installation can result in buckling, cracking and delamination. To insure that tiles adhere properly, avoid installation in cold weather or make sure that the floor is heated for 24 hours after installation.

Colored grouts add a special touch without adding to costs. Don't bother with a colored grout unless the joint is at least ⅛" wide. You may wish to use a grout additive instead of water. This will strengthen the grout and bring out the color. To save time, also consider using a special protective coating applied to

tile prior to grouting. This will allow you to wipe the grout film off the tile easily when the job is done.

If you plan to install tile in kitchens or other large areas, check the height of the installed floor (tile and mortar bed) to ensure that you aren't higher than the adjoining carpet or hardwood floors.

Remember that you have a ½" fudge factor around floor perimeters if you use shoe molding. If you tile yourself, ask your supplier to loan or rent you a tile cutter with a new blade or buy a new blade — this will make a world of difference.

Tiling shower and bath stalls is tricker than tiling floors. You may want to do the floors, but hire a sub for the rest. Use spacers when tiling the floor to keep the tiles straight.

GLAZING

Glazing, while not part of flooring, normally occurs during the flooring phase. Glazing refers to any mirrors and plate glass windows that must be custom cut from sheets of plate glass. No special specifications are needed.

Figure 69.   Base for wood flooring on concrete slab (without an underlying vapor barrier).

Figure 70.   Base for wood flooring and concrete slab (without an underlying vapor barrier).

GLAZING - Steps

GL1 DETERMINE mirror and special glazing requirements. This means all of the following items:

- Mirrors
- Closet door mirrors
- Shower doors
- Fixed picture windows
- Medicine cabinets

GL2 SELECT mirrors and other items. Here you must decide such trivia as beveled edge or non-beveled edge mirror glass, chrome or gold frame for shower doors, etc. Glazing subs will have catalogs for you to look through.

GL3 CONDUCT standard bidding process for glazing sub.

GL4 INSTALL fixed pane picture windows. Check that window has no scratches and is adequately sealed.

GL5 INSTALL shower doors and medicine cabinets. If you can, turn on shower head and point toward the shower door to check for leaks. Door should glide freely along track.

GL6 INSTALL mirrors and closet door mirrors. Mirrors should be installed with a non-abrasive mastic. Check for hairline scratches in the silver coating; this cannot be fixed aside from replacing the mirror.

GL7 INSPECT all glazing installation.

GL8 CORRECT all glazing problems.

GL9 PAY glazier and have him sign an affidavit.

FLOORING and TILE - Steps

FL1 SELECT carpet brands, styles, colors and coverage. Also select your padding. Keep styles and colors to a minimum. This helps your buying power, minimizes scrap and provides for easier resale.

FL2 SELECT hardwood floor type, brand, style, color and coverage.

FL3 SELECT vinyl floor covering brand, style, color and coverage.

FL4 SELECT tile brands, styles, colors and coverage. This includes tile for bath walls, bath floors, shower stalls, patios and kitchen counter tops. Once your sub-floor is in, borrow about a square yard of your favorite tile from your supplier. Lay it down where it will be used and see how it looks.

FL5 CONDUCT standard bidding process For best prices on carpet, go to a carpet specialist or carpet mill. When possible, have the supplier bid for material and labor. If your supplier does not install, ask for installer references.

Tile

FL6 ORDER tile and grout. If you do the job yourself, borrow or rent a tile cutter from the tile supplier. Look for good bargains on "seconds" — tile with slight imperfections — to use as cut pieces. Don't use sanded grout with marble tiles. The sand will scratch the marble surface. Make sure that all tile comes from the same batch. Tile colors can vary from batch to batch.

FL7 PREPARE area to be tiled. Sweep floor clean and nail down all squeaky floor areas with ridged nails.

FL8 INSTALL tile base in shower stalls. This normally involves applying concrete over a wire mesh. In shower stalls, this is done on top of the shower pan. If you have tile in the kitchen do not tile under the cabinets or the island. Prior to tiling around a whirlpool tub, make sure the tub is secure and has been fully wired, grounded and plumbed.

FL9 APPLY tile adhesive. Use a trowel with grooves suitable for your tile and grout. Use large curved, sweeping motions.

FL10 INSTALL tile and marble thresholds. Don't forget to use tile spacers to assure even tile spacing. Make sure tubs are secure in place before tiling. Make sure to save a few extra tiles in case of subsequent damage to floor tiles. This will ensure a perfect color match if repairs are needed.

FL11 APPLY grout over tile. Apply silicone sealant between the tub and tile.

FL12 INSPECT tile. Refer to specifications and inspection criteria.

FL13 CORRECT any problems that need fixing.

FL14 SEAL grout. This should only be done after grout has been in place for about three weeks. Use a penetrating sealer to protect the grout from stains.

FL15 PAY tile sub. Get him to sign an affidavit.

FL16 PAY tile sub retainage after floor has proven to be stable and well glued.

Hardwood

FL17 ORDER hardwood flooring. Hardwood flooring should remain in the room in which it will be installed for several weeks in order for it to expand and contract based on local humidity conditions. You may want to order a few extra bundles of shorter, cheaper lengths to do closets and other small areas.

FL18 PREPARE sub-floor for hardwood flooring. If you have a wood sub-floor, you should put down at least two layers of heavy-duty building paper. Make sure that all dirt and drywall compound are thoroughly cleaned off the floor. The surface must be totally clean and level. If you are laying hardwood on a slab, you have two choices:

- Seal the slab with a liquid sealer and install flooring with an adhesive
- Prepare a sub-floor:
  — Sweep slab
  — Apply 1" x 2" treated wood strips called bottom sleepers with adhesive and 1 ½" concrete nails, 24" apart, perpendicular to the oak strips
  — Lay 6 mil poly vapor barrier over strips
  — Lay second layer of 1" x 2" wood strips over vapor barrier.
  — Nail wood flooring strips to the firring strips.

FL19 INSTALL hardwood flooring. You may want to wait until all drywall and painting work is complete before installing hardwood to protect the finish. Ask installers to leave some scraps. Store them away for repair work or other use.

FL20 SAND hardwood flooring. Although most floors are pre-sanded, you may still need to have them sanded for the smoothest possible finish. Sand only with the grain. Cross-grain sanding will not look bad until the stain is applied. Once floors are sanded, there should be no traffic until after the sealer is dry.

FL21 INSPECT hardwood flooring. Refer to specifications and inspection guidelines.

FL22 CORRECT any problems with hardwood flooring. Common problems are split strips, hammer dents in strip edges, uneven spacing, gaps, squeaks, non-staggered joints and last strip not parallel with wall.

FL23 STAIN hardwood flooring. The floors must be swept very well before this step is performed. Close windows if it is dusty outside.

FL24 SEAL hardwood flooring. Polyurethane is the most popular sealant. You normally have an option of either gloss or satin finish. Place construction paper over dry floors to protect them from construction traffic.

FL25 INSPECT hardwood flooring again, this time primarily for finish work.

FL26 PAY hardwood flooring sub. Have him sign an affidavit.

FL27 PAY hardwood flooring sub retainage.

Vinyl Floor Covering

FL28 PREPARE sub-floor for vinyl floor covering. Sweep floor clean and nail down any last squeaks with ringed nails. Plane down any high spots.

FL29 INSTALL vinyl floor covering and thresholds. Ask installers to leave behind any large scraps that can be used for repair work.

FL30 INSPECT vinyl floor covering. Refer to specifications and inspection guidelines.

FL31 CORRECT any problems with vinyl floor.

FL32 PAY vinyl floor covering sub. Have him sign an affidavit.

FL33 PAY vinyl floor covering sub retainage.

Carpet

FL34 PREPARE sub-floor for carpeting. Sweep floor clean and nail or plane down down any high spots. This is your last chance to fix squeaky floors easily and install hidden speaker wires.

FL35 INSTALL carpet stretcher strips.

FL36 INSTALL carpet padding. You should use an upgraded pad if you use a tongue and groove sub-floor. If you don't use a carpet stretcher on this step, you are doing the job wrong.

FL37 INSTALL carpet. This should be done with a carpet stretcher to get a professional job. Ask installer to leave larger scraps for future repair work.

FL38 INSPECT carpet. Refer to specifications and inspection guidelines.

FL39 CORRECT any problems with carpeting installation.

FL40 PAY carpet sub. Have him sign an affidavit.

FL41 PAY carpet retainage.

FLOORING and TILE — Specifications

Carpet

■ Bid is to furnish and install wall-to-wall carpet in the following rooms:
  • Living room
  • Dining room
  • Master bedroom and closets
  • Second bedroom and closets
  • Third bedroom and closets
  • Second floor stairway
  • Second floor hallway
  • 8" accent border to be installed in master bathroom. Color to be of builder's choice.

■ Full-size upgraded pad is to be provided and installed under all carpet.

■ Stretcher strips are to be installed around carpet perimeters.

■ All seams to be invisible. (This is critical to a good carpet job.) Seams should be located in inconspicuous and low traffic areas.

■ All major carpet and padding scraps to remain on site.

■ All necessary thresholds to be installed.

■ All work to be performed in a professional manner.

Oak Flooring

■ Bid is to provide and install "select and better" grade flooring in the following areas:
  • Foyer and first floor hallway
  • Den

■ Oak strips to be single width, 3¼" strips.

■ Two perpendicular layers of heavy gauge paper to be installed between sub-floor and oak flooring.

■ All oak strips to be nailed in place with flooring nails at a 50° angle. Nails to be installed only with a nailing machine to prevent hammer head damage to floor.

■ Shorter lengths to be used in closets.

■ All oak strips to be staggered randomly so that no two adjacent joint ends are within 6" of each other.

■ Oak flooring and oak staircase treads to be sanded to a smooth surface.

■ Oak flooring and oak staircase treads to be swept, stained, sealed and coated with satin finish polyurethane.

■ Stain to be a medium brown.

■ Ridged or spiral flooring nails to be used exclusively.

■ Only first and last strip to be surface-nailed, concealable by shoe mold.

Parquet Flooring

■ Bid is to provide and install parquet flooring in the following areas:
  • Sunroom

- Sunroom closet

■ Parquet flooring to be stained and waxed.

■ Install marble thresholds in the following areas:
  - Between hallway and living room
  - Between hallway and dining room
  - Between hallway and den
  - Between kitchen and dining room

Vinyl Floor Covering

■ Bid is to provide and install vinyl floor covering in the following areas:
  - Kitchen and kitchen closet
  - Utility room

■ All seams to be invisible.

■ All major scraps to remain on site.

■ All necessary thresholds to be installed.

Tile

■ Bid is to provide and install specified tile flooring in the following areas:
  - Master bath shower stall walls. One course of curved base tile around perimeter. Tile to go all the way to ceiling.
  - Master bath shower floor.
  - Surround and one step for whirlpool bath.
  - Second bath shower stall walls all the way to ceiling.
  - Second bath floor. Per attached diagram.
  - Half bath floor. Per attached diagram. One course of base tile around perimeter.
  - Kitchen floor (per diagram). Tan grout sealed. One course of base tile around perimeter.
  - Kitchen wall backsplash. See drawings attached.
  - Kitchen island top.
  - Hobby room and closet.

■ Grout colors to be as specified by builder.

■ All necessary soap dishes, tissue holders, towel racks and toothbrush holders to be supplied and installed in white unless otherwise specified by builder in writing.

■ Matching formed base and cap tiles to be used as needed to finish edging and corners.

■ ¼" per foot slope toward drain in shower stalls.

■ All necessary tub and shower drains installed.

■ All grout to be sealed three weeks after grout is installed.

■ Extra tile and grout to remain on site.

FLOORING and TILE - Inspection

Carpet

☐ Proper carpet is installed.

☐ No visible seams.

☐ Carpet is stretched tightly and secured by carpet strips.

☐ Colors match as intended. Watch for color variations.

☐ Carpet installed on stairs fits tight on each riser.

Oak Flooring and Parquet

☐ Proper oak strips and/or parquet installed. (Make, color, etc.)

☐ No flooring shifts, creaks or squeaks under pressure.

☐ Even staining and smooth surface.

☐ No scratches, cracks or uneven surfaces. Scratches normally indicate sanding across the grain or using too coarse sandpaper for final pass.

☐ Smaller lengths used in closets to reduce scrap and waste.

☐ All necessary thresholds are installed and are parallel to floor joints.

☐ Only edge boards have visible nails. No other boards have visible nails.

☐ Edge boards are parallel to walls.

☐ No irregular or excessive spacing between boards.

☐ No floor registers covered up by flooring.

Vinyl Floor Covering

☐ Proper vinyl floor covering is installed. (Make, color, pattern, etc.)

☐ Vinyl floor covering has smooth adhesion to floor. No bubbles.

☐ No movement of flooring when placed under pressure.

☐ No visible or excessive seams.

☐ No scratches or irregularities.

☐ All necessary thresholds have been installed and are parallel to floor joints.

☐ All necessary thresholds are of proper height for effective door operation. No more than ⅛" gap under interior doors.

☐ Pattern is parallel or perpendicular to walls as specified.

Tile

☐ Proper tiles and grouts are installed. (Make, style, dimensions, color, pattern, etc.)

☐ Tile joints are smooth, evenly spaced, parallel and perpendicular to each other and walls where applicable.

☐ Tiles are secure and do not move when placed under pressure.

☐ No scratches, cracks, chips or other irregularities.

☐ Grout is sealed as specified.

☐ Grout lines parallel and perpendicular with walls.

☐ Tile pattern matches artistically.

☐ Tiles are laid symmetrically from the center of the room out. Cut pieces on opposite sides of the room are of the same size.

☐ All tile cuts are smooth and even around perimeter and floor register openings.

☐ Marble thresholds are installed level with no cracks or chips.

☐ Marble thresholds parallel with door when closed.

☐ Metal thresholds installed between tile and wood joints.

☐ Marble thresholds are at proper height.

☐ Matching formed tiles used at base of tile walls as specified.

☐ Cap tiles used at top of tile walls.

☐ Proper tile edging for tubs, sinks and shower stalls.

☐ No cracked or damaged tiles.

☐ Tile floor is level.

☐ Extra tile and grout available on site.

MISCELLANEOUS FINISH

Weatherstripping

☐ All exterior doors have weatherstripping and threshold installed.

☐ Doors open and close securely with a tight seal.

☐ No leaks after a heavy rain.

Mirrors and Shower Doors

☐ Door fixtures match faucets.

☐ Doors slide properly with no friction or binding.

☐ No scratches on mirror.

Landscaping

When you consider how much resale value and curb appeal a good landscaping job can add to a home, it is surprising that so many builders scrimp on this important effort. Many builders just throw up a few bushes and then seed or sod. Hopefully you will be willing to spend just a bit more time and effort to do the job right. If you don't want to spend all the money at once, you can devise a two- or three-year implementation plan, beginning with the critical items such as ground coverage.

Important items to keep in mind are:

- Plan for curb appeal. Your lawn should be a show-place.

- Plan for low maintenance. If you don't want to trim hedges and rake leaves forever, be smart about the trees and bushes you install or keep.

- Work with the sun, not against it. Maximize sunlight into the home by careful planning of trees.

- Plan for proper drainage. This is CRITICAL! Water must drain away from dwelling and not collect in any low spots.

- Consider doing much of this work yourself.

- Consider assistance from a landscape architect.

Every lot has one best use and many poor ones. A good landscape architect can help you do more than select grass. Landscape architects can be helpful in:

- Determining best position of the home on the lot.

- Determining attractive driveway patterns.

- Determining which trees should remain and additional trees and/or bushes to plant for privacy and lowest maintenance.

- Determining soil condition and soil additives.

- Determining proper drainage and ground coverings.

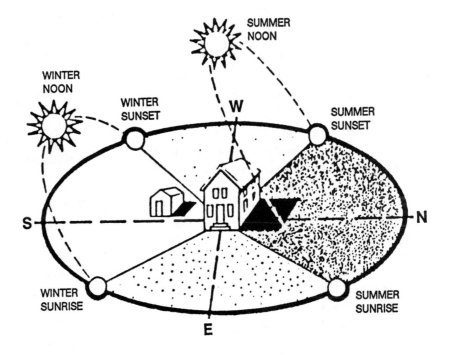

excellent location
good location
poor location

Figure 71. Landscaping orientation

You can normally pay an independent landscape architect by the hour, but if you do a lot of work with him, work up a fixed price. Meet him at your lot with the lot survey. Walk the lot with him, getting his initial impressions and ideas. From there, you may request a site plan. The site plan will normally be a large drawing showing exact home position, driveway layout, existing trees and bushes, sculptured islands and other topographical features.

LANDSCAPING - Steps

Before Construction

LD1 EVALUATE your lot in terms of trees to keep, drainage, privacy, slopes, high and low spots and exposure to morning and afternoon sun. A landscape architect can help you greatly with this step. He can also help you determine if you will have too little or too much soil after excavation and what to do about it. Excavated soil may be used to fill in low spots or otherwise assist in developing a drainage pattern or landscaping feature.

LD2 DETERMINE best possible position for home on lot. Considerations should include:

- Good southern exposure for parts of the house with a lot of glass.
- Best view for most important rooms when at all possible. Don't give your best view to a garage or windowless wall.
- Best angle for curb appeal. Consider angling your home if on a corner lot.

LD3 DEVELOP site plan. This is a bird's-eye view of what you want the finished site to look like, including exact position of home, driveway and all other paved surfaces, such as walks and patios, major trees, islands, grass areas, flower beds, bushes and even an underground watering system if you intend to have one. The site plan should show all baselines and easements. If any portion of your home falls outside a baseline, you will need a land variance. When determining grass areas, consider shade. Most grasses do not grow well or do not grow at all in shade. No amount of fertilizer or lawn care can compensate for a lack of sun.

LD4 CONTACT a landscape architect to critique and/or improve on your design. They normally have more experience and can surprise you with new and interesting ideas. For example, instead of having a driveway go straight from the street to the garage, consider putting a lazy curve in the drive and a slight mound on the street side. This helps hide the expanse of concrete which is not normally a focal point. Landscape architects can recommend specific types of bushes to suit special privacy needs.

LD5 FINALIZE site plan. Make several copies in blueprint form. You will need at least one for yourself, one for a landscaper if you hire one and one for the county.

LD6 SUBMIT site plan to building officials and bank along with your blueprints.

LD7 DELIVER fill dirt, if needed, to site. Choose a spot to pile topsoil from the foundation grading. Do not mix this dirt with fill dirt unless both types are topsoil. Make sure fill dirt is clean and dry. Wet dirt will form lumps and clods as it dries.

LD8 PAY landscape architect (if you used one).

After Construction

LD9 CONDUCT soil tests. Soil samples should be made for every several thousand feet of yard. Soil to be tested should be taken from 6" down. Soil testing will help to determine pH (level of acidity) and the lack of essential nutrients. Most counties have an extension service which will test the samples for you at little or no charge. Good general purpose soil conditioners are peat moss, manure and lime.

LD10 TILL first 4" to 6" of soil, adding soil conditioners as needed. Cut any unwanted trees down and grind stumps before sod is laid down. Rake surface smooth first one way and then another.

LD11 APPLY soil treatments as needed. You may also wish to add a slow release, non-burning fertilizer (no stronger than 6-6-6) to help your young grass grow. Apply gypsum pellets to break down clay.

LD12 INSTALL underground sprinkling system as needed. This normally consists of a network of ½" PVC pipe purchased from a garden supply store.

LD13 PLANT flower bulbs. This is the easiest and best time to plant daffodils, crocus, hyacinths, gladioli, etc.

LD14 APPLY seed or sod, depending upon your choice. Seed is much cheaper, but sod means an instant thriving lawn and elimination of topsoil runoff. Seed is hard to start on a hill or in other adverse conditions. If you do choose seed, use a broadcast spreader or a special seed dispensing device. Cover the seed with hay or straw to protect seeds from washing away with rain. If you sod, this will be a tougher job, but doing it yourself could really save some money. Sod always has at least three prices: direct from a sod farm, delivered by a sod broker or delivered and installed by a sod broker. If you can, buy direct from a sod farm. Visit them if you have time to see before you buy. Have them drop the sod in shady areas all around the grounds to be covered to reduce carrying. Keep sod slightly moist until installed. Have a good crew to help you lay sod because it will only live on pallets for a few days.

LD15 SOAK lawn with water if sod is applied. Sprinkle lightly for long periods of time if a seeded lawn is used. Roll lawn with a heavy metal cylinder.

LD16 INSTALL bushes and trees. If you plan to install trees, please keep them at least 4' from the driveway area. Trees are notorious for breaking up a driveway when the roots begin to spread.

LD17 PREPARE landscaped islands. Place pine bark, pine straw, mulch or gravel in designated areas. Over time, pine straw will kill some grasses, particularly Bermuda. Keep pine straw in islands only.

LD18 INSTALL mailbox if you have the kind that sits on a post. If you have a masonry or large frame mailbox, it will be installed during the framing or masonry stages of construction.

LD19 INSPECT landscaping job. Refer to specifications and checklist.

LD20 CORRECT any problems noted.

LD21 PAY landscaping sub for job. Have him sign an affidavit.

LD22 PAY landscaping sub retainage after grass is fully established without bare areas.

LANDSCAPING - Specifications

■ Bid is to landscape as described below:

■ Loosen soil in yard to a depth of 6" with no dirt clumps larger than 6".

■ Finely rake all area to be seeded or sodded.

■ Install the following soil treatments:

Peat moss	21 cubic feet per 1000 square feet
Sand	500 lbs. per 1000 square feet
Lime	200 lbs. per 1000 square feet
6-6-6	as prescribed by mfr. for new lawns

■ All grass to be lightly fertilized with 6-6-6 and watered heavily immediately to prevent drying.

■ Sod to be Bermuda 419, laid within 48 hours of delivery.

■ Sod pieces to butt each with no gaps with joints staggered.

■ Islands to be naturally shaped by trimming sod.

■ Sod to be rolled after watering.

■ Prepare three pine straw islands as described in attached site plan.

■ Install trees and bushes according to attached planting schedule and site plan.

■ Cover all seeded areas with straw to prevent runoff.

■ Install splash blocks for downspouts.

■ Burlap to be removed from root balls prior to installation.

■ Trees and shrubs to be watered after installation.

LANDSCAPING - Inspection

☐ All areas sodded/seeded as specified.

☐ All trees and bushes installed as specified.

☐ Sod and/or seed is alive and growing.

☐ Sod is smooth and even with no gaps.

☐ Straw covers seed evenly with no bare spots.

☐ All specified bushes and trees are alive and in upright position.

☐ Splash blocks installed.

☐ Grass cut if specified.

☐ No weeds in yard.

☐ No exposed dirt within 16" of siding or brick veneer.

☐ Pine bark or pine straw islands installed as specified.

Sources of Additional Information

The following sources are generally recognized as members of the building industry that have impact on standards and guidelines.

Air Conditioning Contractors of America (ACCA)
1513 16th St. NW
Washington, DC 20036

Aluminum Association (AA)
900 19th St. NW, Ste. 300
Washington, DC 20006
202-862-5100

American Concrete Institute (ACI)
P.O. Box 19150
Detroit, MI 48219

American Hardboard Association
520 N. Hicks Rd.
Palatine, IL 60067
312-934-8800

American Institute of Steel Construction, Inc.
1 E. Wacker Dr., Ste. 3100
Chicago, IL 60601-2001
312-670-2400

American Institute of Timber Construction (AITC)
11818 SE Mill Plain Blvd., Ste. 415
Vancouver, WA 98684
206-254-9132

American Insurance Association (AIA)
1130 Connecticut Ave. NW, Ste. 1000
Washington, DC 20036
202-828-7100

American Iron and Steel Institute (AISI)
1133 15th St. NW
Washington, DC 20005
202-452-7100

American National Standards Institute (ANSI)
11 W. 42nd St., 13th floor
New York, NY 10036
212-642-4900

American Plywood Association (APA)
P.O. Box 11700
Tacoma, WA 98411
206-565-6600

American Society for Testing Materials (ASTM)
1916 Race Street
Philadelphia, PA 19103

American Soc. of Heating, Refrig. and Air Cond. Engineers
1791 Tullie Circle NE
Atlanta, GA 30329
404-636-8400

American Welding Society, Inc. (AWS)
550 LeJeune Rd. NW, P.O. Box 351040
Miami, FL 33135
305-443-9353

American Wood Preservers Bureau (AWPB)
P.O. Box 5283
Springfield, VA 22150
703-339-6660

American Wood Preservers Institute (AWPI)
1945 Old Gallows Rd., Ste. 550
Vienna, VA 22182

American Wood-Preservers Association (AWPA)
P.O. Box 849
Stevensville, MD 21666
301-643-4163

Asphalt Roofing Manufacturers Association
6288 Montrose Rd.
Rockville, MD 20852
301-231-9050

Brick Institute of America (BIA)
11490 Commerce Park Dr.
Reston, VA 22091
703-620-0010

Building Systems Councils of NAHB
15th & M Streets NW
Washington, DC 20005

Cedar Shake and Shingle Bureau
515 116th Ave. NE, Ste. 275
Bellevue, WA 98004

Chemical Manufacturers Association
2501 M St. NW
Washington, DC 20037

Commercial Standards (U.S. Department of Commerce)
Superintendent of Documents
Government Printing Office
Washington, DC 20402

Concrete Reinforcing Steel Institute (CRSI)
933 Plum Grove Rd.
Schaumburg, IL 60173

Federal Specifications (FS)
Superintendent of Documents
Government Printing Office
Washington, DC 20234

Forest Products Research Society
2801 Marshall Court
Madison, WI 53705
608-231-1361

Gypsum Association (GA)
810 1st St. NE, No. 510
Washington, DC 20002
202-289-5440

Hardwood Plywood Manufacturer's Association (HPMA)
1825 Michael Faraday Dr., P.O. Box 2789
Reston, VA 22090

International Masonry Institute
823 15th St. NW
Washington, DC 20005
202-783-3908

Manufactured Housing Institute
1745 Jefferson Davis Hwy., Ste. 511
Arlington, VA 22202

Metal Building Manufacturers Association (MBMA)
2130 Keith Building
Cleveland, OH 44115

Metal Lath/Steel Framing Association Division
600 S. Federal St., Ste. 400
Chicago, IL 60605
312-922-6222

Mineral Insulation Manufacturers Association
1420 King St.
Alexandria, VA 22314

National Association of Home Builders (NAHB)
15th & M Streets NW
Washington, DC 20005

National Bureau of Standards (NBS) (U.S. Department of Commerce)
Superintendent of Documents
Government Printing Office
Washington, DC 20402

National Clay Pipe Institute (NCPI)
P.O. Box 759
Lake Geneva, WI 53147
414-248-9094

National Concrete Masonry Association (NCMA)
P.O. Box 781
Herndon, VA 22070-0781

National Fire Protection Association (NFPA)
1 Batterymarch Park, P.O. Box 9101
Quincy, MA O2269-9101
617-770-3000

National Fire Sprinkler Association
Robin Hill Corp. Pk., Rt. 22, Box 1
Patterson, NY 12563
617-770-3000

National Forest Products Association
1250 Connecticut Ave. NW, Ste. 200
Washington, DC 20036
202-463-2700

National Lime Association (NLA)
3601 N. Fairfax Dr.
Arlington, VA 22201
703-243-5463

National Particleboard Association (NPA)
18928 Premiere Ct.
Gaithersburg, MD 20879
301-670-0604

National Pest Control Association (NPCA)
8100 Oak St.
Dunn Loring, VA 22027
703-573-8330

Perlite Institute (PI)
88 New Dorp Plaza
Staten Island, NY 10306
718-351-5723

Portland Cement Association (PCA)
5420 Old Orchard Road
Skokie, IL 60077

Post-Tensioning Institute (PTI)
1717 W. Northern Ave., Ste. 218
Phoenix, AZ 85021
402-870-7540

Prestressed Concrete Institute (PCI)
175 W. Jackson Blvd.
Chicago, IL 60604
312-786-0300

Sheet Metal & Air Cond.
Contractor's National Association
P.O. Box 70
Merrifield, VA 22116
703-790-9890

Society of the Plastics Industry (SPI)
1275 K St. NW
Washington, DC 20005
202-371-5200

Southern Forest Products Association (SFPA)
P.O. Box 52468
New Orleans, LA 70152

Southern Pine Inspection Bureau (SPIB)
4709 Scenic Hwy.
Pensacola, FL 32504
904-434-2611

Southwest Research & Information Center (SRI)
P.O. Box 4524
Albuquerque, NM 87106
505-262-1862

Steel Joist Institute (SJI)
1205 48th Ave. N., Ste. A
Myrtle Beach, SC 29577

Steel Window Institute (SWI)
% Thomas Assocs., Inc.
2130 Keith Building
Cleveland, OH 44115

The Hydronics Institute (HI)
35 Russo Place, P.O. Box 218
Berkely Heights, NJ O7922

Tile Council of America (TCA)
P.O. Box 326
Princeton, NJ O8542

Truss Plate Institute (TPI)
583 D'Onofrio Dr., Ste. 200
Madison, WI 53719
608-833-5900

Underwriters' Laboratories (UL)
333 Pfingsten Road
Northbrook, IL 60062

Western Wood Products Association (WWPA)
Yeon Building, 522 SW 5th Ave.
Portland, OR 97204-2122
503-224-3930

Appendices

SECTION III: APPENDICES

Appendices

MASTERPLAN

	Masterplan				
STEP	DESCRIPTION	Date Started	Date Complete	Date Inspected	NOTES
	PRE-CONSTRUCTION				
PC1	BEGIN construction project scrapbook				
PC2	DETERMINE size of home				
PC3	EVALUATE alternate house plans				
PC4	SELECT house plan				
PC5	MAKE design changes				
PC6	PERFORM material and labor take-off				
PC7	CUT costs as required				
PC8	UPDATE material and labor take-off				
PC9	ARRANGE temporary housing				
PC10	FORM separate corporation				
PC11	APPLY for business license				
PC12	ORDER business cards				
PC13	OBTAIN free and clear title to land				
PC14	APPLY for construction loan				
PC15	ESTABLISH project checking account				
PC16	CLOSE construction loan				
PC17	OPEN builder accounts				
PC18	OBTAIN purchase order forms				
PC19	OBTAIN building permit				
PC20	OBTAIN builder's risk policy				
PC21	OBTAIN worker's compensation policy				
PC22	ACQUIRE minimum tools				
PC23	VISIT construction sites				
PC24	DETERMINE need for on-site storage				
PC25	NOTIFY all subs and labor				
PC26	OBTAIN compliance bond				

Masterplan

STEP	DESCRIPTION	Date Started	Date Complete	Date Inspected	NOTES
PC27	DETERMINE minimum occupancy requiremnts				
PC28	CONDUCT spot survey of lot				
PC29	MARK all lot boundaries and corners				
PC30	POST construction signs				
PC31	POST building permit on site				
PC32	ARRANGE for portable toilet				
PC33	ARRANGE for site telephone				
	EXCAVATION				
EX1	CONDUCT excavation bidding process				
EX2	LOCATE underground utilities				
EX3	DETERMINE exact dwelling location				
EX4	MARK area to be cleared				
EX5	MARK where curb is to be cut				
EX6	TAKE last picture of site area				
EX7	CLEAR site area				
EX8	EXCAVATE trash pit				
EX9	INSPECT cleared site				
EX10	EXCAVATE foundation/basement area				
EX11	INSPECT site and excavated area				
	BATTER BOARDS				
EX12	LAY OUT corner stakes for 4 corners of house				
EX13	DRIVE 3 batter board stakes at each corner				
EX14	NAIL 1x6 horizontal boards to stakes				
EX15	PULL batter board strings				
EX16	RE-CHECK distance of each string				
EX17	LAY OUT remaining batter boards and re-check				
	DRAINAGE				
EX18	APPLY crusher run to driveway area				
EX19	SET UP silt fence				
EX20	PAY excavator (initial)				

STEP	DESCRIPTION	Date Started	Date Complete	Date Inspected	NOTES
	BACKFILL				
EX21	PLACE supports on foundation wall				
EX22	INSPECT backfill area				
EX23	BACKFILL foundation				
EX24	CUT driveway area				
EX25	COVER septic tank and septic tank line				
EX26	COVER trash pit				
EX27	PERFORM final grade				
EX28	CONDUCT final inspection				
EX29	PAY excavator (final)				
	PEST CONTROL				
PS1	CONDUCT standard bidding process				
PS2	NOTIFY pest control sub for pre-treat				
PS3	APPLY pesticide to foundation				
PS4	APPLY pesticide to perimeter				
PS5	OBTAIN signed pest control warranty				
PS6	PAY pest control sub				
	CONCRETE				
CN1	CONDUCT bidding process (concrete supplier)				
CN2	CONDUCT bidding process (formwork/finishing)				
CN3	CONDUCT bidding process (block masonry)				
	FOOTINGS				
CN4	INSPECT batter boards				
CN5	DIG footings				
CN6	SET footing forms				
CN7	INSPECT footing forms				
CN8	SCHEDULE and complete footing inspection				
CN9	CALL concrete supplier for concrete				
CN10	POUR footings				

	Masterplan				
STEP	**DESCRIPTION**	**Date Started**	**Date Complete**	**Date Inspected**	**NOTES**
CN11	INSTALL key forms				
CN12	FINISH footings as needed				
CN13	REMOVE footing forms				
CN14	INSPECT footings				
CN15	PAY concrete supplier for footings				
	POURED WALL				
CN16	SET poured wall concrete forms				
CN17	SCHEDULE concrete supplier				
CN18	INSPECT poured wall concrete forms				
CN19	POUR foundation walls				
CN20	FINISH poured foundation walls				
CN21	REMOVE poured wall concrete forms				
CN22	INSPECT poured walls				
CN23	BREAK OFF tie ends from walls				
CN24	PAY concrete supplier for walls				
	BLOCK WALL				
CN25	ORDER blocks/schedule masons				
CN26	LAY concrete blocks				
CN27	FINISH concrete blocks				
CN28	INSPECT concrete block work				
CN29	PAY concrete block masons				
CN30	CLEAN up after block masons				
	CONCRETE SLAB				
CN31	SET slab forms				
CN32	PACK slab sub-soil				
CN33	INSTALL stub plumbing				
CN34	SCHEDULE HVAC sub for slab work				
CN35	INSPECT plumbing and gas lines				
CN36	POUR and spread crushed stone				
CN37	INSTALL vapor barrier				

STEP	DESCRIPTION	Date Started	Date Complete	Date Inspected	NOTES
CN38	LAY reinforcing wire as required				
CN39	INSTALL rigid insulation				
CN40	CALL concrete supplier for slab				
CN41	INSPECT slab forms				
CN42	POUR slab				
CN43	FINISH slab				
CN44	INSPECT slab				
CN45	PAY concrete supplier for slab				
	DRIVEWAY				
CN46	COMPACT drive and walkway soil				
CN47	SET drive and walkway forms				
CN48	CALL concrete supplier				
CN49	INSPECT drive and walkway forms				
CN50	POUR drive and walkway				
CN51	FINISH drive and walkway areas				
CN52	INSPECT drive and walkway areas				
CN53	ROPE OFF drive and walkway areas				
CN54	PAY concrete supplier				
CN55	PAY concrete finishers				
CN56	PAY concrete finisher's retainage				
	WATERPROOFING				
WP1	CONDUCT standard bidding process				
WP2	SEAL footing and wall intersection				
WP3	APPLY first coat of portland cement				
WP4	APPLY second coat of portland cement				
WP5	APPLY waterproofing compound				
WP6	APPLY 6 mil poly vapor barrier				
WP7	INSPECT waterproofing (tar/poly)				
WP8	INSTALL gravel bed for drain tile				
WP9	INSTALL drain tile				
WP10	INSPECT drain tile				

STEP	DESCRIPTION	Date Started	Date Complete	Date Inspected	NOTES
	Masterplan				
WP11	APPLY top layer of gravel on drain tile				
WP12	PAY waterproofing sub				
WP13	PAY waterproofing sub retainage				
	FRAMING				
FR1	CONDUCT standard bidding process (material)				
FR2	CONDUCT standard bidding process (labor)				
FR3	DISCUSS aspects of framing with crew				
FR4	ORDER special materials				
FR5	ORDER first load of framing lumber				
FR6	INSTALL sill felt				
FR7	ATTACH sill plate with lag bolts				
FR8	INSTALL support columns				
FR9	SUPERVISE framing process				
FR10	FRAME first floor joists and subfloor				
FR11	FRAME basement stairs				
FR12	POSITION all first floor large items				
FR13	FRAME exterior walls (first floor)				
FR14	PLUMB and line first floor				
FR15	FRAME second floor joists and subfloor				
FR16	POSITION all large second floor items				
FR17	FRAME exterior walls (second floor)				
FR18	PLUMB and line second floor				
FR19	INSTALL second floor ceiling joists				
FR20	FRAME roof				
FR21	INSTALL roof decking				
FR22	PAY framing first installment				
FR23	INSTALL lapped tar paper				
FR24	FRAME chimney chases				
FR25	INSTALL pre-fab fireplaces				
FR26	FRAME dormers and skylights				
FR27	FRAME tray ceilings, skylights, and bays				
FR28	INSTALL sheathing on exterior walls				

STEP	DESCRIPTION	Date Started	Date Complete	Date Inspected	NOTES
	Masterplan				
FR29	INSPECT sheathing				
FR30	REMOVE temporary bracing				
FR31	INSTALL exterior windows and doors				
FR32	APPLY deadwood				
FR33	INSTALL roof ventilators				
FR34	FRAME decks				
FR35	INSPECT framing				
FR36	SCHEDULE loan draw inspection				
FR37	CORRECT any framing problems				
FR38	PAY framing labor (second payment)				
FR39	PAY framing sub retainage				
	ROOFING				
RF1	SELECT shingle style, material, and color				
RF2	PERFORM standard bidding process				
RF3	ORDER shingles and roofing felt				
RF4	INSTALL metal drip edge				
RF5	INSTALL roofing felt				
RF6	INSTALL drip edge on rake				
RF7	INSTALL roofing shingles				
RF8	INSPECT roofing				
RF9	PAY roofing sub				
RF10	PAY roofing sub retainage				
	GUTTERS				
GU1	SELECT gutter type and color				
GU2	PERFORM standard bidding process				
GU3	INSTALL underground drain pipe				
GU4	INSTALL gutters and downspouts				
GU5	INSTALL splashblocks				
GU6	INSPECT gutters				
GU7	INSTALL copper awnings				
GU8	PAY gutter sub				

	Masterplan				
STEP	**DESCRIPTION**	**Date Started**	**Date Complete**	**Date Inspected**	**NOTES**
GU9	PAY gutter sub retainage				
	PLUMBING				
PL1	DETERMINE type and quantity of fixtures				
PL2	CONDUCT standard bidding process				
PL3	WALK THROUGH site with plumber				
PL4	ORDER special plumbing fixtures				
PL5	APPLY for water connection and sewer tap				
PL6	INSTALL stub plumbing for slabs				
PL7	MOVE large plumbing fixtures into place				
PL8	MARK location of all fixtures				
PL9	INSTALL rough-in plumbing				
PL10	INSTALL water meter and spigot				
PL11	INSTALL sewer tap				
PL12	SCHEDULE plumbing inspection				
PL13	INSTALL septic tank and line				
PL14	CONDUCT rough-in plumbing inspection				
PL15	CORRECT rough-in plumbing problems				
PL16	PAY plumbing sub for rough-in				
	PLUMBING FINISH				
PL17	INSTALL finish plumbing				
PL18	TAP into water supply				
PL19	CONDUCT finish plumbing inspection				
PL20	CORRECT finish plumbing problems				
PL21	PAY plumbing sub for finish work				
PL22	PAY plumbing sub retainage				
	HVAC				
HV1	CONDUCT energy audit				
HV2	SHOP for heating and cooling system				
HV3	CONDUCT standard bidding process				
HV4	FINALIZE HVAC design				

STEP	DESCRIPTION	Date Started	Date Complete	Date Inspected	NOTES
	Masterplan				
HV5	ROUGH-IN heating and air system				
HV6	INSPECT heating and air rough-in				
HV7	CORRECT rough-in problems				
HV8	PAY HVAC sub for rough-in				
HV9	INSTALL finish heating and air				
HV10	INSPECT final HVAC installation				
HV11	CORRECT all HVAC problems				
HV12	CALL gas company to install lines				
HV13	DRAW gas line on plat diagram				
HV14	PAY HVAC sub for finish work				
HV15	PAY HVAC sub retainage				
	ELECTRICAL				
EL1	DETERMINE electrical requirements				
EL2	SELECT electrical fixtures and appliances				
EL3	DETERMINE phone installation requirements				
EL4	CONDUCT standard bidding process				
EL5	SCHEDULE phone wiring				
EL6	APPLY for temporary electrical hookup				
EL7	INSTALL temporary electric pole				
EL8	PERFORM rough-in electrical				
EL9	INSTALL phone wiring				
EL10	SCHEDULE rough-in electrical inspection				
EL11	INSPECT rough-in electrical				
EL12	CORRECT rough-in electrical problems				
EL13	PAY electrical sub for rough-in work				
EL14	INSTALL garage door for opener installation				
EL15	INSTALL garage door opener				
EL16	PERFORM finish electrical work				
EL17	CALL phone co. to connect service				
EL18	INSPECT finish electrical				
EL19	CORRECT finish electrical problems				
EL20	CALL electrical utility to connect service				

	Masterplan				
STEP	DESCRIPTION	Date Started	Date Complete	Date Inspected	NOTES
EL21	PAY electrical sub for finish work				
EL22	PAY electrical sub retainage				
	MASONRY				
MA1	DETERMINE brick pattern and color				
MA2	DETERMINE stucco pattern and color				
MA3	PERFORM standard bidding process (masonry)				
MA4	PERFORM standard bidding process (stucco)				
MA5	APPLY flashing				
MA6	ORDER brick, stone, and angle irons				
MA7	LAY bricks				
MA8	FINISH bricks and mortar				
MA9	INSPECT brickwork				
MA10	CORRECT brickwork deficiencies				
MA11	PAY masons				
MA12	CLEAN UP excess bricks				
MA13	INSTALL base for decorative stucco				
MA14	PREPARE stucco test area				
MA15	APPLY stucco lath				
MA16	APPLY first coat of stucco				
MA17	APPLY second coat of stucco				
MA18	INSPECT stucco work				
MA19	CORRECT stucco deficiencies				
MA20	PAY stucco sub				
MA21	PAY masonry sub retainage				
MA22	PAY stucco sub retainage				
	SIDING/CORNICE				
SC1	SELECT siding material and color				
SC2	CONDUCT standard bidding process				
SC3	ORDER window and doors				
SC4	INSTALL windows and doors				
SC5	INSTALL flashing				

	Masterplan				
STEP	DESCRIPTION	Date Started	Date Complete	Date Inspected	NOTES
SC6	INSTALL siding				
SC7	INSTALL siding trim around corners				
SC8	CAULK siding joints				
SC9	INSPECT siding				
SC10	PAY sub for siding work				
SC11	INSTALL cornice				
SC12	INSPECT cornice work				
SC13	CORRECT any cornice problems				
SC14	PAY cornice sub				
SC15	CORRECT siding problems				
SC16	ARRANGE for painter to caulk and paint				
SC17	PAY siding sub retainage				
SC18	PAY cornice sub retainage				
	INSULATION				
IN1	DETERMINE insulation requirements				
IN2	CONDUCT standard bidding process				
IN3	INSTALL exterior wall insulation				
IN4	INSTALL soundproofing				
IN5	INSTALL floor insulation				
IN6	INSTALL attic insulation				
IN7	INSPECT insulation				
IN8	CORRECT insulation work as needed				
IN9	PAY insulation sub				
IN10	PAY insulation sub retainage				
	DRYWALL				
DR1	PERFORM standard bidding process				
DR2	ORDER and receive drywall				
DR3	HANG drywall on all walls				
DR4	FINISH drywall				
DR5	INSPECT drywall				
DR6	TOUCH UP and repair drywall				

Masterplan

STEP	DESCRIPTION	Date Started	Date Complete	Date Inspected	NOTES
DR7	PAY drywall sub				
DR8	PAY drywall sub retainage				
	TRIM				
TR1	DETERMINE trim requirments				
TR2	SELECT molding and millwork				
TR3	INSTALL windows after framing				
TR4	CONDUCT standard bidding process				
TR5	INSTALL interior doors				
TR6	INSTALL window casing and aprons				
TR7	INSTALL trim around cased openings				
TR8	INSTALL staircase openings				
TR9	INSTALL crown molding				
TR10	INSTALL base and base cap molding				
TR11	INSTALL chair rail molding				
TR12	INSTALL picture molding				
TR13	INSTALL, sand, and stain paneling				
TR14	CLEAN all sliding door tracks				
TR15	INSTALL thresholds and weather stripping				
TR16	INSTALL shoe molding				
TR17	INSTALL door and window hardware				
TR18	INSPECT trimwork				
TR19	CORRECT trim and stain work				
TR20	PAY trim sub				
	PAINTING AND WALLCOVERING				
PT1	SELECT paint schemes				
PT2	PERFORM standard bidding process				
PT3	PURCHASE all painting materials				
	Exterior				
PT4	PRIME and caulk exterior surfaces				
PT5	PAINT exterior siding and trim				

STEP	DESCRIPTION	Date Started	Date Complete	Date Inspected	NOTES
	Masterplan				
PT6	PAINT cornice work				
PT7	PAINT gutters				
	Interior				
PT8	PREPARE painting surfaces				
PT9	PRIME walls and trim				
PT10	PAINT or stipple ceilings				
PT11	PAINT walls				
PT12	PAINT or stain trim				
PT13	REMOVE paint from windows				
PT14	INSPECT paint job				
PT15	TOUCH UP paint job				
PT16	CLEAN UP				
PT17	PAY painter				
PT18	PAY painter retainage				
	CABINETRY				
CB1	CONFIRM kitchen design				
CB2	SELECT cabinetry/countertop				
CB3	COMPLETE cabinet layout diagram				
CB4	PERFORM standard bidding process				
CB5	PURCHASE cabinetry and countertops				
CB6	STAIN or paint cabinetry				
CB7	INSTALL bathroom vanities				
CB8	INSTALL kitchen wall cabinets				
CB9	INSTALL kitchen base cabinets				
CB10	INSTALL kitchen and bath countertops				
CB11	INSTALL cabinet hardware				
CB12	INSTALL utility room cabinetry				
CB13	CAULK cabinet joints as needed				
CB14	INSPECT cabinetry and countertops				
CB15	TOUCH UP and repair as needed				
CB16	PAY cabinet sub				

STEP	DESCRIPTION	Date Started	Date Complete	Date Inspected	NOTES
	Masterplan				
	GLAZING				
GL1	DETERMINE mirror and glass requirements				
GL2	SELECT mirrors and glass				
GL3	CONDUCT standard bidding process				
GL4	INSTALL fixed pane picture windows				
GL5	INSTALL shower doors				
GL6	INSTALL mirrors				
GL7	INSPECT all glazing installation				
GL8	CORRECT all glazing problems				
GL9	PAY glazier				
	FLOORING AND TILE				
FL1	SELECT carpet color, style, and coverage				
FL2	SELECT hardwood floor type				
FL3	SELECT vinyl floor covering				
FL4	SELECT tile type and coverage				
FL5	CONDUCT standard bidding process				
	Tile				
FL6	ORDER tile and grout				
FL7	PREPARE area to be tiled				
FL8	INSTALL tile base in shower stalls				
FL9	APPLY tile adhesive				
FL10	INSTALL tile and marble thresholds				
FL11	APPLY grout over tile				
FL12	INSPECT tile				
FL13	CORRECT tile problems				
FL14	SEAL grout				
FL15	PAY tile sub				
FL16	PAY tile sub retainage				

Masterplan

STEP	DESCRIPTION	Date Started	Date Complete	Date Inspected	NOTES
	Hardwood				
FL17	ORDER hardwood flooring				
FL18	PREPARE sub floor for hardwood flooring				
FL19	INSTALL hardwood flooring				
FL20	SAND hardwood flooring				
FL21	INSPECT hardwood flooring				
FL22	CORRECT hardwood flooring problems				
FL23	STAIN hardwood flooring				
FL24	SEAL hardwood flooring				
FL25	INSPECT hardwood flooring (final)				
FL26	PAY hardwood flooring sub				
FL27	PAY hardwood flooring sub retainage				
	Vinyl Floor Covering				
FL28	PREPARE sub floor for vinyl floor covering				
FL29	INSTALL vinyl floor covering				
FL30	INSPECT vinyl floor covering				
FL31	CORRECT vinyl floor covering problems				
FL32	PAY vinyl floor covering sub				
FL33	PAY vinyl floor covering sub retainage				
	Carpet				
FL34	PREPARE subfloor for carpeting				
FL35	INSTALL carpet stretcher strips				
FL36	INSTALL carpet padding				
FL37	INSTALL carpet				
FL38	INSPECT carpet				
FL39	CORRECT carpet problems				
FL40	PAY carpet sub				
FL41	PAY carpet sub retainage				
	LANDSCAPING				
LD1	EVALUATE lot				

Masterplan

STEP	DESCRIPTION	Date Started	Date Complete	Date Inspected	NOTES
LD2	DETERMINE best house location				
LD3	DEVELOP site plan				
LD4	CONTACT landscape architect				
LD5	FINALIZE site plan				
LD6	SUBMIT site plan				
LD7	DELIVER fill dirt				
LD8	PAY landscape architect				
	After Construction				
LD9	CONDUCT soil test				
LD10	TILL topsoil				
LD11	APPLY soil treatments				
LD12	INSTALL underground sprinkling system				
LD13	PLANT flower bulbs				
LD14	APPLY seed or sod				
LD15	SOAK lawn with water				
LD16	INSTALL bushes and trees				
LD17	PREPARE landscaped islands				
LD18	INSTALL mailbox				
LD19	INSPECT landscaping job				
LD20	CORRECT any landscaping problems				
LD21	PAY landscaping sub				
LD22	PAY landscaping sub retainage				
	TOTAL COMPLETION TIME				

Project Schedule

HOW TO USE THE PROJECT SCHEDULE

The Project Schedule that follows on the next page gives you a visual representation of your entire project over a span of eighteen months.

The time span of your project may vary considerably from this length, so adjust your timing accordingly. The length of each project bar includes some slack time and starts at the earliest possible date. The **shaded** boxes represent the critical path of the project. In other words, each preceding task must be completed before the next CRITICAL TASK can begin. Step numbers correspond directly to the steps in the Project Management section and in the Master Plan.

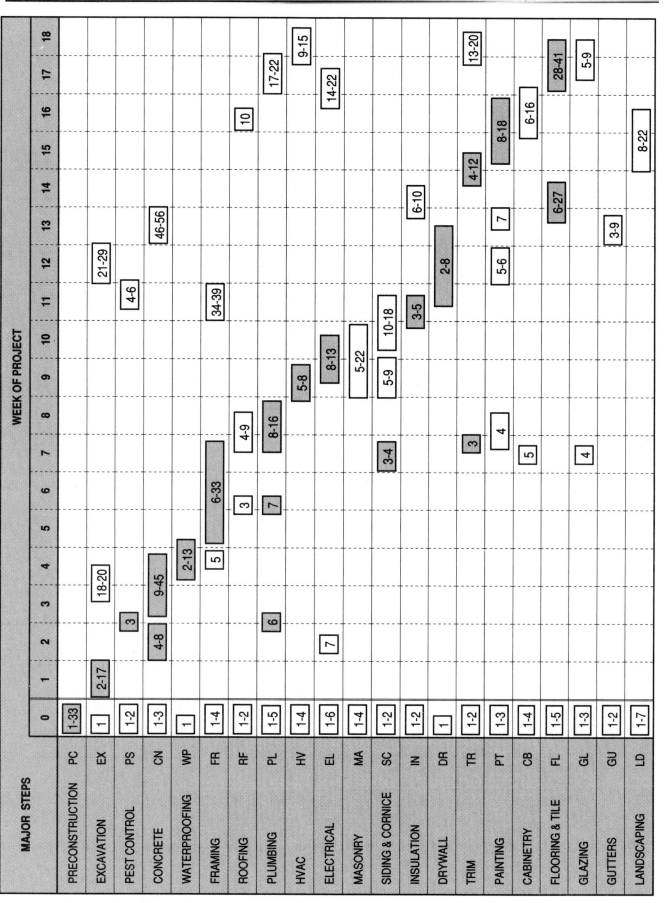

WEEK OF PROJECT

MAJOR STEPS		0	1	2	3	4	5	6	7	8	9	10	11	12	13	14	15	16	17	18
PRECONSTRUCTION	PC	1-33																		
EXCAVATION	EX	1	2-17		18-20									21-29						
PEST CONTROL	PS	1-2		3									4-6							
CONCRETE	CN	1-3	4-8		9-45										46-56					
WATERPROOFING	WP	1				2-13														
FRAMING	FR	1-4				5		6-33					34-39							
ROOFING	RF	1-2						3		4-9								10		
PLUMBING	PL	1-5		6				7		8-16									17-22	
HVAC	HV	1-4									5-8									9-15
ELECTRICAL	EL	1-6		7								8-13							14-22	
MASONRY	MA	1-4										5-22								
SIDING & CORNICE	SC	1-2							3-4		5-9		10-18							
INSULATION	IN	1-2											3-5		6-10					
DRYWALL	DR	1												2-8						
TRIM	TR	1-2							3							4-12			13-20	
PAINTING	PT	1-3								4				5-6	7		8-18			
CABINETRY	CB	1-4							5									6-16		
FLOORING & TILE	FL	1-5													6-27				28-41	
GLAZING	GL	1-3															5-9			
GUTTERS	GU	1-2							4						3-9					
LANDSCAPING	LD	1-7															8-22			

SUPPLIERS/SUB-CONTRACTORS REFERENCE SHEET

NAME	PHONE	TYPE PRODUCT
ADDRESS	CALL WHEN	DATE
	PRODUCTS	
	WORKER'S COMP?	BONDED?

REFERENCE NAME	PHONE	COMMENTS

PRICES/COMMENTS

NAME	PHONE	TYPE PRODUCT
ADDRESS	CALL WHEN	DATE
	PRODUCTS	
	WORKER'S COMP?	BONDED?

REFERENCE NAME	PHONE	COMMENTS

PRICES/COMMENTS

SUPPLIERS/SUB-CONTRACTORS REFERENCE SHEET

NAME	PHONE	TYPE PRODUCT
ADDRESS	CALL WHEN	DATE
	PRODUCTS	
	WORKER'S COMP?	BONDED?

REFERENCE NAME	PHONE	COMMENTS

PRICES/COMMENTS

NAME	PHONE	TYPE PRODUCT
ADDRESS	CALL WHEN	DATE
	PRODUCTS	
	WORKER'S COMP?	BONDED?

REFERENCE NAME	PHONE	COMMENTS

PRICES/COMMENTS

PLAN ANALYSIS CHECKLIST

PROPERTY:_____

PLAN NUMBER: _____

DESCRIPTION	YES	NO
CIRCULATION: Is there access between the following without going through another room?		
Living room to bathroom		
Family room to bathroom		
Each bedroom to bathroom		
Kitchen to dining room		
Living room to dining room		
Kitchen to outside door		
Can get from auto to kitchen without getting wet if raining		
ROOM SIZE AND SHAPE		
Are all rooms adequate size and reasonable shape based on planned use?		
Can living room wall accomodate sofa and end tables (minimum 10 ft.)?		
Can wall of den take sofa and end tables (minimum 10 ft.)?		
Can wall of master bedroom(s) take double bed and end tables?		
STORAGE AND CLOSETS		
Guest closet near front entry		
Linen closet near baths		
Broom closet near kitchen		
Tool and lawnmower storage		
Space for washer and dryer		
EXTERIOR:		
Is the house style "normal" architecture?		
Is the house style compatible with surrounding architecture?		
SITE ANALYSIS		
Does the house conform to the neighborhood?		
Is the house suited to the lot?		
Is the topography good?		
Will water drain away from the house?		
Will grade of driveway be reasonable?		
Is the lot wooded?		
Is the subject lot as good as others in the neighborhood?		
Totals		

LIGHTING AND APPLIANCE ORDER

JOB _____   STORE NAME _____

DATE _____   LIGHTING BUDGET _____

DESCRIPTION	STYLE NO.	QTY.	UNIT PRICE	TOTAL PRICE
Front Entrance				
Rear Entrance				
Dining Room				
Living Room				
Den				
Family Room				
Kitchen				
Kitchen Sink				
Breakfast Area				
Dinette				
Utility Room				
Basement				
Master Bath				
Hall Bath 1				
Guest Bath				
Hall 1				
Hall 2				
Stairway				
Master Bedroom				
Bedroom 2				
Bedroom 3				
Bedroom 4				
Closets				
OUTDOOR				
Front Porch				
Rear Porch				
Porch/Patio				
Carport/Garage				
Post/Lantern				
Floodlights				
Chimes				
Pushbuttons				
APPLIANCES				
Ovens				
Hood				

ITEM ESTIMATE WORKSHEET

VENDOR NAME	DESCRIPTION	MEASURING		CONVERSION FACTOR	ORDERING		PRICE EACH	COST	TAX	TOTAL COST	COST TYPE
		QTY.	UNIT		QTY.	UNIT					

EXPENSE CATEGORY	MATERIAL COST	LABOR COST	SUBCONTRACTOR COST	TOTAL COST

COST ESTIMATE SUMMARY

DESCRIPTION	MATERIAL	LABOR	SUB-CONTR.	TOTAL
EXCAVATION				
PEST CONTROL				
CONCRETE				
WATERPROOFING				
FRAMING				
ROOFING				
PLUMBING				
HVAC				
ELECTRIC				
MASONRY				
SIDING & CORNICE				
INSULATION				
DRYWALL				
TRIM				
PAINTING				
CABINETRY				
TILE				
CARPET				
OTHER FLOORING				
GLAZING				
GUTTERS				
LANDSCAPING				
SUB-TOTAL				
APPLIANCES				
LUMBER				
OTHER MATERIALS				
TOOLS/RENTAL				
LOAN/LEGAL				
INSURANCE				
PERMITS/LICENSE				
SUB-TOTAL				
			GRAND TOTAL	

COST ESTIMATE CHECKLIST

CODE NO.	DESCRIPTION	QTY.	MATERIAL		LABOR		SUB-CONTR.		TOTAL
			UNIT PRICE	TOTAL MATL.	UNIT PRICE	TOTAL LABOR	UNIT PRICE	TOTAL SUB	
SUB-TOTALS									
						GRAND TOTALS			

SUB-CONTRACTOR BID CONTROL LOG

SUB/LABOR	NAME	BID	GOOD UNTIL	NAME	BID	GOOD UNTIL	NAME	BID	GOOD UNTIL	BEST BID	NAME
EXCAVATION											
CONCRETE											
PEST CONTROL											
FRAMING											
ROOFING											
PLUMBING											
HVAC											
ELECTRICAL											
MASONRY											
SIDING											
INSULATION											
DRYWALL											
TRIM											
PAINTING											
CABINETRY											
FLOORING											
TILE											
GLASS											
LANDSCAPING											
GUTTERS											
ASPHALT											

PURCHASE ORDER CONTROL LOG

PO NO.	DATE ORDERED	DESCRIPTION	VENDOR NAME	DATE DELIVERED	DISCOUNT		PAYMENTS				TOTAL PAID
					RATE	DUE	CHK.#	AMT.	CHK.#	AMT.	

PURCHASE ORDER

P/O NO.	PAGE NO.
DATE OF ORDER	JOB NO.
SALESMAN	REQ. NO.
DELIVER TO	

TO:

REQUESTED BY	DELIVER BY	SHIP VIA	TERMS

B/O	QTY. ORDERED	QTY. RECEIVED	DESCRIPTION	UNIT PRICE	TOTAL

PLEASE SEND A COPY OF THIS PO WITH DELIVERED MATERIAL. CALL IF UNABLE TO MAKE DELIVERY DEADLINE.

PURCHASE ORDER cont.

P/O NO.	PAGE NO.

B/O	QTY. ORDERED	QTY. RECEIVED	DESCRIPTION	UNIT PRICE	TOTAL

PLEASE SEND A COPY OF THIS PO WITH DELIVERED
MATERIAL. CALL IF UNABLE TO MAKE DELIVERY DEADLINE.

CHANGE ORDER

CHANGE ORDER NO.

DATE OF CHANGE ORDER	JOB NO.
JOB PHONE	CONTRACT DATE
JOB LOCATION	

TO (CONTRACTOR):

You are directed to make the following changes in this Contract:

Contract time will be ☐ increased ☐ decreased by:

Days

New Completion Date

ACCEPTED — The above prices and specifications are satisfactory and are hereby accepted. All work to be done under same terms and conditions as original contract unless otherwise stipulated.

Original Contract Price	
Previously Authorized Change Orders	
New Contract Price	
This Change Order	
New Authorized Contract Price	

AUTHORIZED BY

SUB-CONTRACTOR

SIGNATURE　　　　DATE

SIGNATURE　　　　DATE

SUB-CONTRACTOR'S AGREEMENT

Sub. Name _____

Address _____

_____

_____

Phone _____

Have Worker's Comp? ☐Yes ☐No

Worker's Comp. No. _____

Expiration Date _____

Tax Id No. _____

Date _____

Job No. _____

Job Address _____

_____

_____

Plan No. _____

Bid Amount _____

Bid Good Until _____

Payment to be made as follows:

_____

_____

_____

_____

Deduct _____ % for worker's compensation.
Deduct _____ % for retainage.

All material is guaranteed to be as specified. All work to be completed in a timely manner, according to standard practices. Any alteration or deviation from specifications below involving extra costs will be executed only upon written order (refer to Change Order Form).

SPECIFICATIONS: (Attach extra sheets if necessary)

_____

_____

_____

_____

_____

_____

_____

_____

_____

Agreement

_____

Sub-contractor   (date)

PAYMENTS

DATE	CHECK NO.	AMOUNT PAID	AMOUNT DUE

SUB-CONTRACTOR'S AFFIDAVIT

STATE OF: _____

COUNTY OF: _____

Personally appeared before the undersigned attesting officer,
_____,
who being duly sworn, on oath says that he was the contractor in charge of improving the property
owned by _____,
located at _____.

Contractor says that all work, labor, services and materials used in such improvements were furnished and performed at the contractor's instance; that said contractor has been paid or partially paid the full contract price for such improvements; that all work done or material furnished in making the improvements have been paid for at the agreed price, or reasonable value, and there are no unpaid bills for labor and services performed or materials furnished; and that no person has any claim or lien by reason of said improvements.

_____

(Seal)

Sworn to and subscribed before me,
this _____ day of _____, 19_____.

_____
Notary Public

CONSTRUCTION LOAN DRAW SCHEDULE

JOB DESCRIPTION _____ **JOB NO.** _____

BANK _____

ADDRESS _____

_____

	AMOUNT
AMOUNT OF CONSTRUCTION LOAN	
CONSTRUCTION LOAN CLOSING COSTS	
TOTAL CONSTRUCTION LOAN COST	

DRAW NO.	DESCRIPTION	DATE	AMOUNT
1			
2			
3			
4			
5			
6			
7			
8			
		TOTAL OF LOAN DRAWS	

BUILDING CONTRACT

(date)_____

1. The undersigned owner authorizes the undersigned builder to construct and deliver to said owner a dwelling in accordance with the plans and specifications which are attached hereto and made a part hereof, on all that tract or parcel of land lying and being in Land:

    Lot _____ of the _____ District
    of _____ County, _____(state), and being known as
    _____

2. Except as proved in the paragraph dealing with allowances hereafter, the total cost to the owner (excluding the cost of the land and additional arranged work), shall be:

    _____ DOLLARS ($_____).
    Said amount shall be paid as follows:

    SAMPLE BUILDING CONTRACT

3. Builder shall commence construction of the house in accordance with the attached plans and specifications after the construction loan has been closed. The construction of the house shall be completed within _____ days from the time that the construction is commenced.

4. The improvements shall be deemed fully completed when approved by the mortgagee for loan purposes.

5. Builder agrees to give possession of the improvements to the purchaser immediately after the full payment to the builder of any cash balance due. At that time, the builder agrees to furnish the purchaser a notarized affidavit that there are no outstanding liens for unpaid material or labor.

6. It is the understanding of the parties that the purchase price above described includes builder's allowances for items hereinafter described. The amounts are listed at builder's cost. It is the understanding of the parties that the purchase price shall be equal to the price described in Paragraph 2 above, provided the costs of the items below listed do not exceed the amounts shown. In the event that the builder's cost exceeds any item hereinafter listed, the purchase price shall be increased by the amount above the allowance shown. The allowances are as follows:

    _____
    _____
    _____
    _____
    _____

_____
_____
_____
_____
_____
_____
_____
_____
_____
_____

7. The cost of any alterations, additions, omissions or deviations at the request of the owner shall be added to the agreed purchase price. No such changes will be made unless stipulated in writing and signed by both parties hereto.

8. Builder shall provide to owner, in writing, a twelve (12) month construction guarantee.

9. Every effort will be exerted on the part of the builder to complete the construction within the period described above. However, builder assumes no responsibilities for delays occasioned by causes beyond his control. In the event of a delay of construction caused by weather, purchaser's selections, etc., the period of delay is to be added to the construction period allotted to builder.

10. This contract shall inure to the benefit of, and shall be binding upon, the parties hereto, their heirs, successors, administrators, executors and assigns.

11. This contract constitutes the sole and entire agreement between the parties hereto and no modification of this contract shall be binding unless attached hereto and signed by all parties to the agreement. No representation, promise, or inducement to this agreement not included in this contract shall be binding upon any party hereto.

The parties do set their hands and seals the day and year first above written.

_____
(Owner)

_____
(Owner)

_____
(Builder)

VETERANS ADMINISTRATION, U.S.D.A. FARMERS HOME ADMINISTRATION, AND
U.S. DEPARTMENT OF HOUSING AND URBAN DEVELOPMENT
HOUSING - FEDERAL HOUSING COMMISSIONER

OMB No. 2505-0192 (Exp. 6-30-87)

For accurate register of carbon copies, form may be separated along above fold. Staple completed sheets together in original order.

DESCRIPTION OF MATERIALS

No. _____
(To be inserted by HUD, VA or FmHA)

☐ Proposed Construction

☐ Under Construction

Property address _____ City _____ State _____

Mortgagor or Sponsor _____
(Name) _____ (Address)

Contractor or Builder _____
(Name) _____ (Address)

INSTRUCTIONS

1. For additional information on how this form is to be submitted, number of copies, etc., see the instructions applicable to the HUD Application for Mortgage Insurance, VA Request for Determination of Reasonable Value, or FmHA Property Information and Appraisal Report, as the case may be.

2. Describe all materials and equipment to be used, whether or not shown on the drawings, by marking an X in each appropriate check-box and entering the information called for each space. If space is inadequate, enter "See misc." and describe under item 27 or on an attached sheet. THE USE OF PAINT CONTAINING MORE THAN THE PERCENTAGE OF LEAD BY WEIGHT PERMITTED BY LAW IS PROHIBITED.

3. Work not specifically described or shown will not be considered unless required, then the minimum acceptable will be assumed. Work exceeding minimum requirements cannot be considered unless specifically described.

4. Include no alternates, "or equal" phrases, or contradictory items. (Consideration of a request for acceptance of substitute materials or equipment is not thereby precluded.)

5. Include signatures required at the end of this form.

6. The construction shall be completed in compliance with the related drawings and specifications, as amended during processing. The specifications include this Description of Materials and the applicable Minimum Property Standards.

1. EXCAVATION:

Bearing soil, type _____

2. FOUNDATIONS:

Footings: concrete mix _____ ; strength psi _____ Reinforcing _____

Foundation wall: material _____ Reinforcing _____

Interior foundation wall: material _____

Columns: material and sizes _____ Party foundation wall _____

Girders: material and sizes _____ Piers: material and reinforcing _____

Basement entrance areaway _____ Sills: material _____

Waterproofing _____ Window areaways _____

Termite protection _____ Footing drains _____

Basementless space: ground cover _____ ; insulation _____ ; foundation vents _____

Special foundations _____

Additional information: _____

3. CHIMNEYS:

Material _____ Prefabricated (*make and size*) _____

Flue lining: material _____ Heater flue size _____ Fireplace flue size _____

Vents (*material and size*): gas or oil heater _____ ; water heater _____

Additional information: _____

4. FIREPLACES:

Type: ☐ solid fuel; ☐ gas-burning; ☐ circulator (*make and size*) _____ Ash dump and clean-out _____

Fireplace: facing _____ ; lining _____ ; hearth _____ ; mantel _____

Additional information: _____

5. EXTERIOR WALLS:

Wood frame: wood grade, and species _____ ☐ Corner bracing. Building paper or felt _____

Sheathing _____ ; thickness _____ ; width _____ ; ☐ solid; ☐ spaced _____ " o. c.; ☐ diagonal;

Siding _____ ; grade _____ ; type _____ ; size _____ ; exposure _____ "; fastening _____

Shingles _____ ; grade _____ ; type _____ ; size _____ ; exposure _____ "; fastening _____

Stucco _____ ; thickness _____ "; Lath _____ ; weight _____ lb.

Masonry veneer _____ Sills _____ Lintels _____ Base flashing _____

Masonry: ☐ solid ☐ faced ☐ stuccoed; total wall thickness _____ "; facing thickness _____ "; facing material _____

Backup material _____ ; thickness _____ "; bonding _____

Door sills _____ Window sills _____ Lintels _____ Base flashing _____

Interior surfaces: dampproofing, _____ coats of _____ ; furring _____

Additional information: _____

Exterior painting: material _____ ; number of coats _____

Gable wall construction: ☐ same as main walls; ☐ other construction _____

6. FLOOR FRAMING:

Joists: wood, grade, and species _____ ; other _____ ; bridging _____ ; anchors _____

Concrete slab: ☐ basement floor; ☐ first floor; ☐ ground supported; ☐ self-supporting; mix _____ ; thickness _____ ";

reinforcing _____ ; insulation _____ ; membrane _____

Fill under slab: material _____ ; thickness _____ ". Additional information: _____

7. SUBFLOORING: (*Describe underflooring for special floors under item 21.*)

Material: grade and species _____ ; size _____ ; type _____

Laid: ☐ first floor; ☐ second floor; ☐ attic _____ sq. ft.; ☐ diagonal; ☐ right angles. Additional information: _____

8. FINISH FLOORING: (*Wood only. Describe other finish flooring under item 21.*)

LOCATION	ROOMS	GRADE	SPECIES	THICKNESS	WIDTH	BLDG. PAPER	FINISH
First floor							
Second floor							
Attic floor	_____ sq. ft.						

Additional information: _____

Previous Edition is Obsolete

DESCRIPTION OF MATERIALS
HUD-92005(10-84) HUD HB 4145.1

DESCRIPTION OF MATERIALS

9. PARTITION FRAMING:

Studs: wood, grade, and species _____ size and spacing _____ Other _____

Additional information: _____

10. CEILING FRAMING:

Joists: wood, grade, and species _____ Other _____ Bridging _____

Additional information: _____

11. ROOF FRAMING:

Rafters: wood, grade, and species _____ Roof trusses (see detail): grade and species _____

Additional information: _____

12. ROOFING:

Sheathing: wood, grade, and species _____ ; ☐ solid; ☐ spaced _____ " o.c.

Roofing _____ ; grade _____ ; size _____ ; type _____

Underlay _____ ; weight or thickness _____ ; size _____ ; fastening _____

Built-up roofing _____ ; number of plies _____ ; surfacing material _____

Flashing: material _____ ; gage or weight _____ ; ☐ gravel stops; ☐ snow guards

Additional information: _____

13. GUTTERS AND DOWNSPOUTS:

Gutters: material _____ ; gage or weight _____ ; size _____ ; shape _____

Downspouts: material _____ ; gage or weight _____ ; size _____ ; shape _____ ; number _____

Downspouts connected to: ☐ Storm sewer; ☐ sanitary sewer; ☐ dry-well. ☐ Splash blocks: material and size _____

Additional information: _____

14. LATH AND PLASTER

Lath ☐ walls, ☐ ceilings: material _____ ; weight or thickness _____ Plaster: coats _____ ; finish _____

Dry-wall ☐ walls, ☐ ceilings: material _____ ; thickness _____ ; finish _____

Joint treatment _____

15. DECORATING: *(Paint, wallpaper, etc.)*

Rooms	Wall Finish Material and Application	Ceiling Finish Material and Application
Kitchen		
Bath		
Other		

Additional information: _____

16. INTERIOR DOORS AND TRIM:

Doors: type _____ ; material _____ ; thickness _____

Door trim: type _____ Base: type _____ ; material _____ ; size _____

Finish: doors _____ ; trim _____

Other trim *(item, type and location)* _____

Additional information: _____

17. WINDOWS:

Windows: type _____; make _____; material _____

Glass: grade _____; □ sash weights; □ balances, type _____; head flashing _____

Trim: type _____; material _____ Paint _____; number coats _____

Weatherstripping: type _____; material _____ Storm sash, number _____

Screens: □ full; □ half; type _____; number _____; screen cloth material _____

Basement windows: type _____; material _____; screens, number _____; Storm sash, number _____

Special windows _____

Additional information: _____

18. ENTRANCES AND EXTERIOR DETAIL:

Main entrance door: material _____; width _____"; thickness _____". Frame: material _____; thickness _____"

Other entrance doors: material _____; width _____"; thickness _____". Frame: material _____; thickness _____"

Head flashing _____ Weatherstripping: type _____; saddles _____

Screen doors: thickness _____"; number _____; screen cloth material _____ Storm doors: thickness _____"; number _____

Combination storm and screen doors: thickness _____"; number _____; screen cloth material _____

Shutters: □ hinged; □ fixed. Railings _____ Attic louvers _____

Exterior millwork: grade and species _____ Paint _____; number coats _____

Additional information: _____

19. CABINETS AND INTERIOR DETAIL:

Kitchen cabinets, wall units: material _____; lineal feet of shelves _____; shelf width _____

Base units: material _____; counter top _____; edging _____

Back and end splash _____ Finish of cabinets _____; number coats _____

Medicine cabinets: make _____; model _____

Other cabinets and built-in furniture _____

Additional information: _____

20. STAIRS:

STAIR	TREADS		RISERS		STRINGS		HANDRAIL		BALUSTERS	
	Material	Thickness	Material	Thickness	Material	Size	Material	Size	Material	Size
Basement										
Main										
Attic										

Disappearing: make and model number _____

Additional information: _____

21. SPECIAL FLOORS AND WAINSCOT: *(Describe Carpet as listed in Certified Products Directory)*

FLOORS

LOCATION	MATERIAL, COLOR, BORDER, SIZES, GAGE, ETC.	THRESHOLD MATERIAL	WALL BASE MATERIAL	UNDERFLOOR MATERIAL
Kitchen				
Bath				

WAINSCOT

LOCATION	MATERIAL, COLOR, BORDER, CAP. SIZES, GAGE, ETC.	HEIGHT	HEIGHT OVER TUB	HEIGHT IN SHOWERS (FROM FLOOR)
Bath				

Bathroom accessories: ☐ Recessed; material _____ ; number _____ ; ☐ Attached; material _____ ; number _____

Additional information: _____

22. PLUMBING:

FIXTURE	NUMBER	LOCATION	MAKE	MFR'S FIXTURE IDENTIFICATION NO.	SIZE	COLOR
Sink						
Lavatory						
Water closet						
Bathtub						
Shower over tub △						
Stall shower △						
Laundry trays						

△ ☐ Curtain rod   △ ☐ Door   ☐ Shower pan: material _____

Water supply: ☐ public; ☐ community system; ☐ individual (private) system. ★

Sewage disposal: ☐ public; ☐ community system; ☐ individual (private) system. ★

★ *Show and describe individual system in complete detail in separate drawings and specifications according to requirements.*

House drain (inside): ☐ cast iron; ☐ tile; ☐ other _____   House sewer (outside): ☐ cast iron; ☐ tile; ☐ other _____

Water piping: ☐ galvanized steel; ☐ copper tubing; ☐ other _____   Sill cocks, number _____

Domestic water heater: type _____ ; make and model _____ ; heating capacity _____

_____ gph. 100° rise. Storage tank: material _____ ; capacity _____ gallons.

Gas service: ☐ utility company; ☐ liq. pet. gas; ☐ other _____   Gas piping: ☐ cooking; ☐ house heating.

Footing drains connected to: ☐ storm sewer; ☐ sanitary sewer; ☐ dry well. Sump pump; make and model _____

_____ ; capacity _____ ; discharges into _____

DESCRIPTION OF MATERIALS

23. HEATING:

□ Hot water. □ Steam. □ Vapor. □ One-pipe system. □ Two-pipe system.

□ Radiators. □ Convectors. □ Baseboard radiation. Make and model _____

Radiant panel: □ floor; □ wall; □ ceiling. Panel coil: material _____

□ Circulator. □ Return pump. Make and model _____ ; capacity _____ gpm.

Boiler: make and model _____ Output _____ Btuh.; net rating _____ Btuh.

Additional information: _____

Warm air: □ Gravity. □ Forced. Type of system _____

Duct material: supply _____ ; return _____ Insulation _____ , thickness _____ □ Outside air intake.

Furnace: make and model _____ Input _____ Btuh.; output _____ Btuh.

Additional information: _____

□ Space heater; □ floor furnace; □ wall heater. Input _____ Btuh.; output _____ Btuh.; number units _____

Make, model _____ Additional information: _____

Controls: make and types _____

Additional information: _____

Fuel: □ Coal; □ oil; □ gas; □ liq. pet. gas; □ electric; □ other _____ ; storage capacity _____

Additional information: _____

Firing equipment furnished separately: □ Gas burner, conversion type. □ Stoker: hopper feed □; bin feed □

Oil burner: □ pressure atomizing; □ vaporizing

Make and model _____ Control _____

Additional information: _____

Electric heating system: type _____ Input _____ watts; @ _____ volts; output _____ Btuh.

Additional information: _____

Ventilating equipment: attic fan, make and model _____ ; capacity _____ cfm.

kitchen exhaust fan, make and model _____

Other heating, ventilating, or cooling equipment _____

24. ELECTRIC WIRING:

Service: □ overhead; □ underground. Panel: □ fuse box; □ circuit-breaker; make _____ AMP's _____ No. circuits _____

Wiring: □ conduit: □ armored cable; □ nonmetallic cable; □ knob and tube; □ other _____

Special outlets: □ range; □ water heater; □ other _____

□ Doorbell. □ Chimes. Push-button locations _____ Additional information: _____

25. LIGHTING FIXTURES:

Total number of fixtures _____ Total allowance for fixtures, typical installation, $ _____

Nontypical installation _____

Additional information: _____

DESCRIPTION OF MATERIALS

26. INSULATION:

Location	Thickness	Material, Type, and Method of Installation	Vapor Barrier
Roof			
Ceiling			
Wall			
Floor			

27. MISCELLANEOUS: *(Describe any main dwelling materials, equipment, or construction items not shown elsewhere; or use to provide additional information where the space provided was inadequate. Always reference by item number to correspond to numbering used on this form.)*

HARDWARE: *(make, material, and finish.)*

SPECIAL EQUIPMENT: *(State material or make, model and quantity. Include only equipment and appliances which are acceptable by local law, custom and applicable FHA standards. Do not include items which, by established custom, are supplied by occupant and removed when he vacates premises or chattles prohibited by law from becoming realty.)*

PORCHES:

TERRACES:

_____

_____

GARAGES:

_____

_____

WALKS AND DRIVEWAYS:

Driveway: width _____; base material _____; thickness _____"; surfacing material _____; thickness _____"

Front walk: width _____; material _____; thickness _____". Service walk: width _____; material _____; thickness _____"

Steps: material _____; treads _____"; risers _____". Check walls _____

OTHER ONSITE IMPROVEMENTS:

(Specify all exterior onsite improvements not described elsewhere, including items such as unusual grading, drainage structures, retaining walls, fence, railings, and accessory structures.)

_____

_____

_____

LANDSCAPING, PLANTING, AND FINISH GRADING:

Topsoil _____" thick: ☐ front yard; ☐ side yards; ☐ rear yard to _____ feet behind main building.

Lawns _(seeded, sodded, or sprigged)_: ☐ front yard _____; ☐ side yards _____; ☐ rear yard _____

Planting: ☐ as specified and shown on drawings; ☐ as follows:

_____ Shade trees, deciduous, _____" caliper.

_____ Low flowering trees, deciduous, _____' to _____'

_____ High-growing shrubs, deciduous, _____' to _____'

_____ Medium-growing shrubs, deciduous, _____' to _____'

_____ Low-growing shrubs, deciduous, _____' to _____'

_____ Evergreen trees. _____' to _____', B & B:

_____ Evergreen shrubs. _____' to _____', B & B.

_____ Vines, 2-year _____

IDENTIFICATION.—This exhibit shall be identified by the signature of the builder, or sponsor, and/or the proposed mortgagor if the latter is known at the time of application.

Date _____ Signature _____

Signature _____

*U.S. GOVERNMENT PRINTING OFFICE: 1989-731-036/IV-00448 Region 4.

BUILDING CHECKLIST

JOB _____

DATE STARTED _____   ESTIMATED COMPLETION DATE_____

(**Bold faced** numbered items indicate critical tasks that must be done befor continuing.)

DATE DONE   NOTES

A. PRE-CLOSING
☐ 1. Take-off   _____   _____
☐ 2. Spec sheet   _____   _____
☐ 3. Contract   _____   _____
☐ 4. Submit loan   _____   _____
☐ 5. Survey   _____   _____
☐ 6. Insurance   _____   _____
☐ 7. Closing   _____   _____

B. POST-CLOSING
☐ 1. Business license   _____   _____
☐ 2. Compliance bond   _____   _____
☐ 3. Sewer tap   _____   _____
☐ 4. Water tap   _____   _____
☐ 5. Perk test (if necessary) _____   _____
☐ 6. Miscellaneous permits _____   _____
☐ 7. Building permit   _____   _____
☐ 8. Temporary services: _____   _____
☐   a.   Electrical   _____   _____
☐   b.   Water   _____   _____
☐   c.   Phone   _____   _____

C. CONSTRUCTION
☐ 1. Rough layout   _____   _____
☐ 2. Rough grading   _____   _____
☐ 3. Water   _____   _____
☐   a.   Meter   _____   _____
☐   b.   Well   _____   _____
☐ 4. **Set temporary pole**   _____   _____
☐ 5. Crawl or basement   _____   _____
☐   a.   Batter boards   _____   _____
☐   b.   **Footings dug**   _____   _____
☐   c.   **Footings poured**   _____   _____
☐   d.   Lay block/pour   _____   _____
☐ 6. Pre-treat   _____   _____

DATE DONE   NOTES

- [ ] 7. Slab
- [ ]   a. Form boards
- [ ]   b. **Plumbing**
- [ ]   c. Miscellaneous pipes
- [ ]   d. Gravel
- [ ]   e. Poly
- [ ]   f. **Re-wire**
- [ ]   g. Pour concrete
- [ ] 8. Spot survey
- [ ] 9. Waterproof
- [ ] 10. Fiberglass tubs
- [ ] 11. Framing
- [ ]   a. Basement walls
- [ ]   b. First floor
- [ ]   c. Walls—1st floor
- [ ]   d. Second floor
- [ ]   e. Walls—2nd floor
- [ ]   f. Sheathing
- [ ]   g. Ceiling joists
- [ ]   h. Rafters/trussed
- [ ]   i. Decking
- [ ]   j. Felt
- [ ] 12. Roofing
- [ ] 13. Set fireplace
- [ ] 14. Set doors
- [ ] 15. Set windows
- [ ] 16. Siding and cornice
- [ ] 17. **Rough plumbing**
- [ ] 18. **Rough HVAC**
- [ ] 19. Rough electrical
- [ ] 20. Measure cabinets
- [ ] 21. Rough phone/cable
- [ ] 22. Rough miscellaneous
- [ ] 23. Insulation
- [ ] 24. Framing inspection
- [ ] 25. Clean interior
- [ ] 26. Drywall
- [ ] 27. Clean interior

DATE DONE   NOTES

- [ ] 28. Stucco
- [ ] 29. Brick
- [ ] 30. Clean exterior
- [ ] 31. Septic tank
- [ ] 32. Utility lines
- [ ]   a.   Gas line
- [ ]   b.   Sewer line
- [ ]   c.   Phone line
- [ ]   d.   Electric line
- [ ] 33. Backfill
- [ ] 34. Pour garage
- [ ] 35. Drives and walks
- [ ] 36. Landscape
- [ ] 37. Gutters
- [ ] 38. Garage door
- [ ] 39. Paint/stain
- [ ] 40. Cabinets
- [ ] 41. Trim
- [ ] 42. Tile
- [ ] 43. Rock
- [ ] 44. Hardwood floors
- [ ] 45. Wallpaper
- [ ] 46. **Plumbing (final)**
- [ ] 47. **HVAC (final)**
- [ ] 48. **Electrical (final)**
- [ ] 49. Mirrors
- [ ] 50. Clean interior
- [ ] 51. Vinyl/carpet
- [ ] 52. Final trim
- [ ] 53. Bath accessories
- [ ] 54. Paint touch up
- [ ] 55. Final touch up
- [ ] 56. Connect utilities

- [ ]   **DATE COMPLETED**

Index

More Great Ideas for All Your Do-It-Yourself Projects!

The Complete Guide to Being Your Own Remodeling Contractor—This helpful guide will ensure that remodeling jobs get done right! Checklists will help you spot work that's not up to snuff, plus you'll control your costs with handy materials lists. *#70246/$18.99/288 pages/150 b&w illus./paperback*

The Complete Guide to Designing Your Own Home—Soon-to-be homeowners—create a place that's uniquely yours. Learn about every step in the home design process—from site selection to financing and decorating. *#70267/$17.99/144 pages/33 b&w illus./paperback*

Home Improvements: Making Investments in Your Home That Pay for Themselves—In a friendly, understandable text, R. Dodge Woodson tells about virtually every kind of home improvement and what they're worth, including landscaping, outside recreational improvements, exterior home improvements and decks, room additions, window and door replacement, bathroom and kitchen remodeling, attic and basement projects and much more! *#70207/$16.95/160 pages/paperback*

Quick & Easy Remodeling Projects to Customize Your Home—Homeowners—learn to build decks, install hardwood flooring and complete other projects to increase your home's character and value. *#70245/$17.99/144 pages/35 illus./paperback*

The Complete Guide to Making Your Home Safe—Discover where household hazards are and how to easily eradicate them, making homes safer and healthier places to live. *#70265/$17.99/240 pages/80 b&w illus./paperback*

The Complete Guide to Home Security—You'll learn tips, techniques and secrets to theft-proofing your home. From doors and windows, to lighting and landscaping, you'll get a complete review of home security. *#70029/$14.95/190 pages/48 photos/illus./paperback*

Gary Branson's Home Repairs and Improvements on a Budget—Save money with step-by-step instructions that show you how to quiet floor noises, prevent drain clogs, locate wall studs, and hundreds of other easy do-it-yourself projects! *#70247/$16.99/160 pages/128 b&w illus./paperback*

The Complete Guide to Four Season Home Maintenance: How to Prevent Costly Problems Before They Occur—With some simple tips and techniques, you'll minimize costly repairs and replacements all year round! *#70192/$18.95/160 pages/92 illus./paperback*

The Home Buyer's Inspection Guide—Don't' get caught in a money-pit! Let an expert building inspector teach you all the critical structural and functional aspects of residential property before you buy. *#70049/$12.99/176 pages/paperback*

Legal Aspects of Buying, Owning, & Selling a Home—In this easy-to-read guide you'll find the answers to all your legal questions concerning buying, selling and occupying a home. *#70151/$12.95/176 pages/11 illus./paperback*

The Complete Guide to Buying Your First Home—This information-packed guide shows you how to plan and organize your buy, and how to avoid common pitfalls for first-time home buyers. *#70023/$16.99/224 pages/41 illus./paperback*

The Complete Guide to Landscape Design, Renovation, and Maintenance—Discover the secrets of beautifying your home through landscaping. Four major sections cover all you need to know about pruning, renovating the overgrown yard, designing and installing a new landscape, and maintaining the yard. *#70030/$14.95/192 pages/85 photos/illus./paperback*

The Complete Guide to Home Plumbing Repair and Replacement—Why pay huge plumber's fees when you can do it yourself. This fully illustrated guide shows you precisely how to troubleshoot, repair and replace your home plumbing system. *#70141/$16.95/224 pages/50 illus./paperback*

Rehab Your Way to Riches—Let a real estate mogul show you how to generate real estate income in ways that limit risk and maximize profits. *#70156/$14.95/208 pages/paperback*

The Complete Guide to Building and Outfitting an Office in Your Home—You'll discover how to convert basements and attics, determine space needs, create layouts—even specifics like how to keep house sounds out! *#70244/$18.99/176 pages/105 b&w illus./paperback*

The Complete Guide to Decorative Landscaping with Brick and Masonry—Beautify your home with patios, walks, brick garden borders, barbecues and dozens of other step-by-step projects. *#70027/$11.95/160 pages/50 photos/illus./paperback*

The Complete Guide to Manufactured Housing—See if manufactured housing will work for you! You'll explore its advantages disadvantages, and practical applications. *#70142/$14.95/160 pages/50 photos/illus./paperback*

The Complete Guide to Home Automation—Simplify your life with energy management, automated lighting, security, appliances, entertainment systems and much more! *#70206/$16.95/176 pages/paperback*

The Complete Guide to Home Roofing Installation and Maintenance—Dozens of insider tips will help you save labor and ensure quality installation and maintenance of an asphalt shingle roof. *#70191/$16.95/176 pages/20+ illus. + 161 photos/paperback*

The Complete Guide to Log and Cedar Homes—Scores of illustrations lead you through all aspects of purchasing or building your log or cedar home—including all phases of construction. *#70190/$16.95/168 pages/18 illus., 56 photos/paperback*

Building and Restoring the Hewn Log House—If you yearn for the rustic life, this practical guide will help you build or restore the traditional log cabin. *#70228/$18.95/176 pages/220 b&w, 45 color illus./paperback*

3131